MAKER
COMICS

SURVIVE IN THE OUTDOORS!

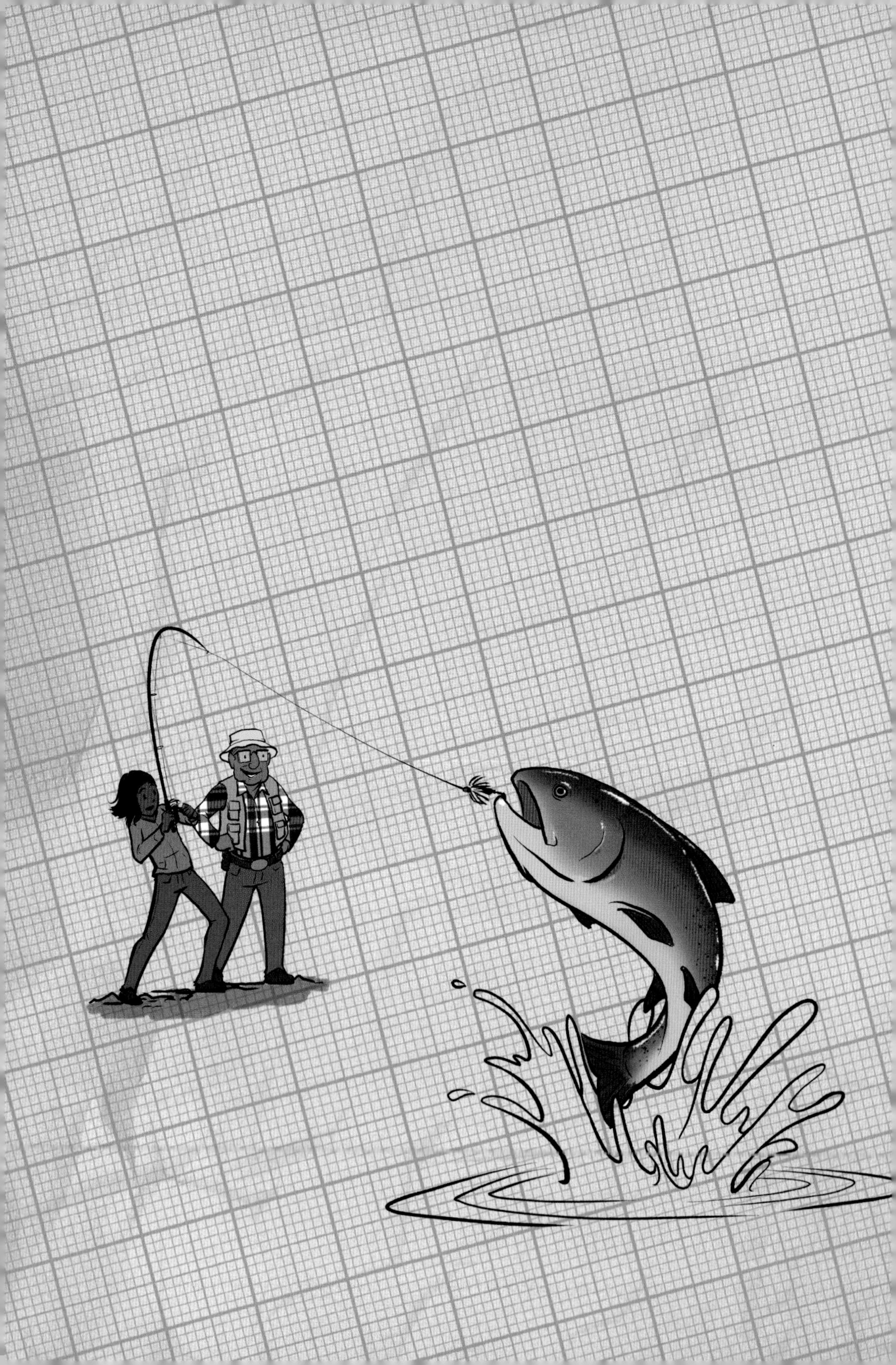

# SURVIVE IN THE OUTDOORS!

## Mike Lawrence

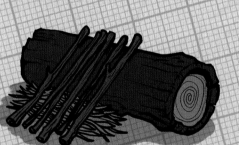

:01

First Second
New York

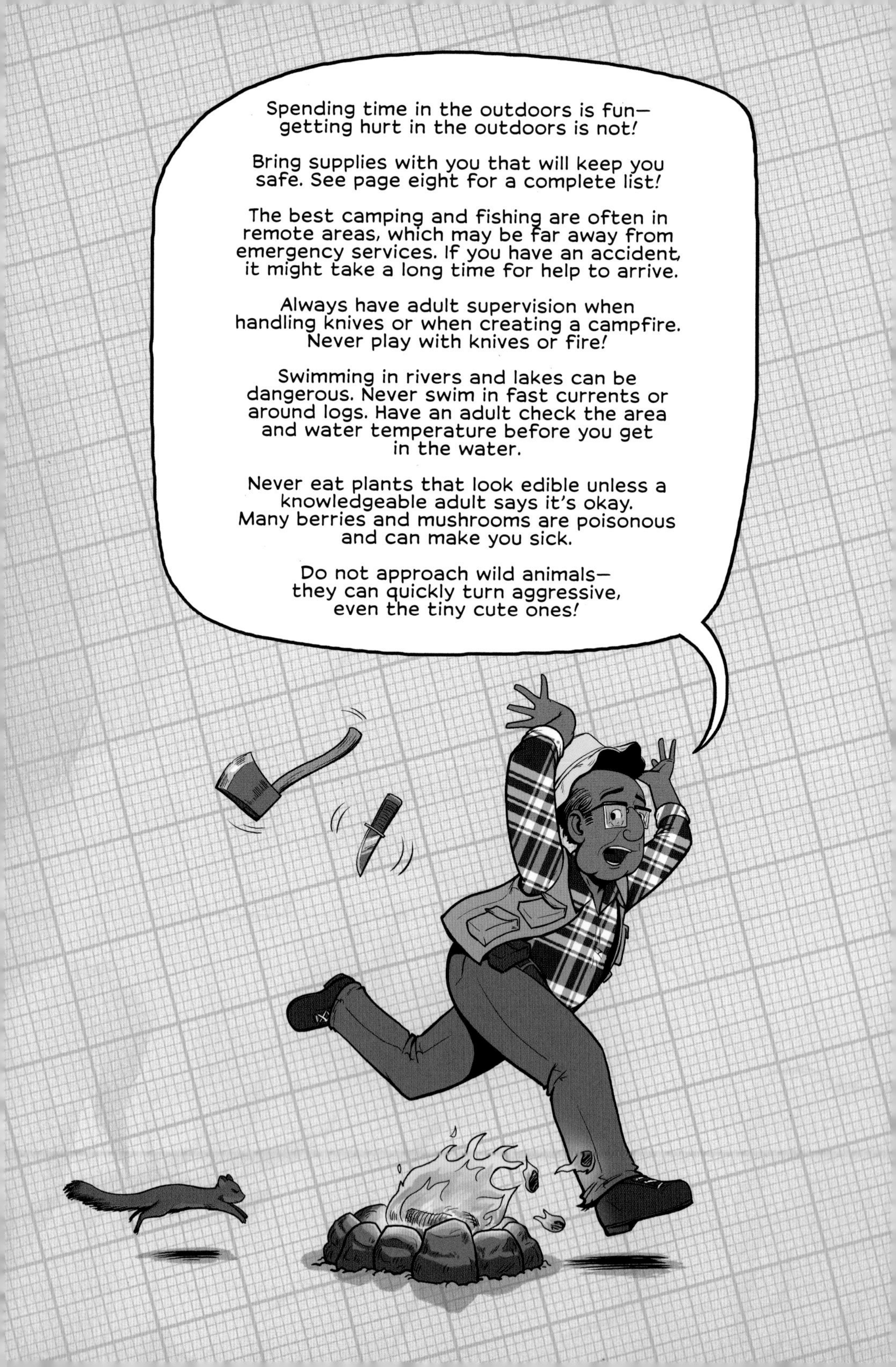
Spending time in the outdoors is fun—getting hurt in the outdoors is not!
Bring supplies with you that will keep you safe. See page eight for a complete list!
The best camping and fishing are often in remote areas, which may be far away from emergency services. If you have an accident, it might take a long time for help to arrive.
Always have adult supervision when handling knives or when creating a campfire. Never play with knives or fire!
Swimming in rivers and lakes can be dangerous. Never swim in fast currents or around logs. Have an adult check the area and water temperature before you get in the water.
Never eat plants that look edible unless a knowledgeable adult says it's okay. Many berries and mushrooms are poisonous and can make you sick.
Do not approach wild animals—they can quickly turn aggressive, even the tiny cute ones!

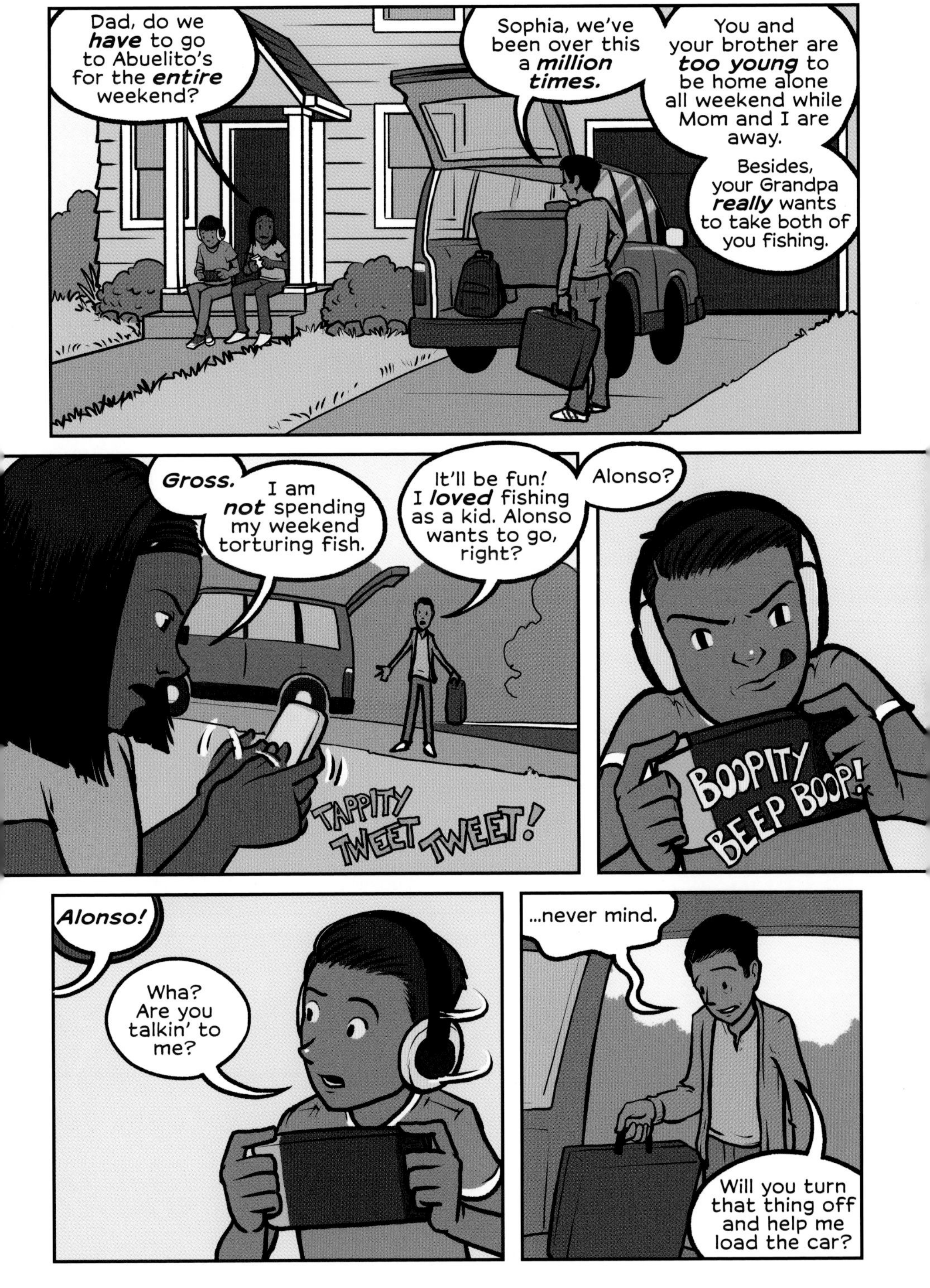

Dad, do we *have* to go to Abuelito's for the *entire* weekend?
Sophia, we've been over this a *million times.*
You and your brother are *too young* to be home alone all weekend while Mom and I are away.
Besides, your Grandpa *really* wants to take both of you fishing.
*Gross.*
I am *not* spending my weekend torturing fish.
It'll be fun! I *loved* fishing as a kid. Alonso wants to go, right?
TAPPITY TWEET TWEET!
Alonso?
BOOPITY BEEP BOOP!
*Alonso!*
Wha? Are you talkin' to me?
...never mind.
Will you turn that thing off and help me load the car?

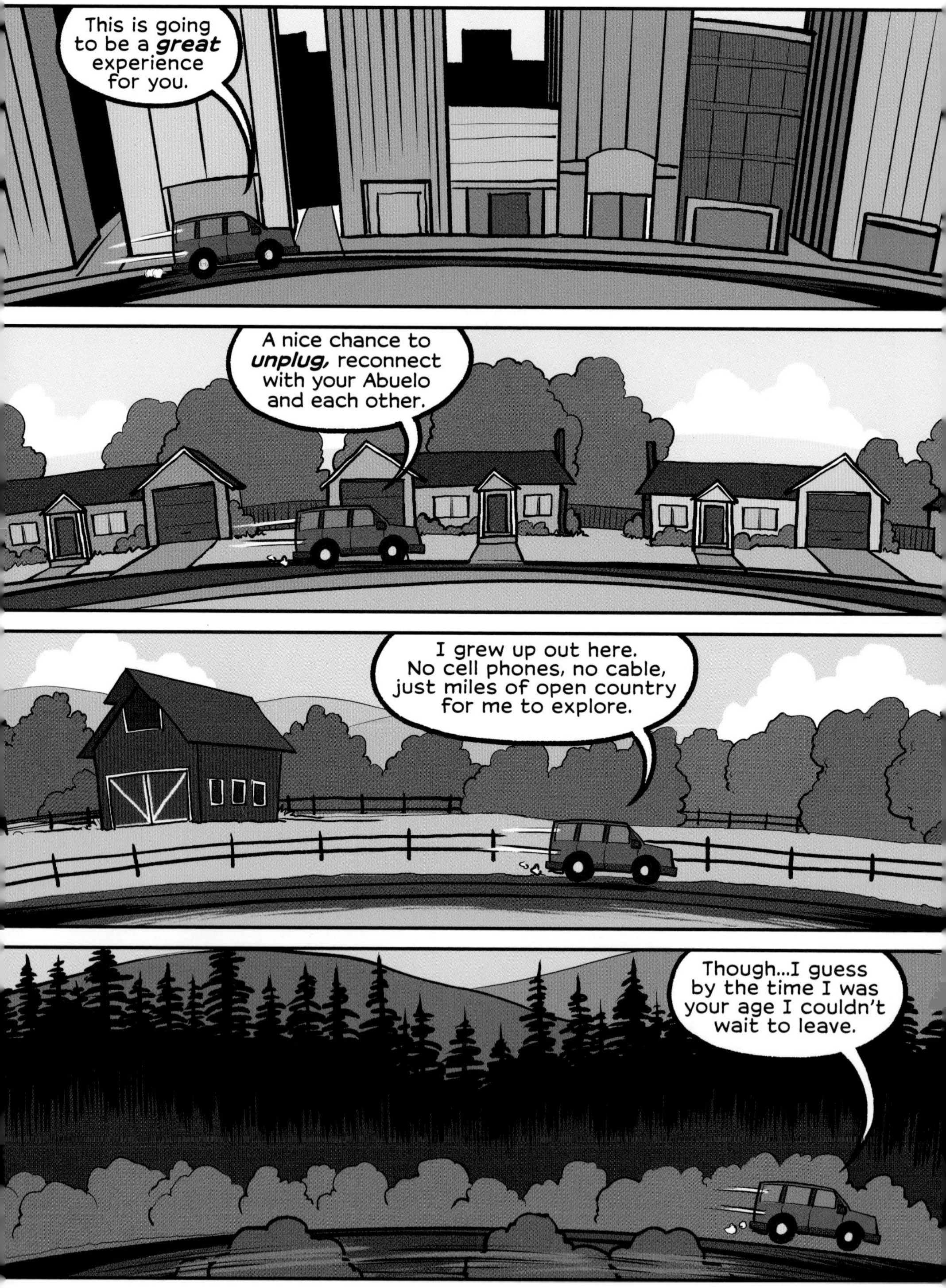
This is going to be a ***great*** experience for you.
A nice chance to ***unplug,*** reconnect with your Abuelo and each other.
I grew up out here. No cell phones, no cable, just miles of open country for me to explore.
Though...I guess by the time I was your age I couldn't wait to leave.

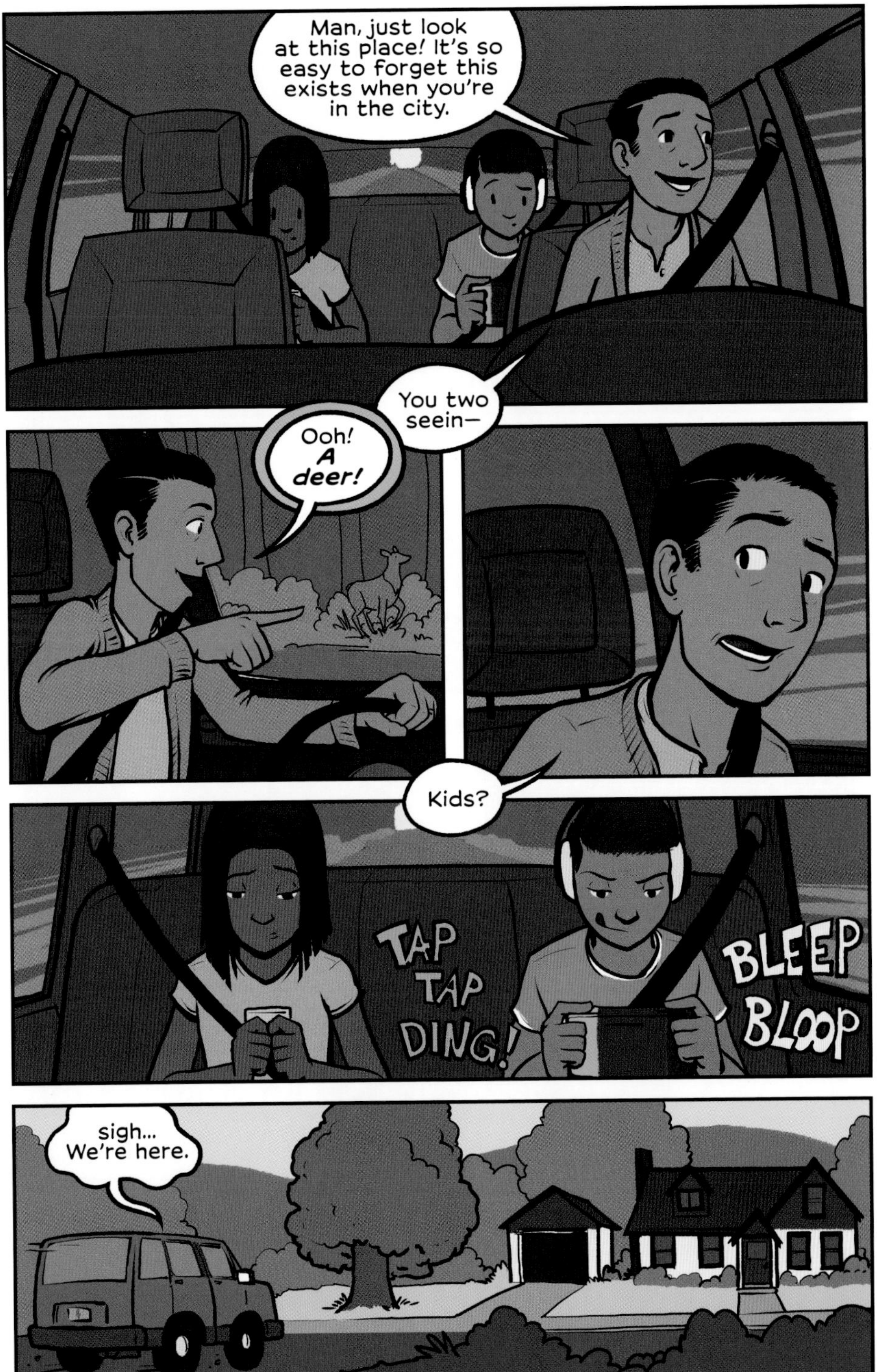
Man, just look at this place! It's so easy to forget this exists when you're in the city.
You two seein—
Ooh! A deer!
Kids?
TAP TAP DING!
BLEEP BLOOP
sigh... We're here.

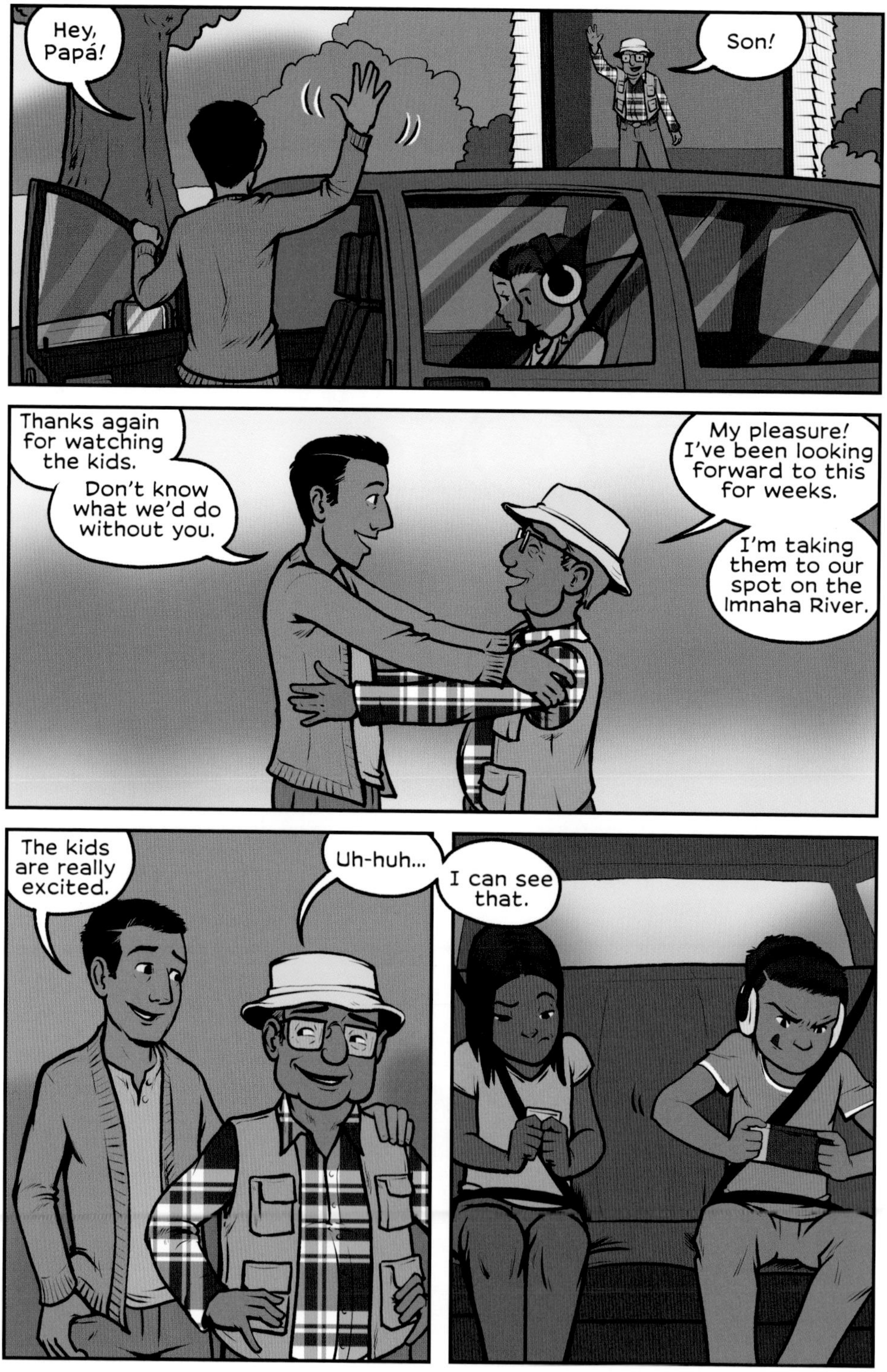
Hey, Papá!
Son!
Thanks again for watching the kids.
Don't know what we'd do without you.
My pleasure! I've been looking forward to this for weeks.
I'm taking them to our spot on the Imnaha River.
The kids are really excited.
Uh-huh...
I can see that.

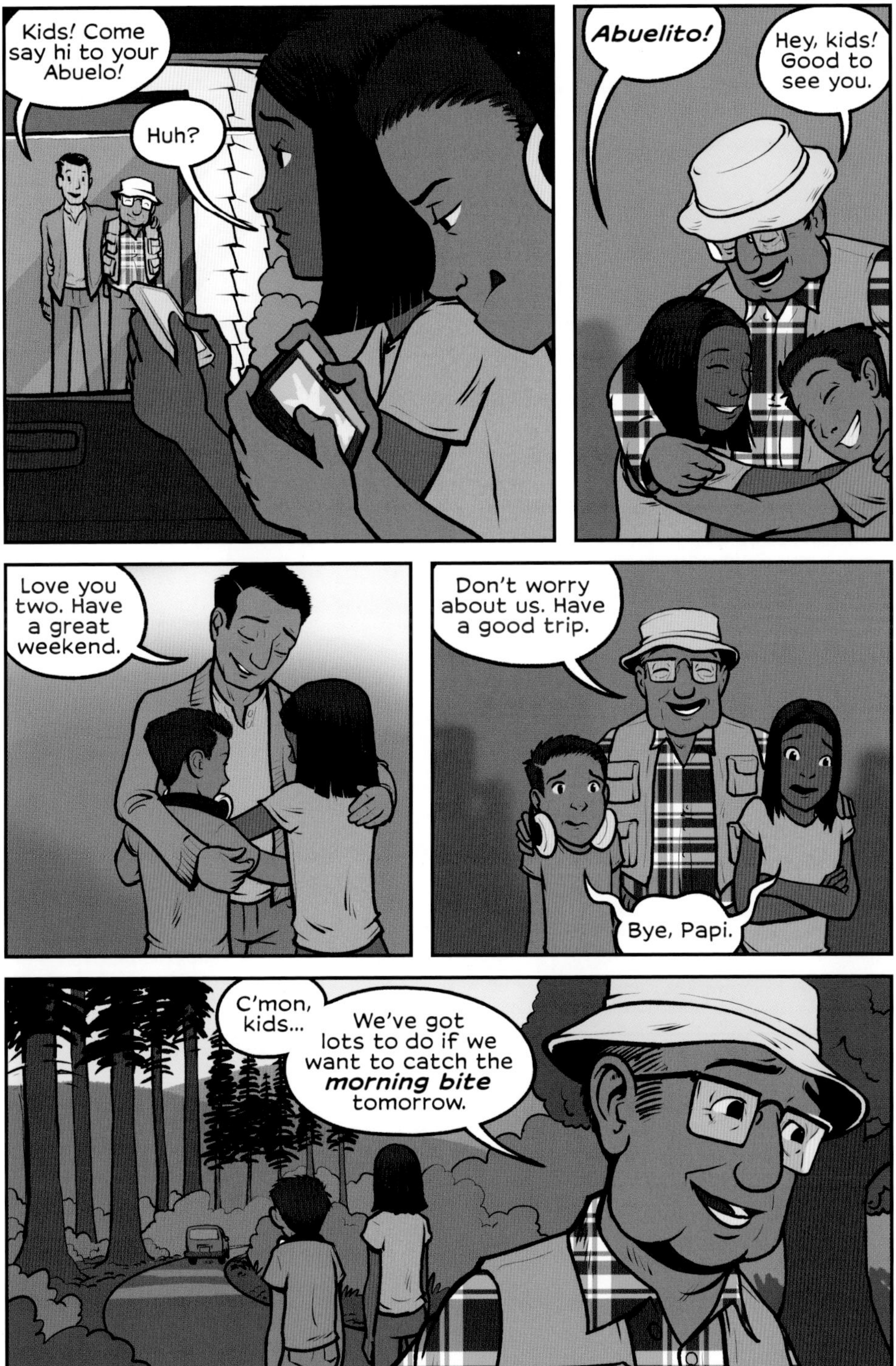
Kids! Come say hi to your Abuelo!
Huh?
Abuelito!
Hey, kids! Good to see you.
Love you two. Have a great weekend.
Don't worry about us. Have a good trip.
Bye, Papi.
C'mon, kids...
We've got lots to do if we want to catch the ***morning bite*** tomorrow.

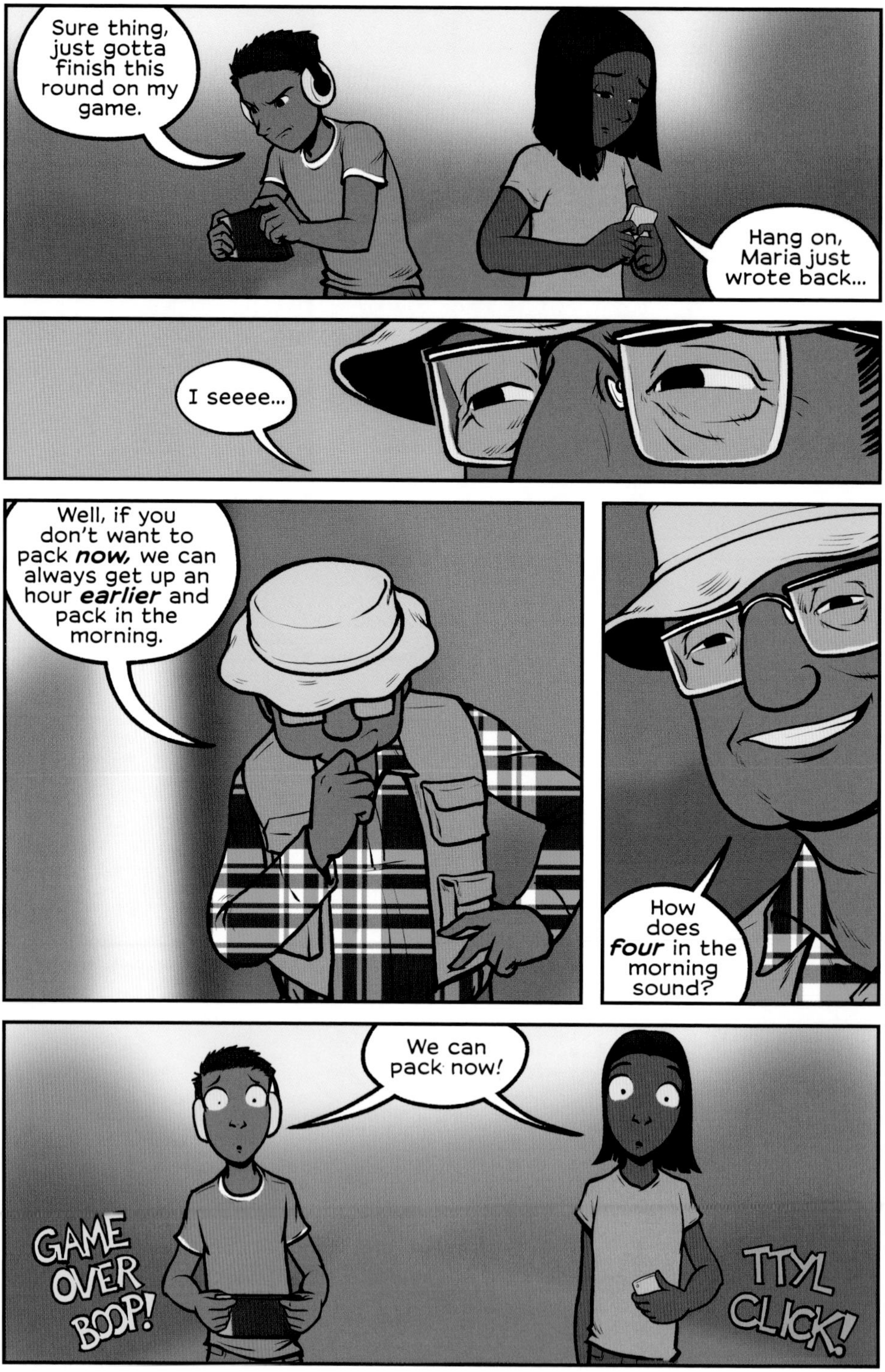
Sure thing, just gotta finish this round on my game.
Hang on, Maria just wrote back...
I seeee...
Well, if you don't want to pack *now,* we can always get up an hour *earlier* and pack in the morning.
How does *four* in the morning sound?
We can pack now!
GAME OVER BOOP!
TTYL CLICK!

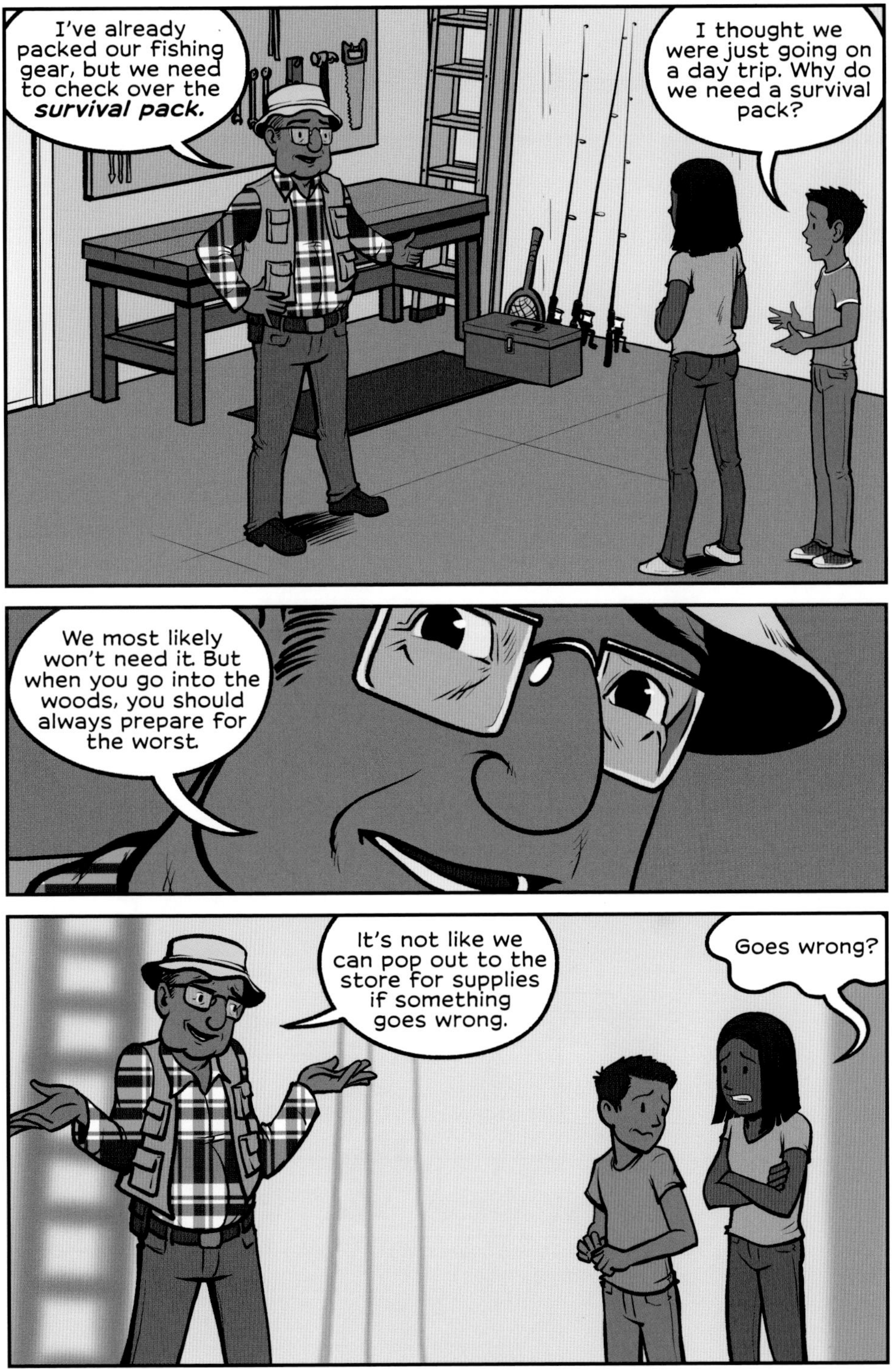
I've already packed our fishing gear, but we need to check over the ***survival pack.***
I thought we were just going on a day trip. Why do we need a survival pack?
We most likely won't need it. But when you go into the woods, you should always prepare for the worst.
It's not like we can pop out to the store for supplies if something goes wrong.
Goes wrong?

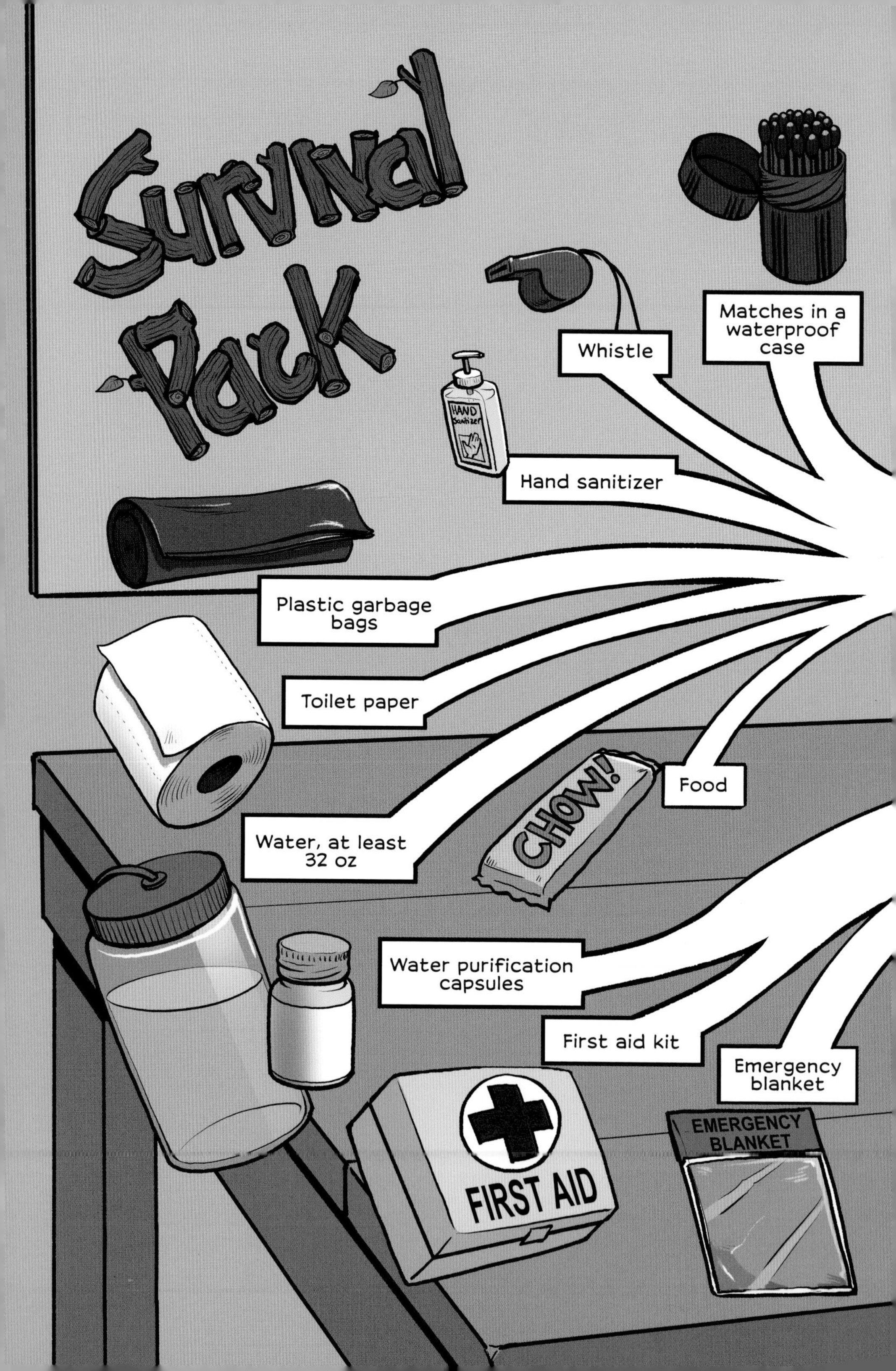

Survival Pack
Matches in a waterproof case
Whistle
HAND Sanitizer
Hand sanitizer
Plastic garbage bags
Toilet paper
CHOW!
Food
Water, at least 32 oz
Water purification capsules
First aid kit
Emergency blanket
FIRST AID
EMERGENCY BLANKET

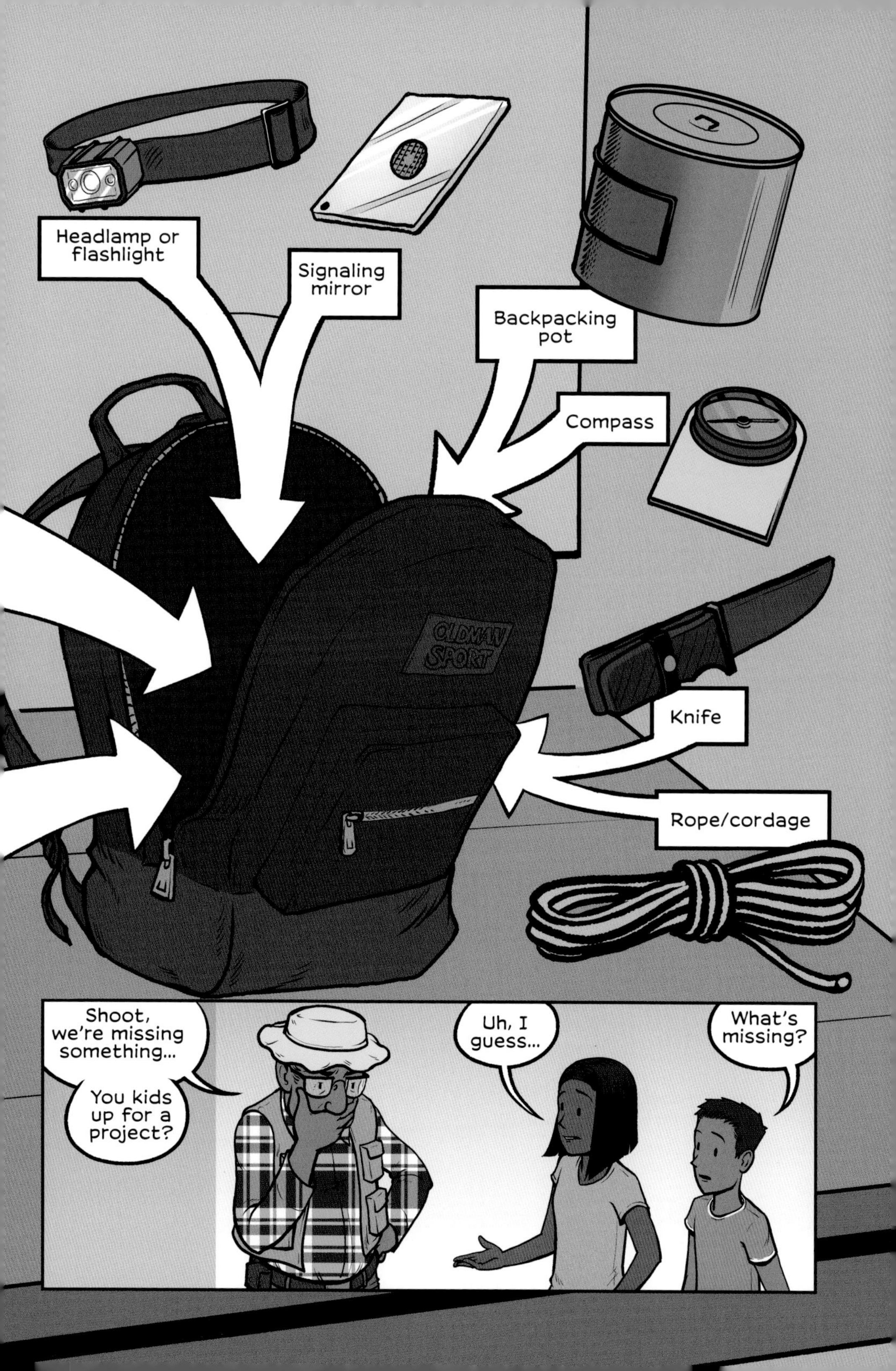

Headlamp or flashlight
Signaling mirror
Backpacking pot
Compass
OLDMAN SPORT
Knife
Rope/cordage
Shoot, we're missing something...
You kids up for a project?
Uh, I guess...
What's missing?

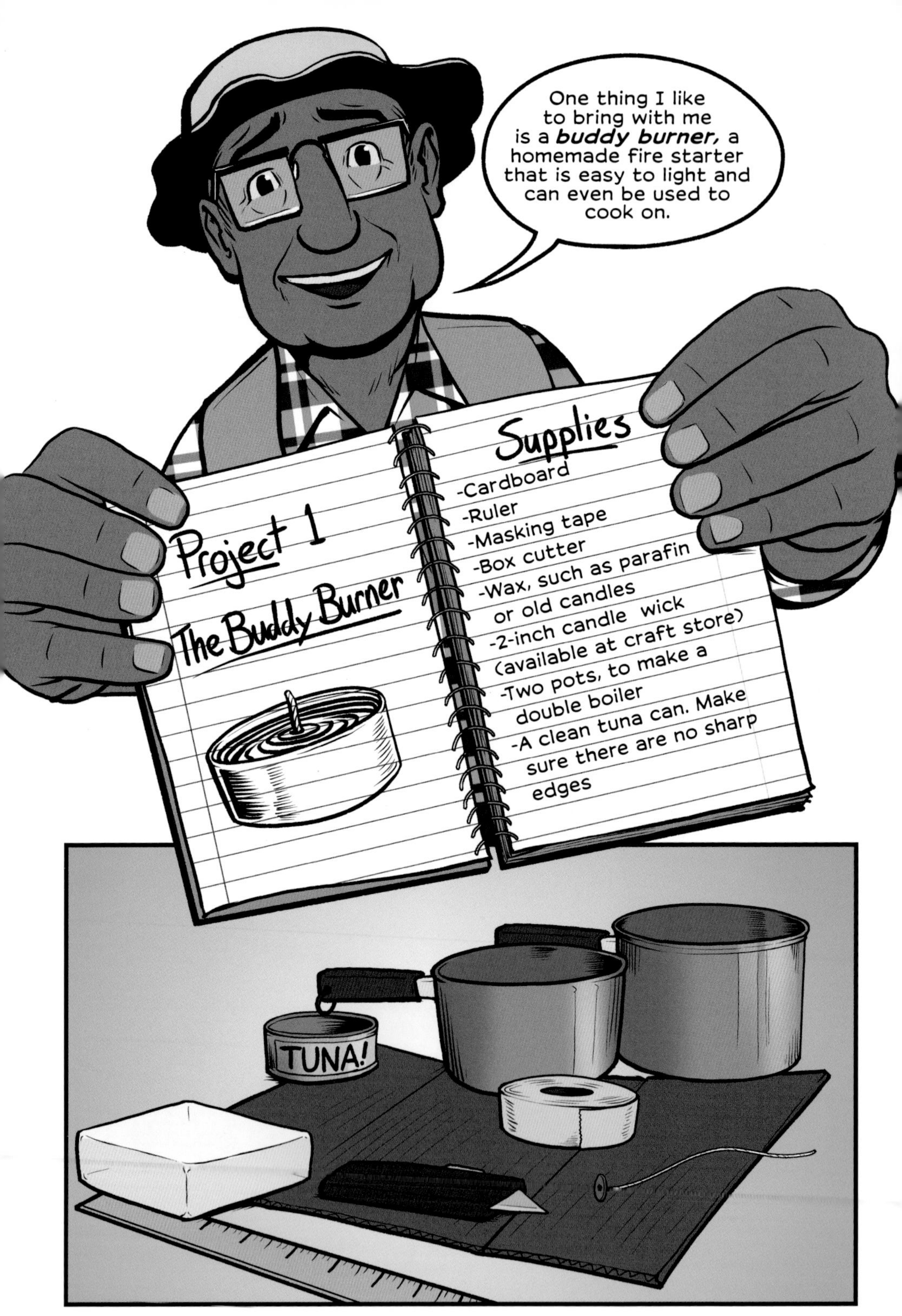
One thing I like to bring with me is a ***buddy burner,*** a homemade fire starter that is easy to light and can even be used to cook on.
Project 1
The Buddy Burner
Supplies
-Cardboard
-Ruler
-Masking tape
-Box cutter
-Wax, such as parafin or old candles
-2-inch candle wick (available at craft store)
-Two pots, to make a double boiler
-A clean tuna can. Make sure there are no sharp edges
TUNA!

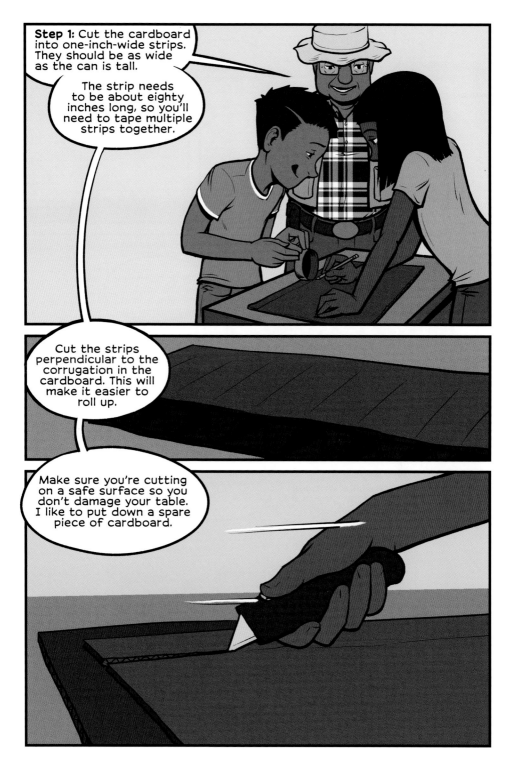

**Step 1:** Cut the cardboard into one-inch-wide strips. They should be as wide as the can is tall.

The strip needs to be about eighty inches long, so you'll need to tape multiple strips together.

Cut the strips perpendicular to the corrugation in the cardboard. This will make it easier to roll up.

Make sure you're cutting on a safe surface so you don't damage your table. I like to put down a spare piece of cardboard.

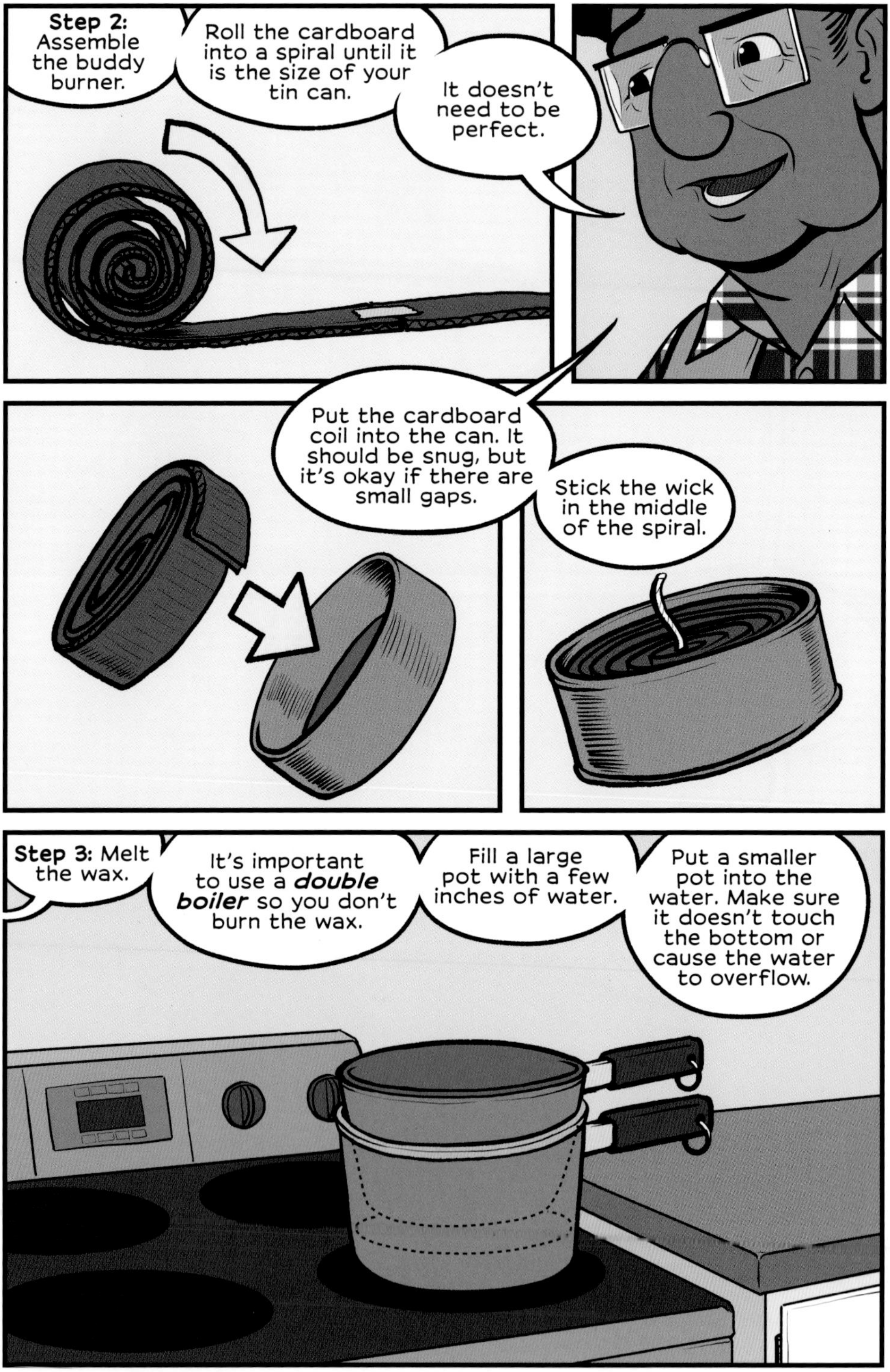
Step 2: Assemble the buddy burner.
Roll the cardboard into a spiral until it is the size of your tin can.
It doesn't need to be perfect.
Put the cardboard coil into the can. It should be snug, but it's okay if there are small gaps.
Stick the wick in the middle of the spiral.
Step 3: Melt the wax.
It's important to use a *double boiler* so you don't burn the wax.
Fill a large pot with a few inches of water.
Put a smaller pot into the water. Make sure it doesn't touch the bottom or cause the water to overflow.

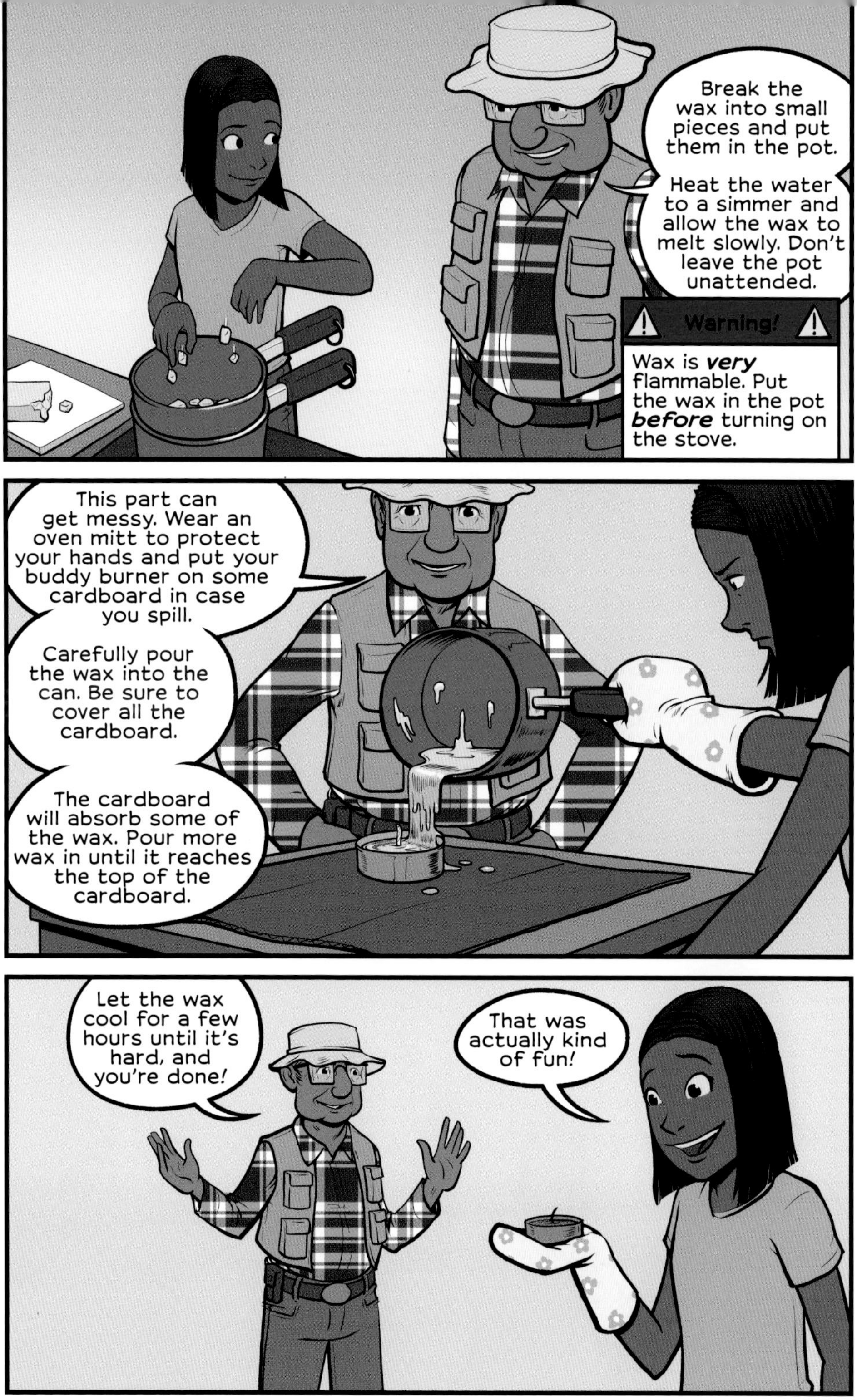
Break the wax into small pieces and put them in the pot.
Heat the water to a simmer and allow the wax to melt slowly. Don't leave the pot unattended.
Warning!
Wax is ***very*** flammable. Put the wax in the pot ***before*** turning on the stove.
This part can get messy. Wear an oven mitt to protect your hands and put your buddy burner on some cardboard in case you spill.
Carefully pour the wax into the can. Be sure to cover all the cardboard.
The cardboard will absorb some of the wax. Pour more wax in until it reaches the top of the cardboard.
Let the wax cool for a few hours until it's hard, and you're done!
That was actually kind of fun!

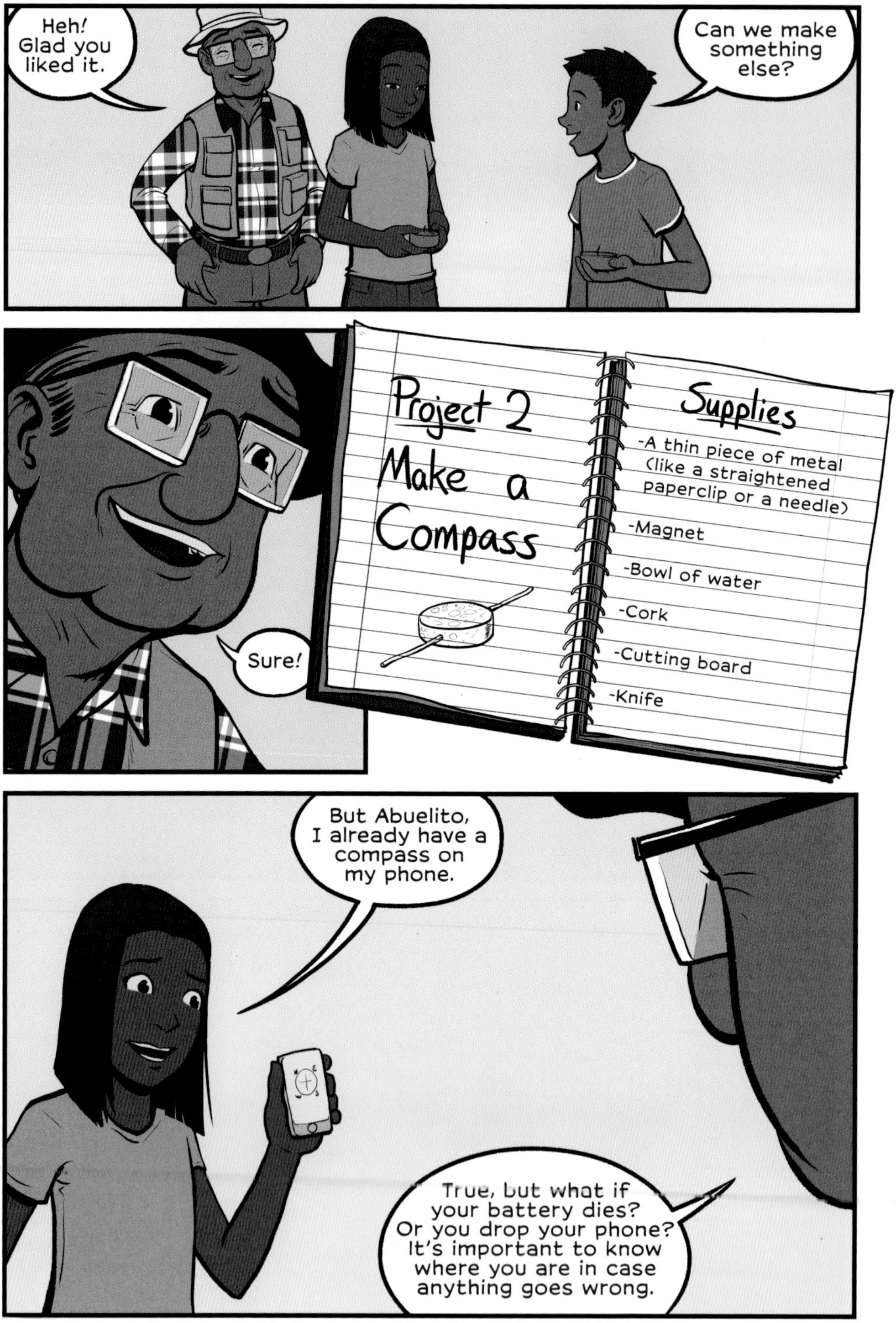
Heh! Glad you liked it.
Can we make something else?
Sure!
Project 2
Make a Compass
Supplies
-A thin piece of metal (like a straightened paperclip or a needle)
-Magnet
-Bowl of water
-Cork
-Cutting board
-Knife
But Abuelito, I already have a compass on my phone.
True, but what if your battery dies? Or you drop your phone? It's important to know where you are in case anything goes wrong.

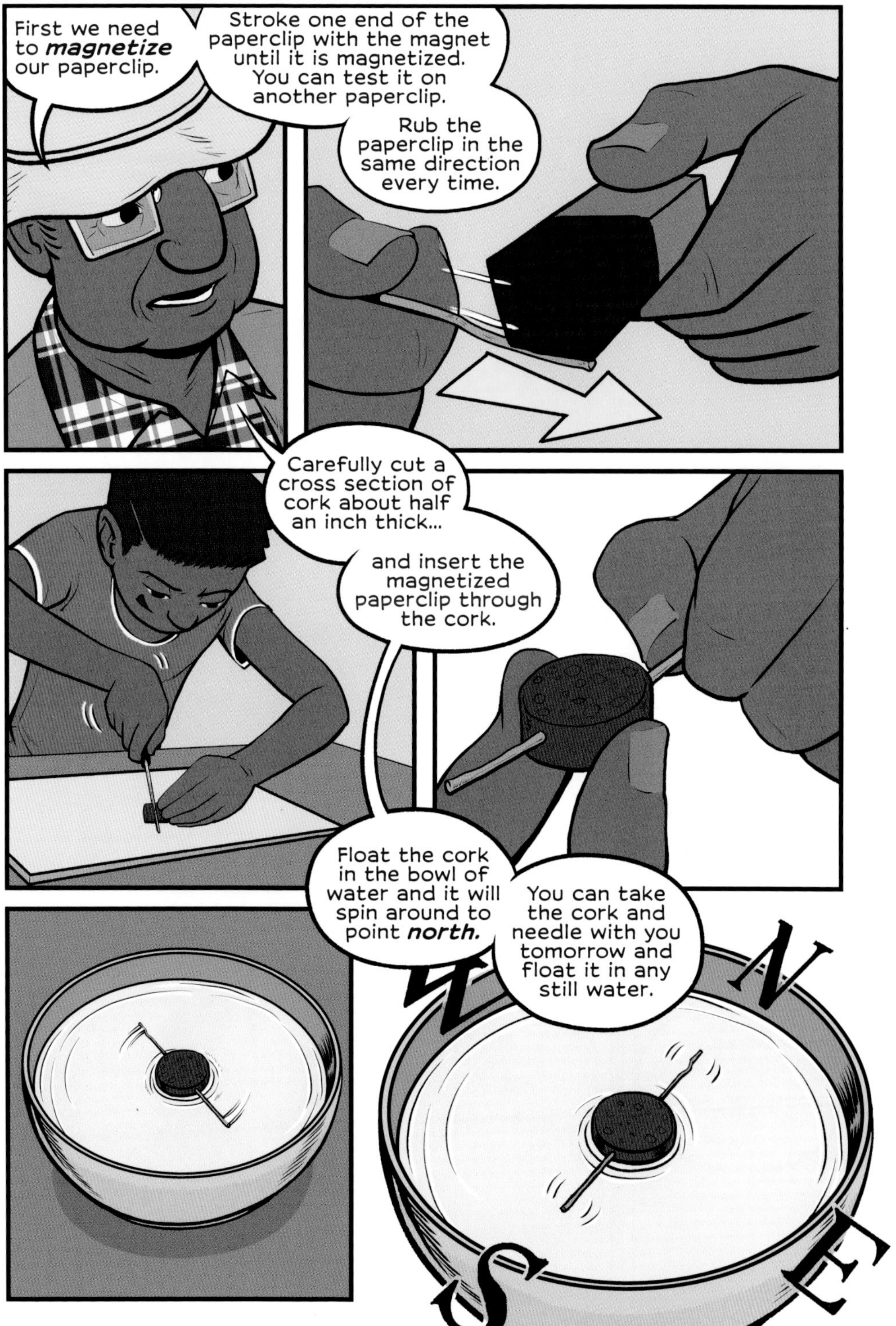

First we need to *magnetize* our paperclip.
Stroke one end of the paperclip with the magnet until it is magnetized. You can test it on another paperclip.
Rub the paperclip in the same direction every time.
Carefully cut a cross section of cork about half an inch thick...
and insert the magnetized paperclip through the cork.
Float the cork in the bowl of water and it will spin around to point *north.*
You can take the cork and needle with you tomorrow and float it in any still water.
N
W
S
E

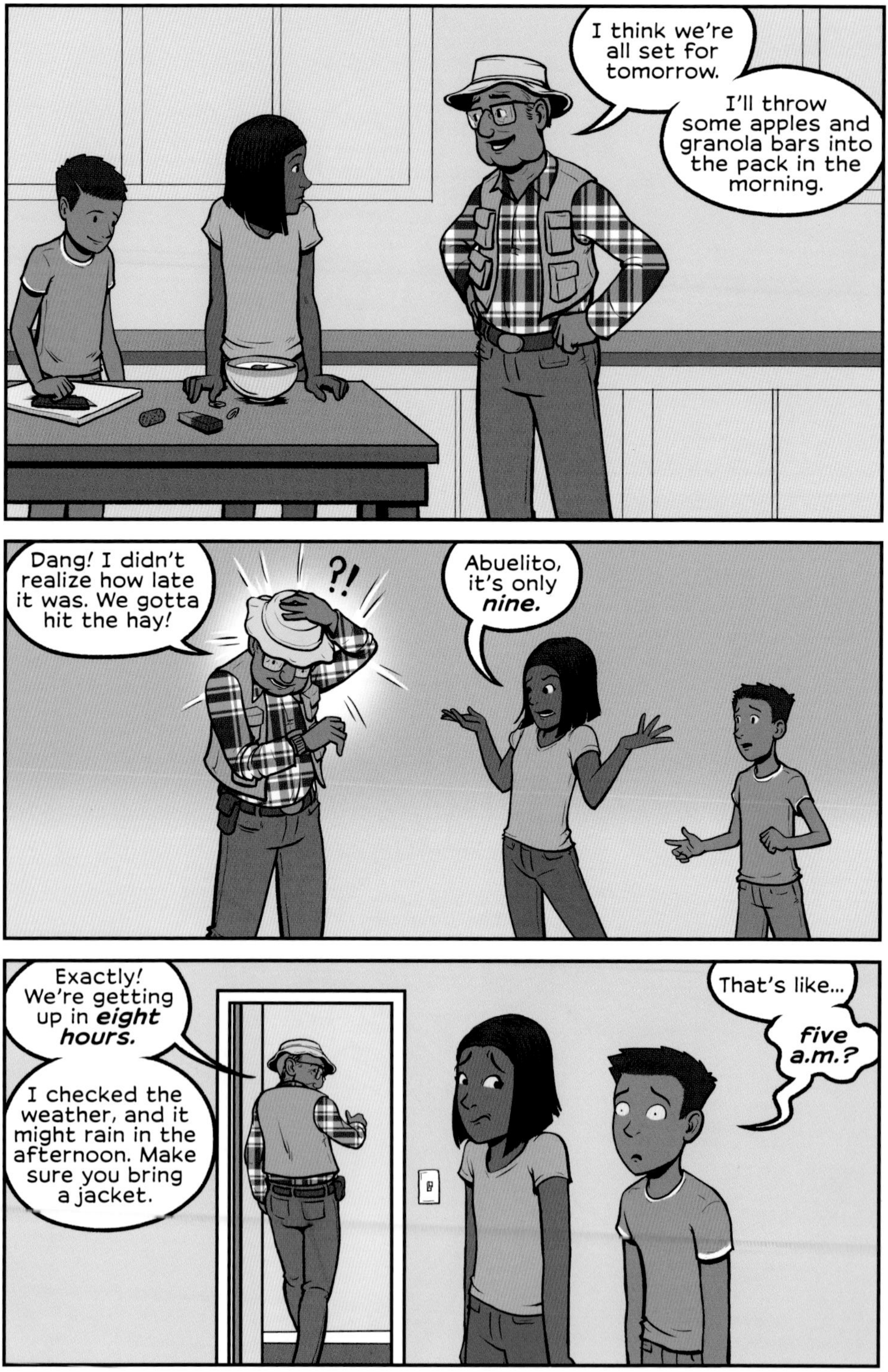
I think we're all set for tomorrow.
I'll throw some apples and granola bars into the pack in the morning.
Dang! I didn't realize how late it was. We gotta hit the hay!
?!
Abuelito, it's only *nine.*
Exactly! We're getting up in *eight hours.*
I checked the weather, and it might rain in the afternoon. Make sure you bring a jacket.
That's like...
*five a.m.?*

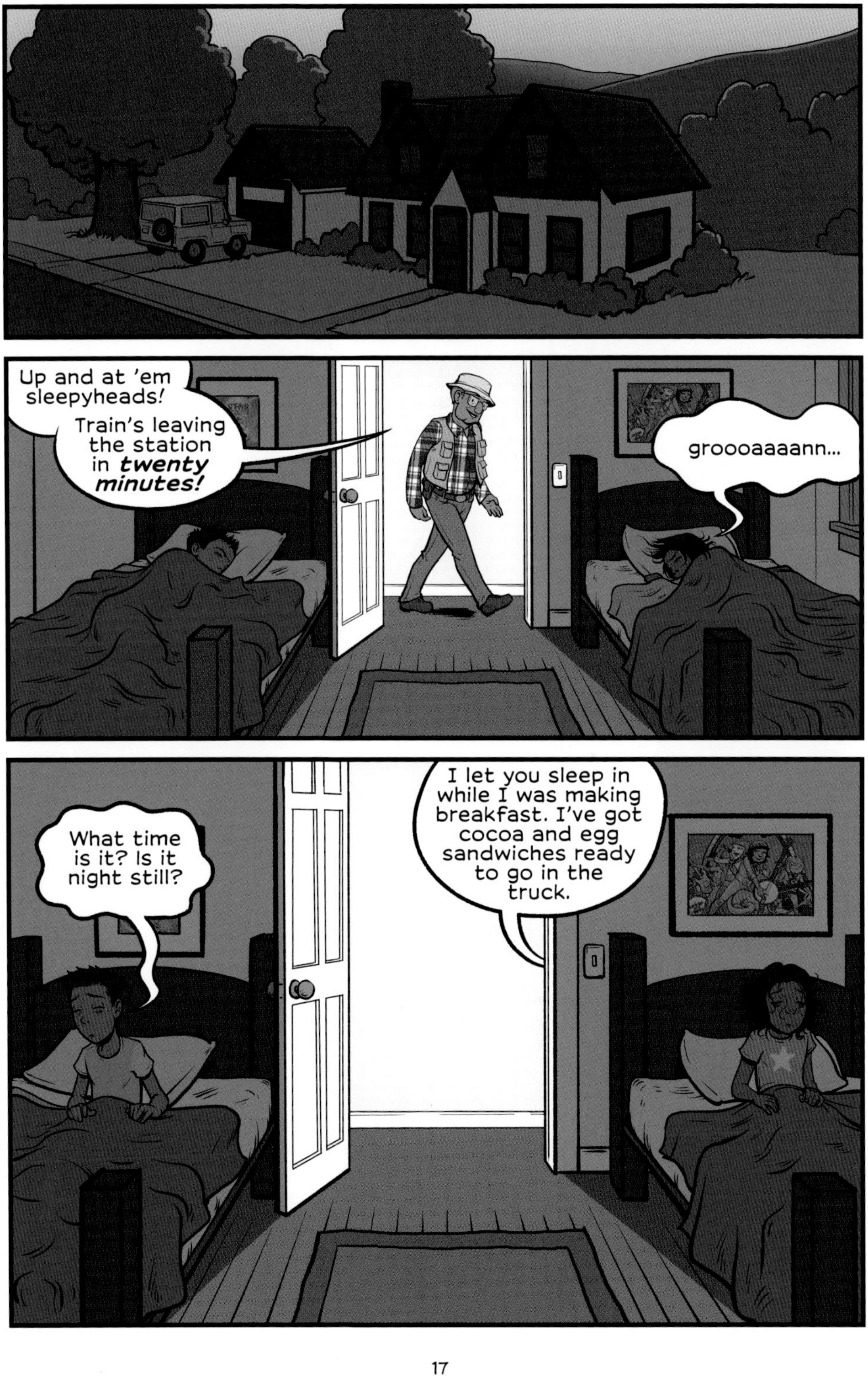
Up and at 'em sleepyheads!
Train's leaving the station in ***twenty minutes!***
groooaaaann...
What time is it? Is it night still?
I let you sleep in while I was making breakfast. I've got cocoa and egg sandwiches ready to go in the truck.

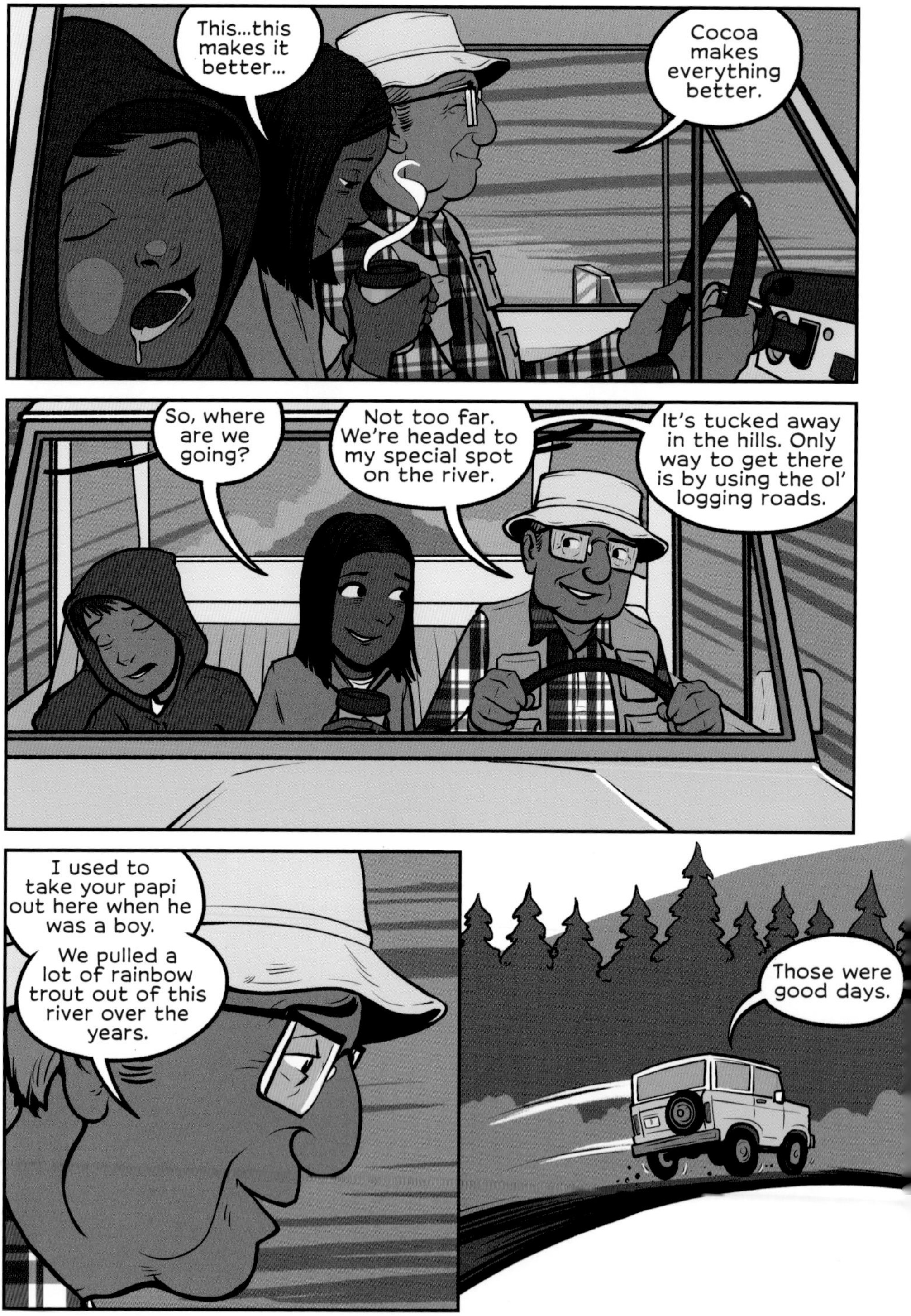
This...this makes it better...
Cocoa makes everything better.
So, where are we going?
Not too far. We're headed to my special spot on the river.
It's tucked away in the hills. Only way to get there is by using the ol' logging roads.
I used to take your papi out here when he was a boy.
We pulled a lot of rainbow trout out of this river over the years.
Those were good days.

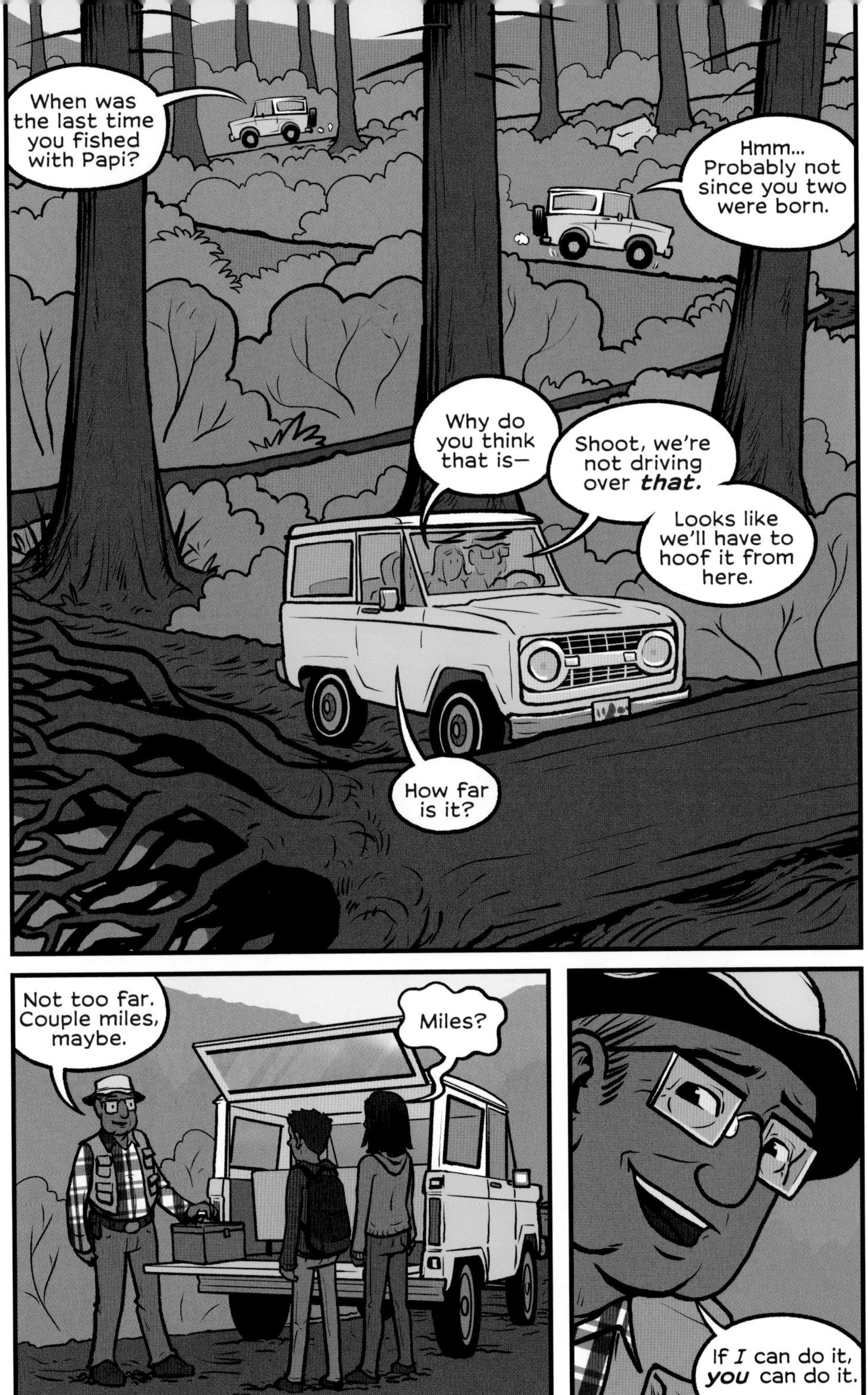
When was the last time you fished with Papi?
Hmm... Probably not since you two were born.
Why do you think that is—
Shoot, we're not driving over *that.*
Looks like we'll have to hoof it from here.
How far is it?
Not too far. Couple miles, maybe.
Miles?
If *I* can do it, *you* can do it.

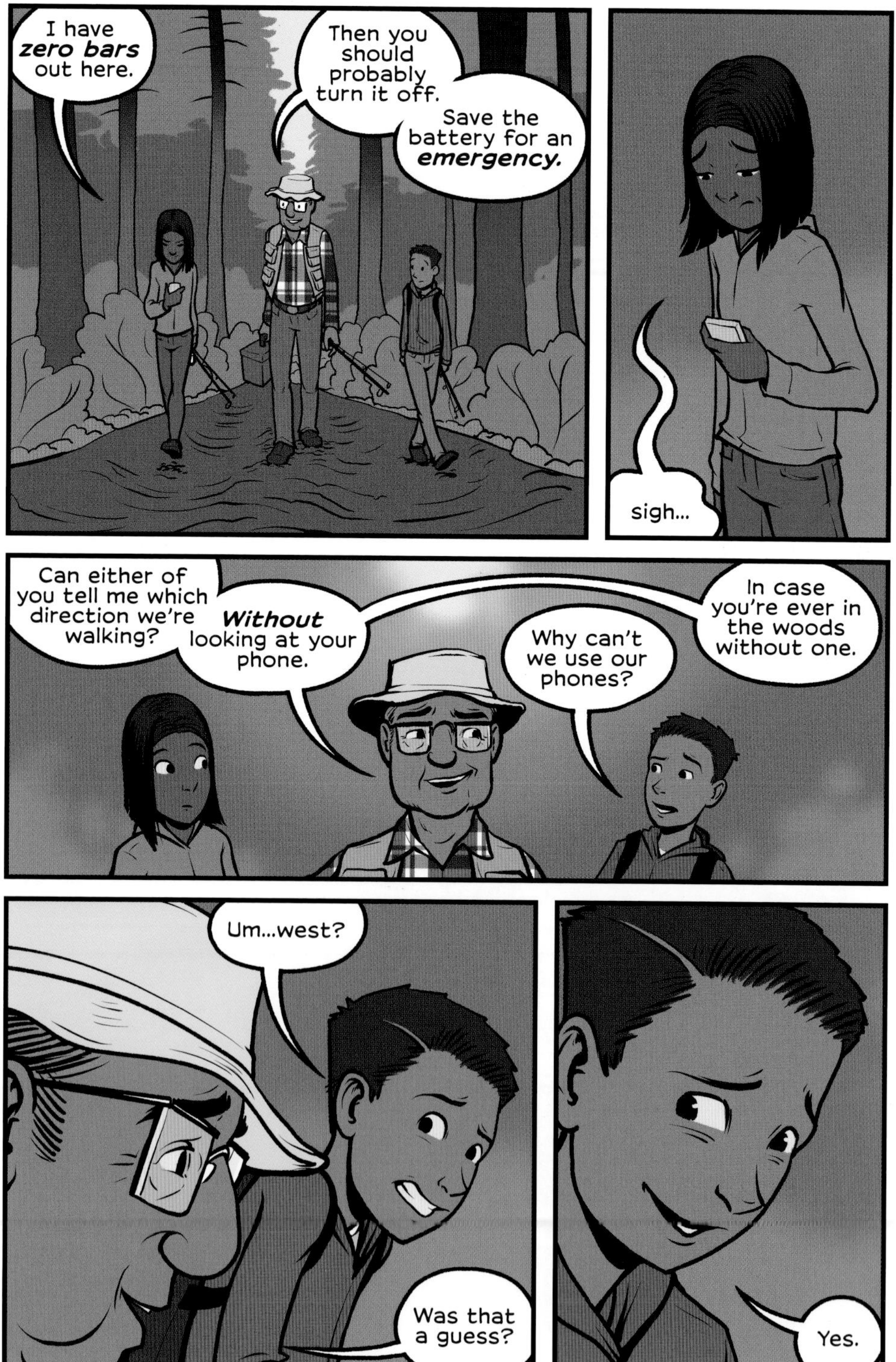
I have *zero bars* out here.
Then you should probably turn it off.
Save the battery for an *emergency.*
sigh...
Can either of you tell me which direction we're walking?
*Without* looking at your phone.
Why can't we use our phones?
In case you're ever in the woods without one.
Um...west?
Was that a guess?
Yes.

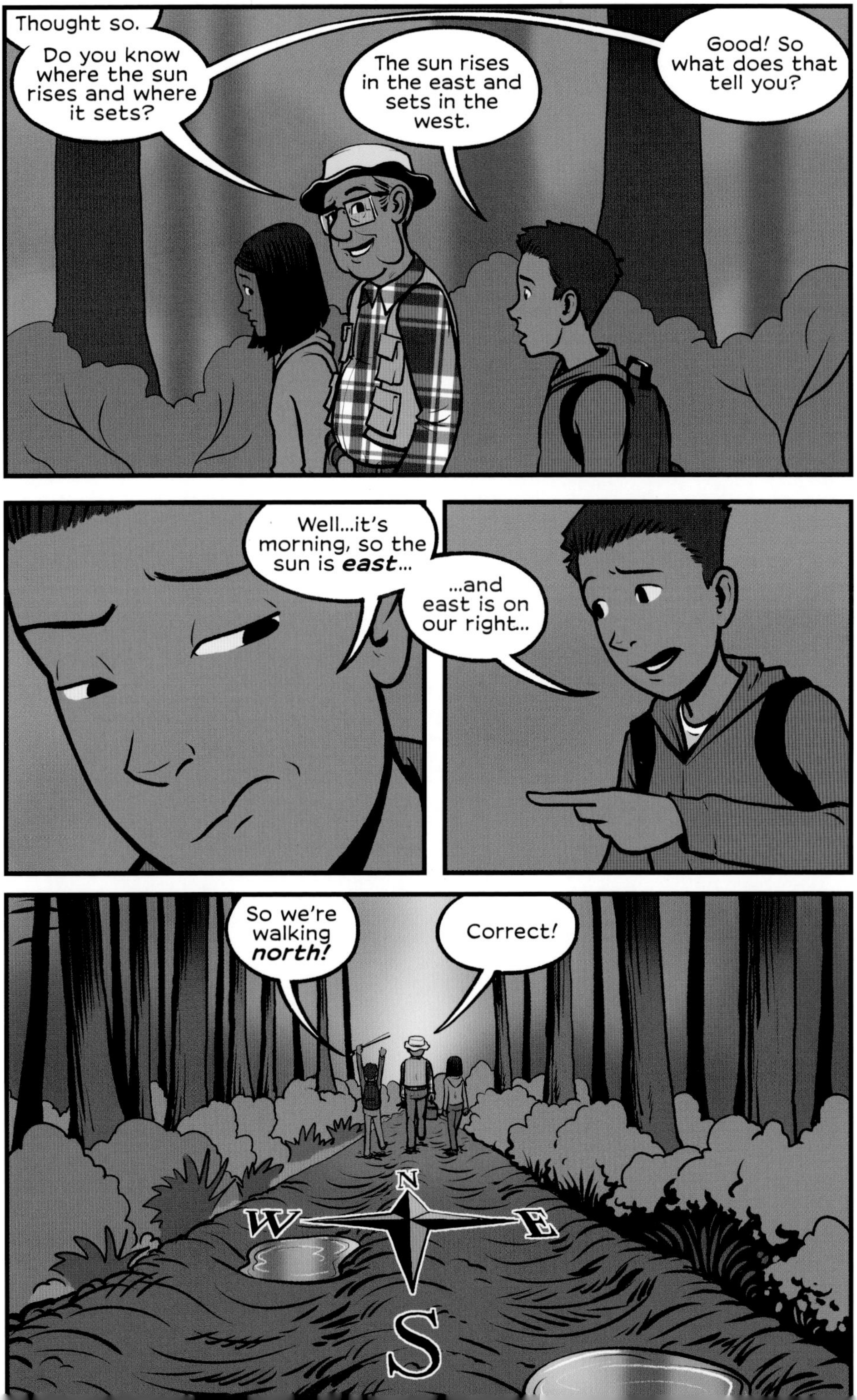
Thought so.
Do you know where the sun rises and where it sets?
The sun rises in the east and sets in the west.
Good! So what does that tell you?
Well...it's morning, so the sun is ***east***...
...and east is on our right...
So we're walking ***north!***
Correct!
N
W
E
S

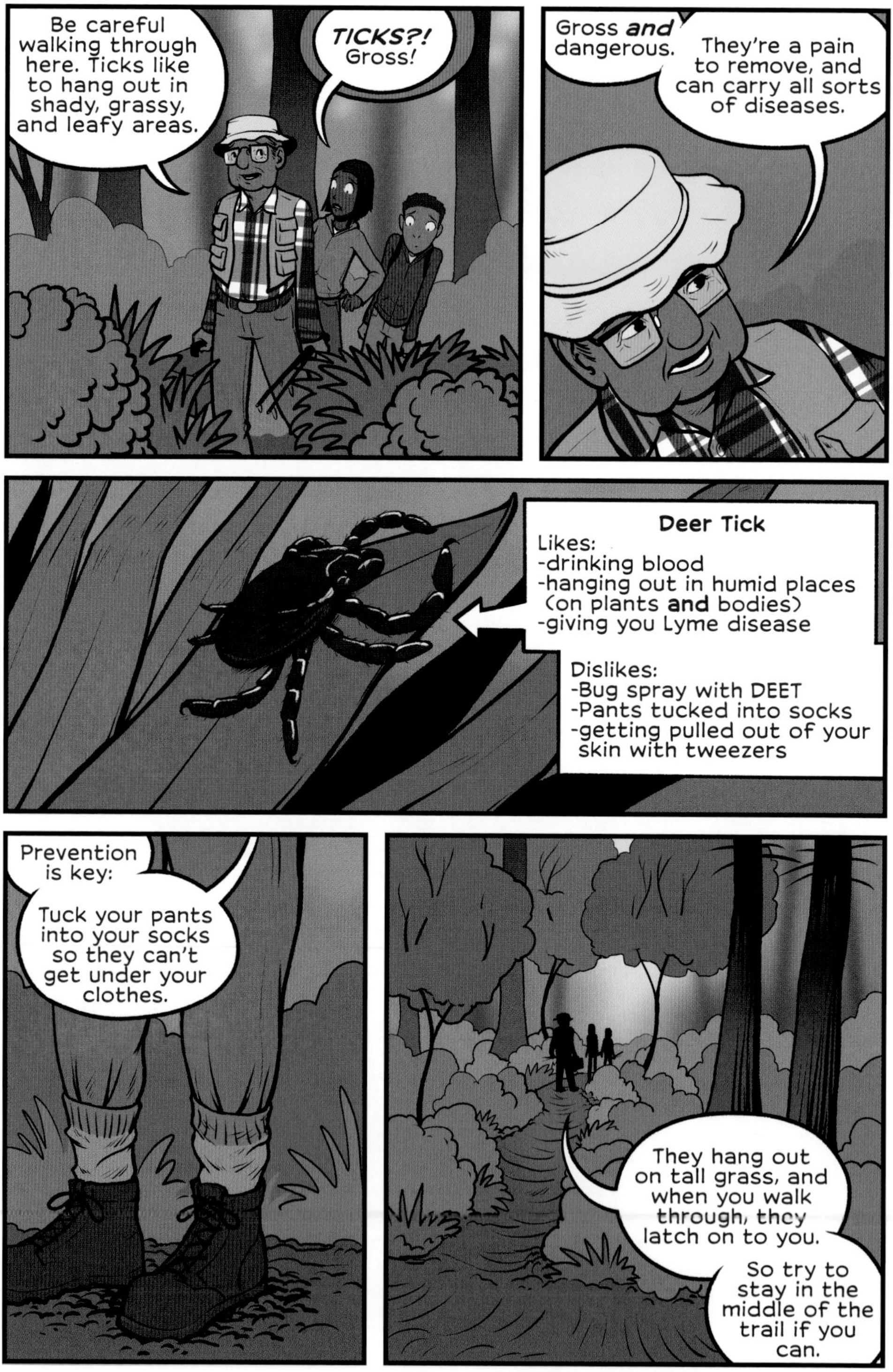
Be careful walking through here. Ticks like to hang out in shady, grassy, and leafy areas.
TICKS?! Gross!
Gross and dangerous.
They're a pain to remove, and can carry all sorts of diseases.
Deer Tick
Likes:
-drinking blood
-hanging out in humid places (on plants and bodies)
-giving you Lyme disease
Dislikes:
-Bug spray with DEET
-Pants tucked into socks
-getting pulled out of your skin with tweezers
Prevention is key:
Tuck your pants into your socks so they can't get under your clothes.
They hang out on tall grass, and when you walk through, they latch on to you.
So try to stay in the middle of the trail if you can.

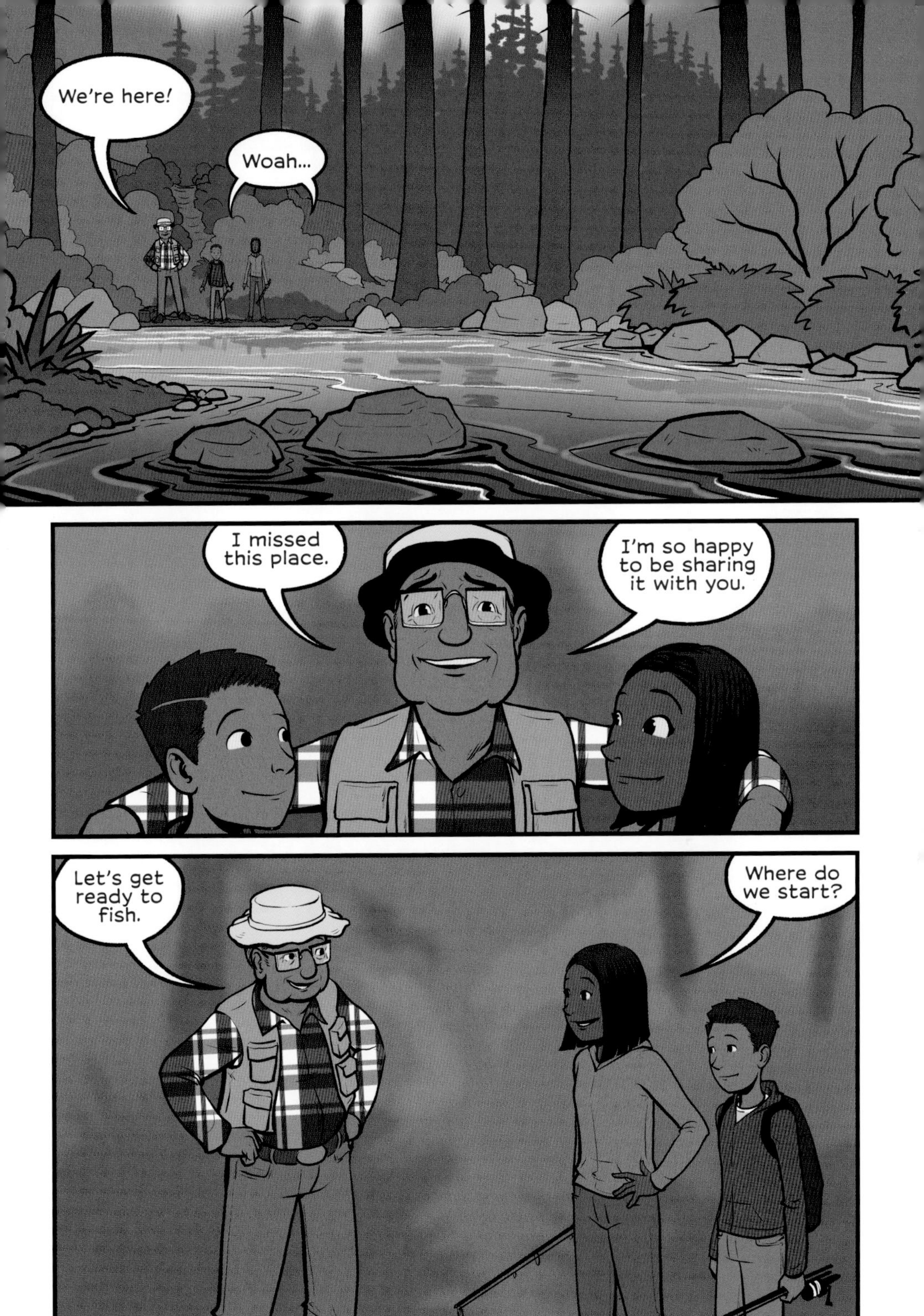
We're here!
Woah...
I missed this place.
I'm so happy to be sharing it with you.
Let's get ready to fish.
Where do we start?

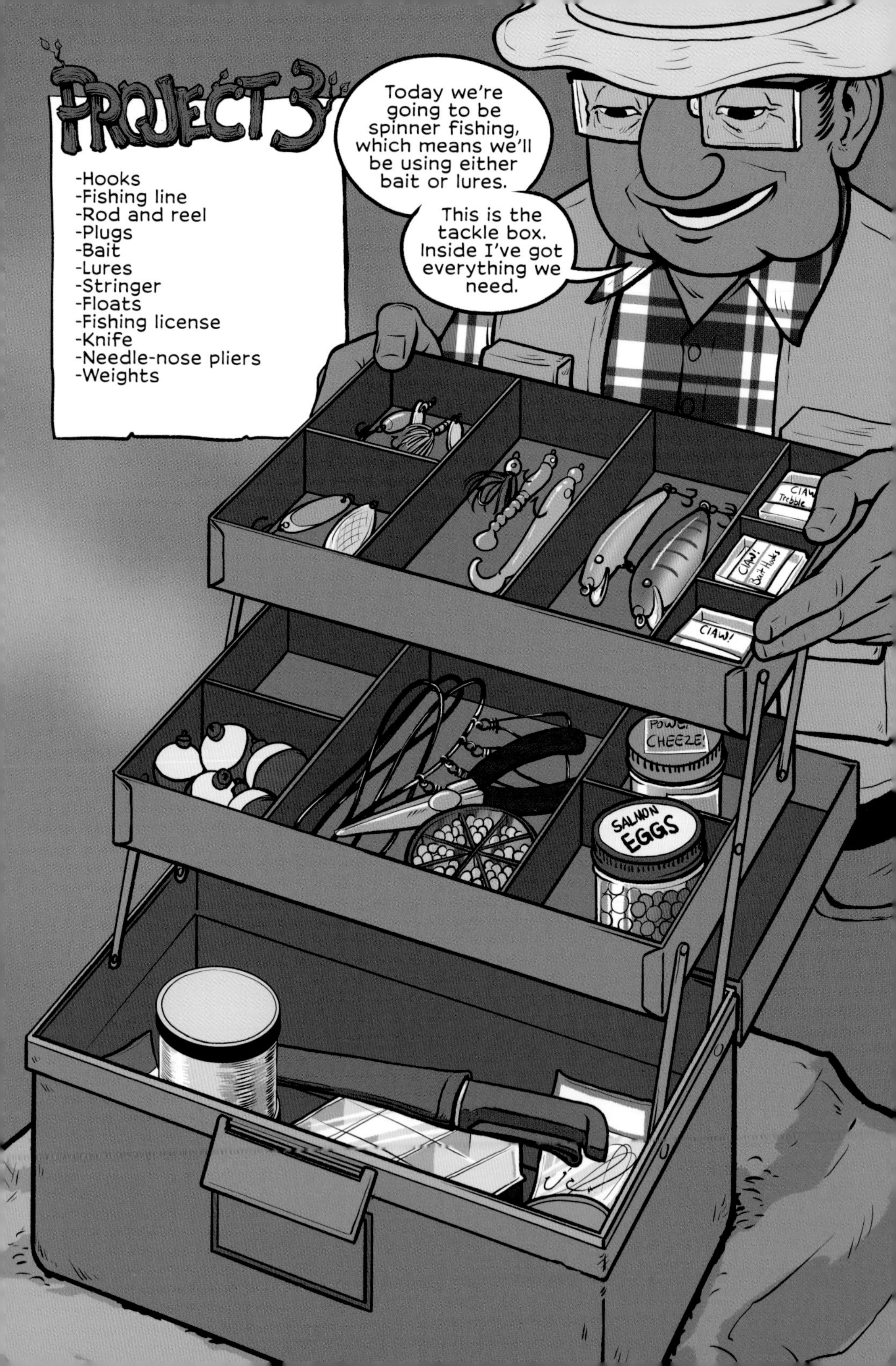
PROJECT 3
-Hooks
-Fishing line
-Rod and reel
-Plugs
-Bait
-Lures
-Stringer
-Floats
-Fishing license
-Knife
-Needle-nose pliers
-Weights
Today we're going to be spinner fishing, which means we'll be using either bait or lures.
This is the tackle box. Inside I've got everything we need.
CLAW Trebble
CLAW! Bait Hooks
CLAW!
CHEEZE!
SALMON EGGS

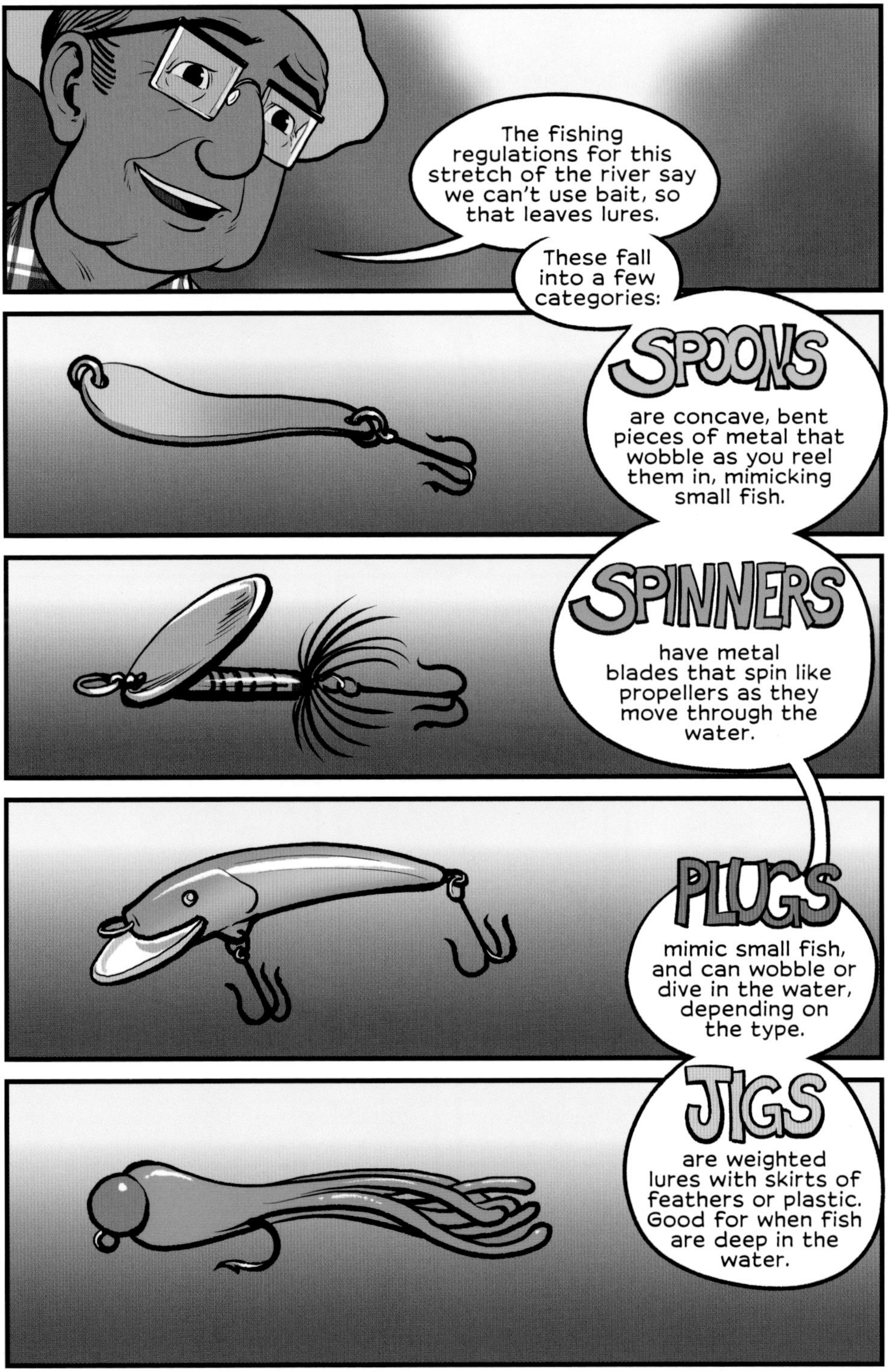
The fishing regulations for this stretch of the river say we can't use bait, so that leaves lures.
These fall into a few categories:
SPOONS
are concave, bent pieces of metal that wobble as you reel them in, mimicking small fish.
SPINNERS
have metal blades that spin like propellers as they move through the water.
PLUGS
mimic small fish, and can wobble or dive in the water, depending on the type.
JIGS
are weighted lures with skirts of feathers or plastic. Good for when fish are deep in the water.

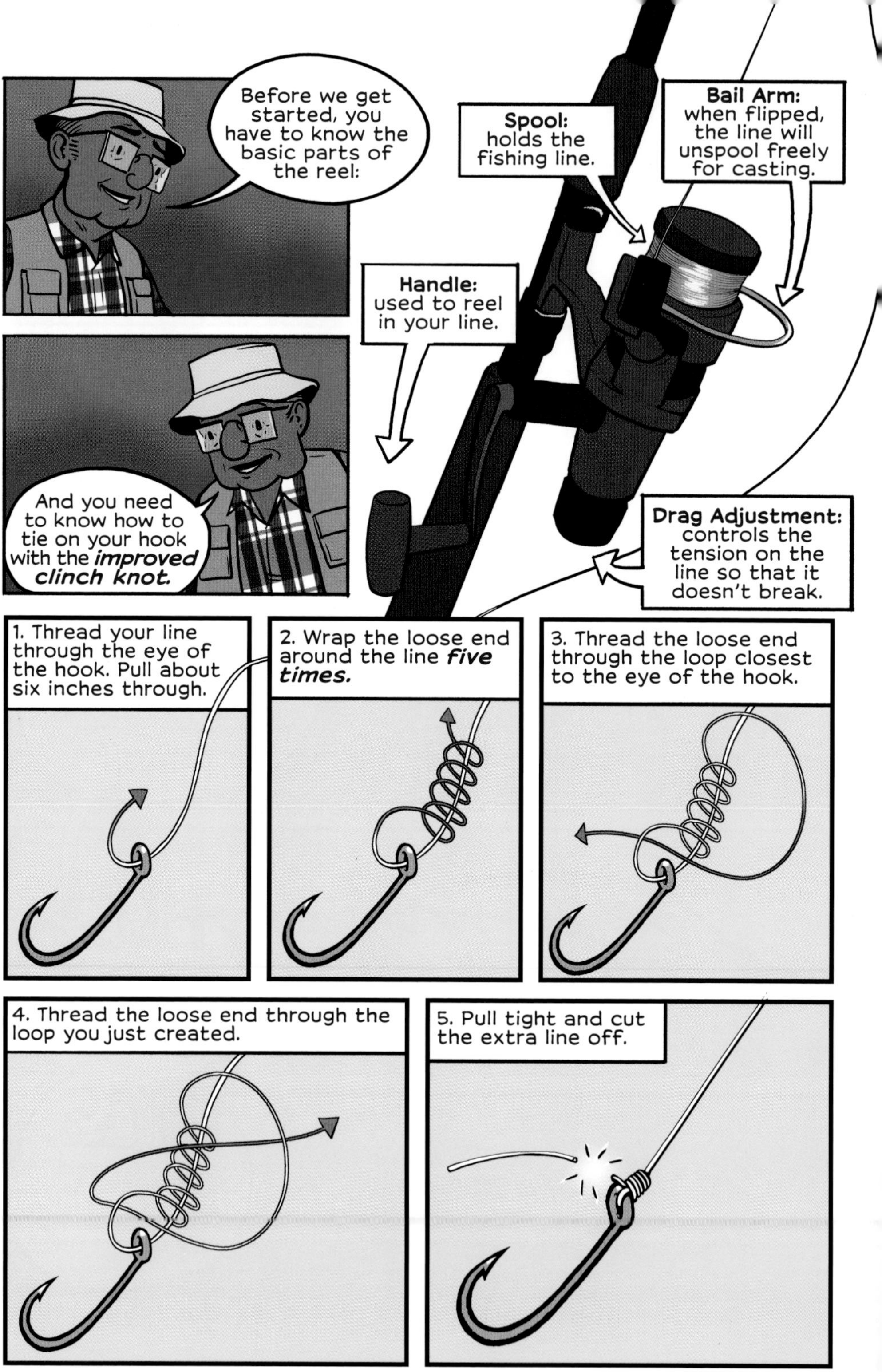
Before we get started, you have to know the basic parts of the reel:
And you need to know how to tie on your hook with the ***improved clinch knot.***
**Spool:** holds the fishing line.
**Bail Arm:** when flipped, the line will unspool freely for casting.
**Handle:** used to reel in your line.
**Drag Adjustment:** controls the tension on the line so that it doesn't break.
1. Thread your line through the eye of the hook. Pull about six inches through.
2. Wrap the loose end around the line ***five times.***
3. Thread the loose end through the loop closest to the eye of the hook.
4. Thread the loose end through the loop you just created.
5. Pull tight and cut the extra line off.

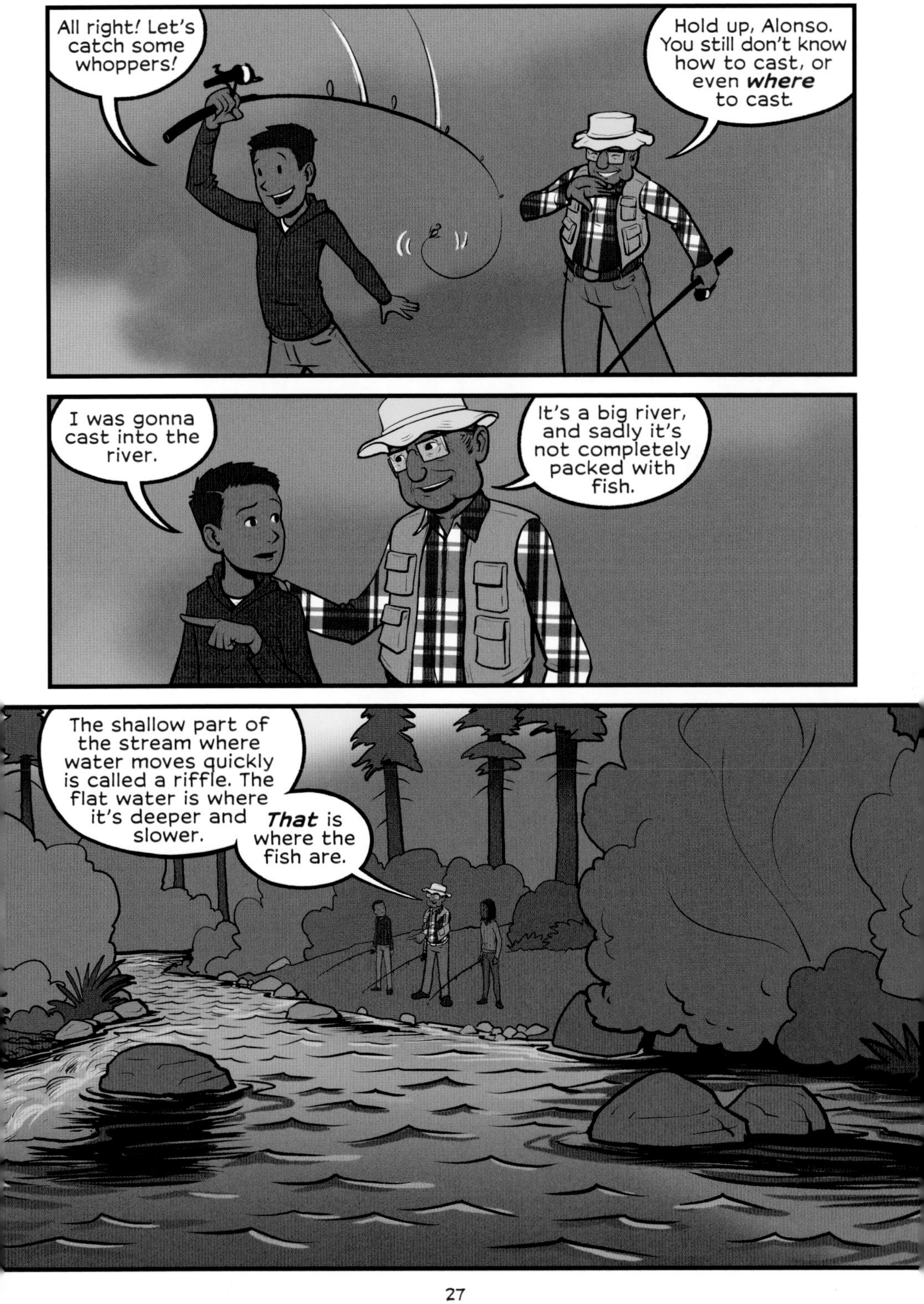
All right! Let's catch some whoppers!
Hold up, Alonso. You still don't know how to cast, or even ***where*** to cast.
I was gonna cast into the river.
It's a big river, and sadly it's not completely packed with fish.
The shallow part of the stream where water moves quickly is called a riffle. The flat water is where it's deeper and slower.
***That*** is where the fish are.

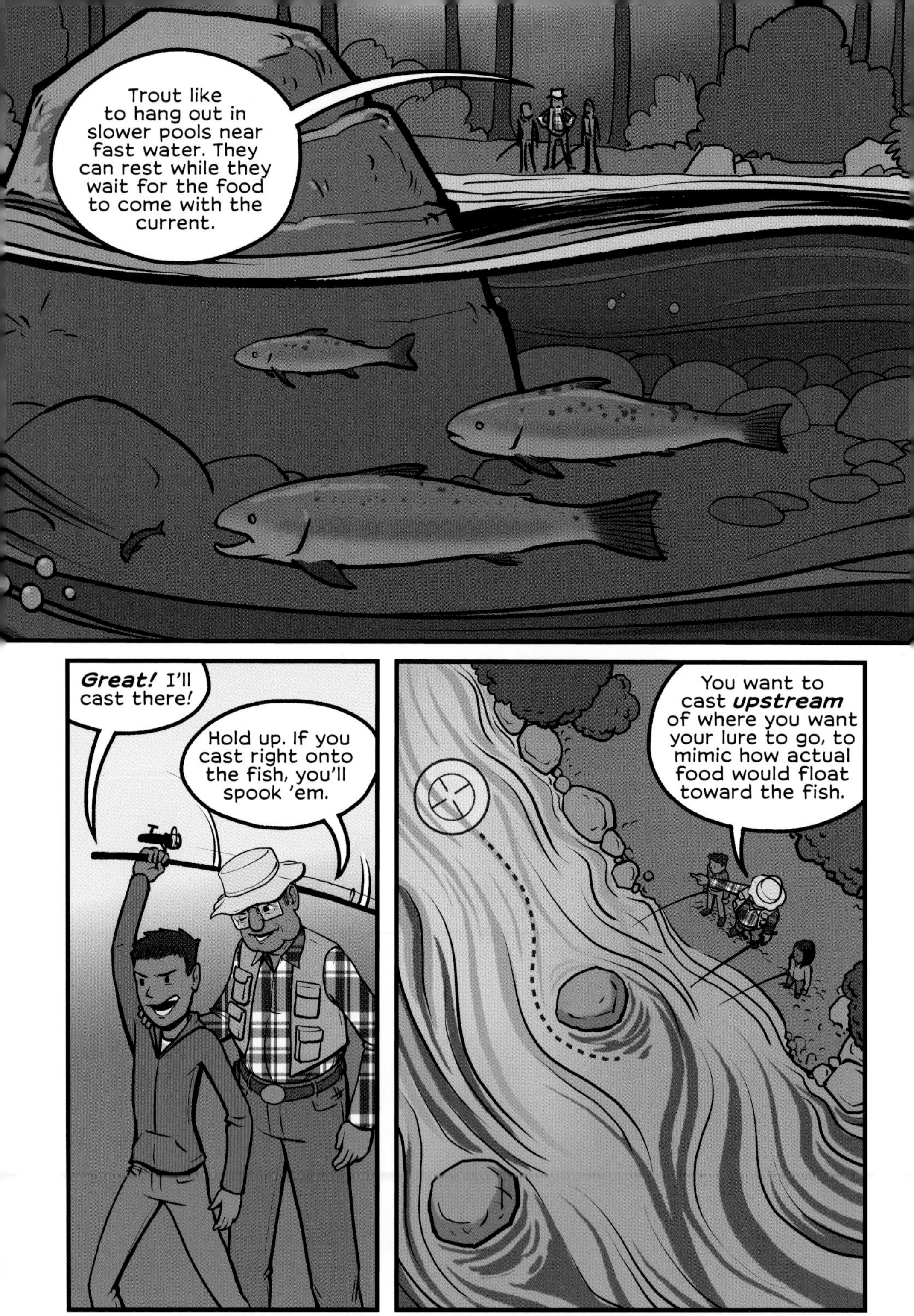
Trout like to hang out in slower pools near fast water. They can rest while they wait for the food to come with the current.
*Great!* I'll cast there!
Hold up. If you cast right onto the fish, you'll spook 'em.
You want to cast ***upstream*** of where you want your lure to go, to mimic how actual food would float toward the fish.

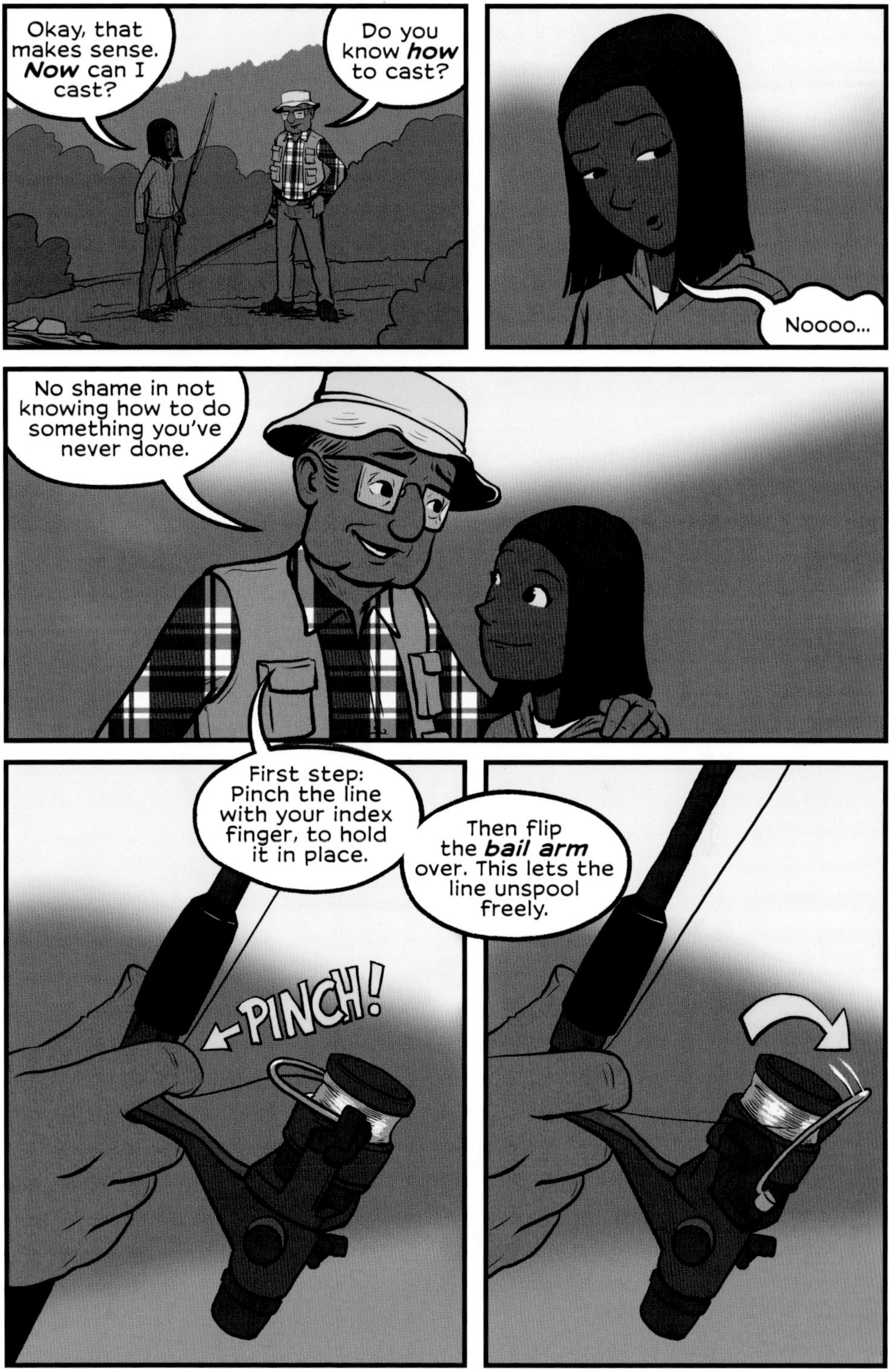

Okay, that makes sense. *Now* can I cast?
Do you know *how* to cast?
Noooo...
No shame in not knowing how to do something you've never done.
First step: Pinch the line with your index finger, to hold it in place.
PINCH!
Then flip the *bail arm* over. This lets the line unspool freely.

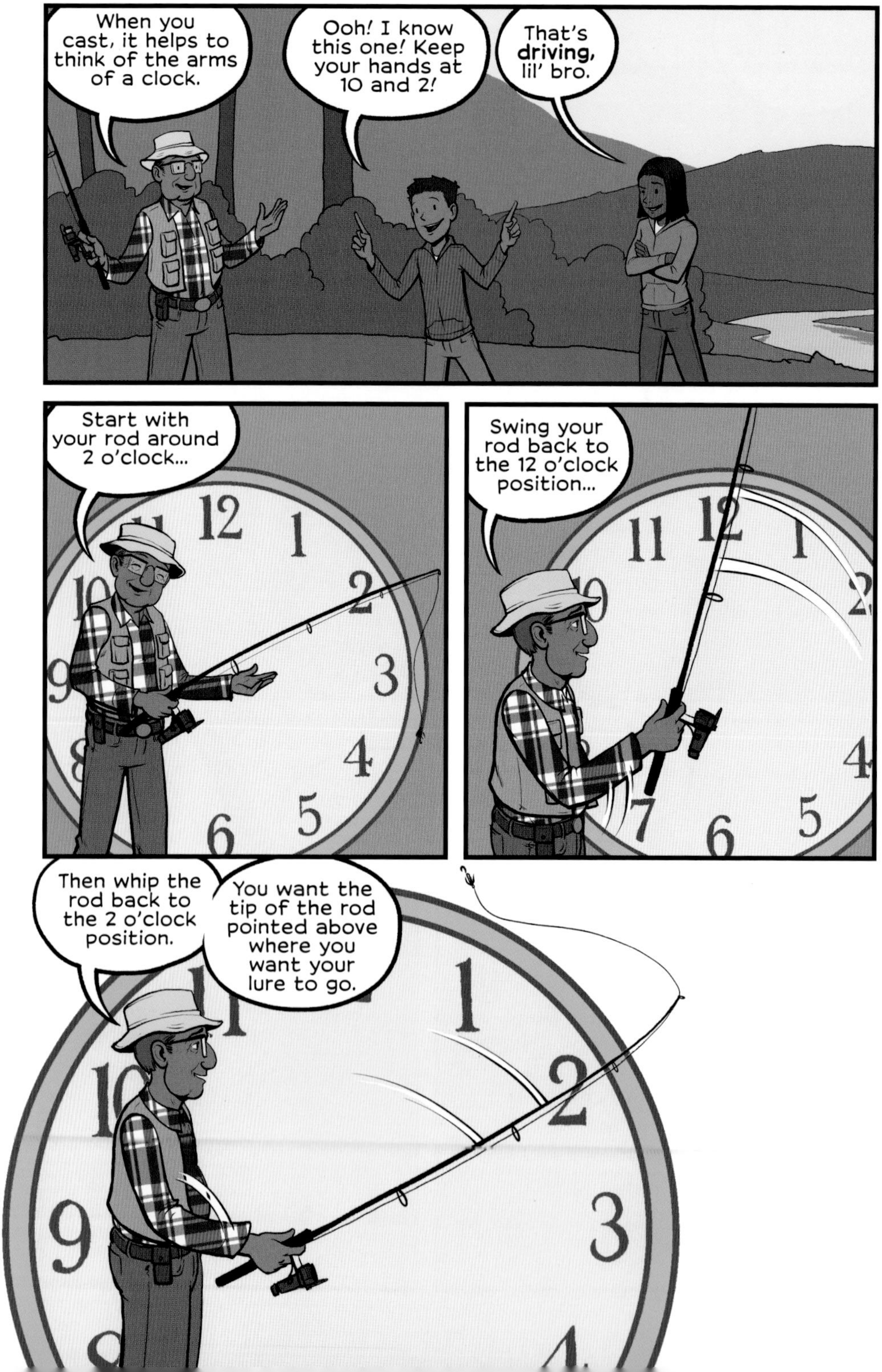
When you cast, it helps to think of the arms of a clock.
Ooh! I know this one! Keep your hands at 10 and 2!
That's **driving,** lil' bro.
Start with your rod around 2 o'clock...
Swing your rod back to the 12 o'clock position...
Then whip the rod back to the 2 o'clock position.
You want the tip of the rod pointed above where you want your lure to go.

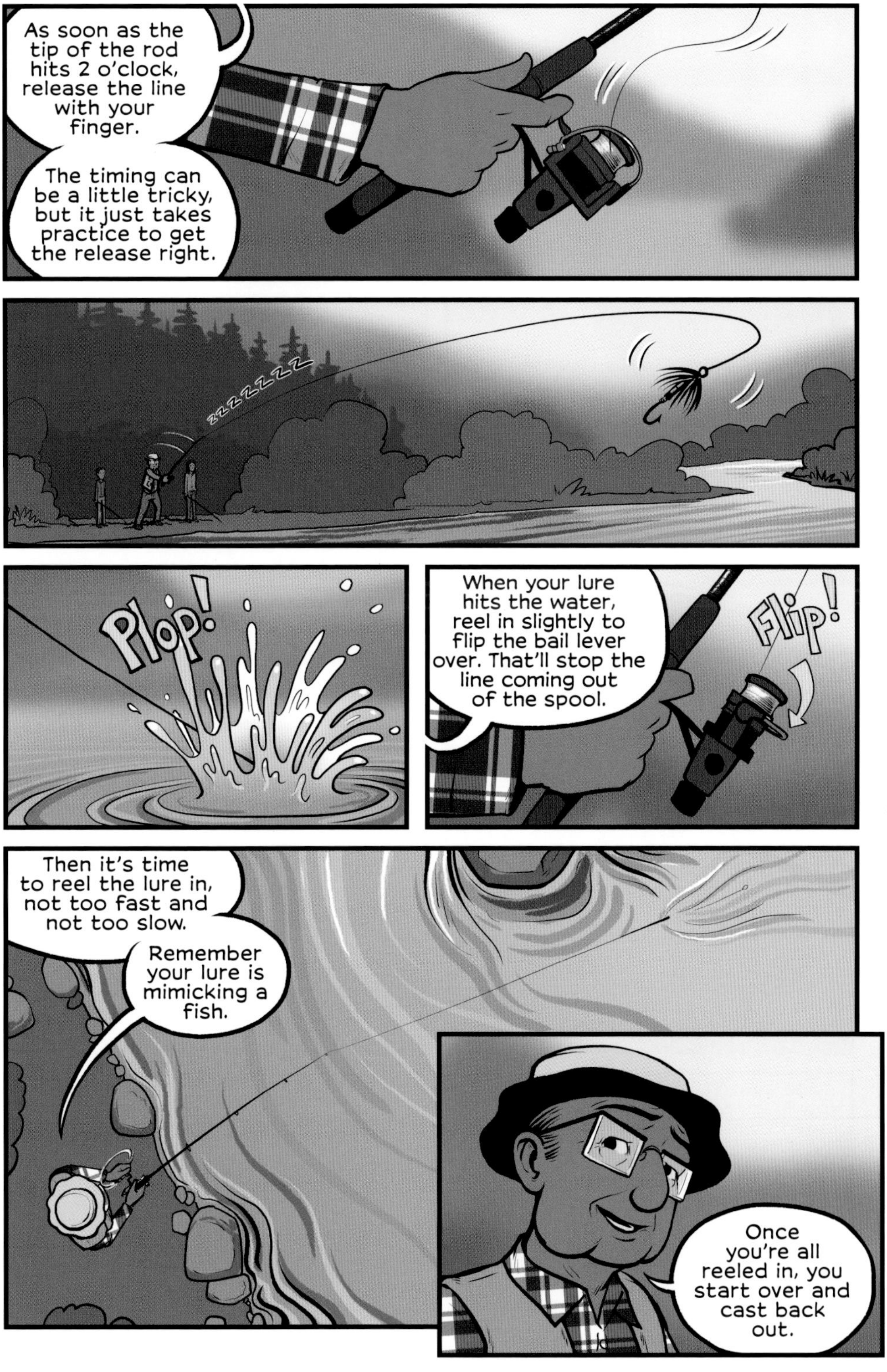
As soon as the tip of the rod hits 2 o'clock, release the line with your finger.
The timing can be a little tricky, but it just takes practice to get the release right.
ZZZZZZZ
Plop!
When your lure hits the water, reel in slightly to flip the bail lever over. That'll stop the line coming out of the spool.
Flip!
Then it's time to reel the lure in, not too fast and not too slow.
Remember your lure is mimicking a fish.
Once you're all reeled in, you start over and cast back out.

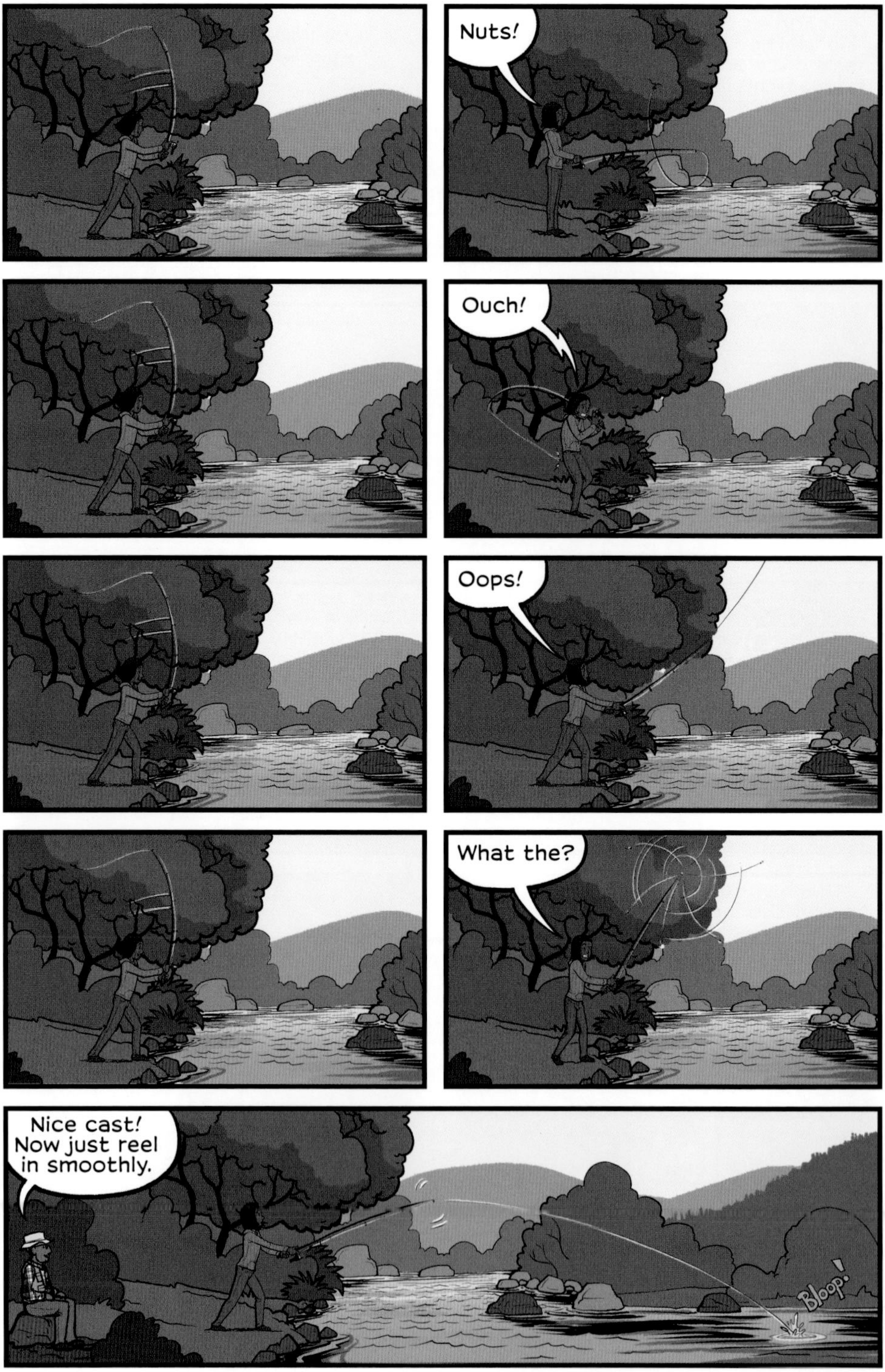
Nuts!
Ouch!
Oops!
What the?
Nice cast! Now just reel in smoothly.
Bloop!

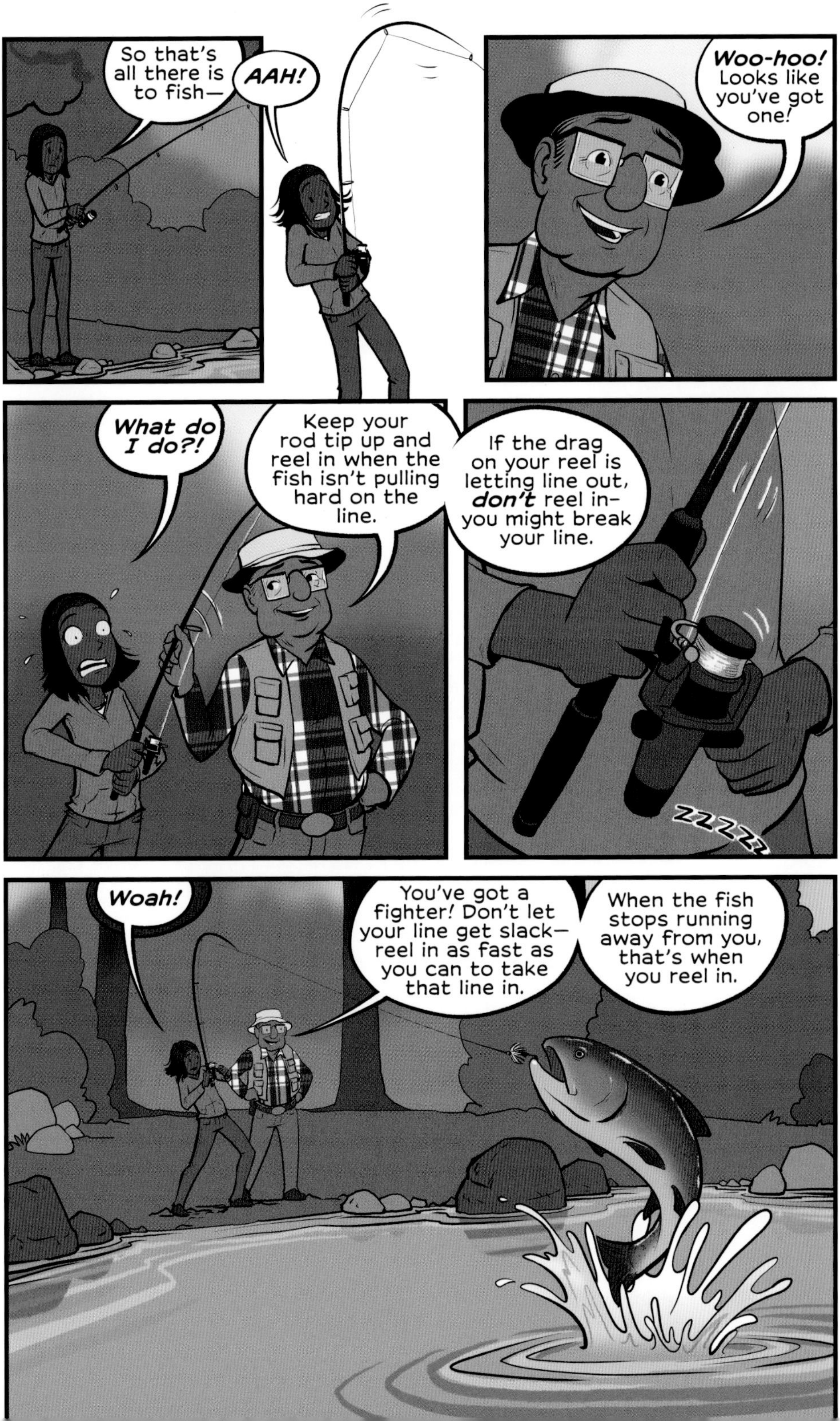
So that's all there is to fish—
AAH!
Woo-hoo! Looks like you've got one!
What do I do?!
Keep your rod tip up and reel in when the fish isn't pulling hard on the line.
If the drag on your reel is letting line out, don't reel in—you might break your line.
ZZZZZ
Woah!
You've got a fighter! Don't let your line get slack—reel in as fast as you can to take that line in.
When the fish stops running away from you, that's when you reel in.

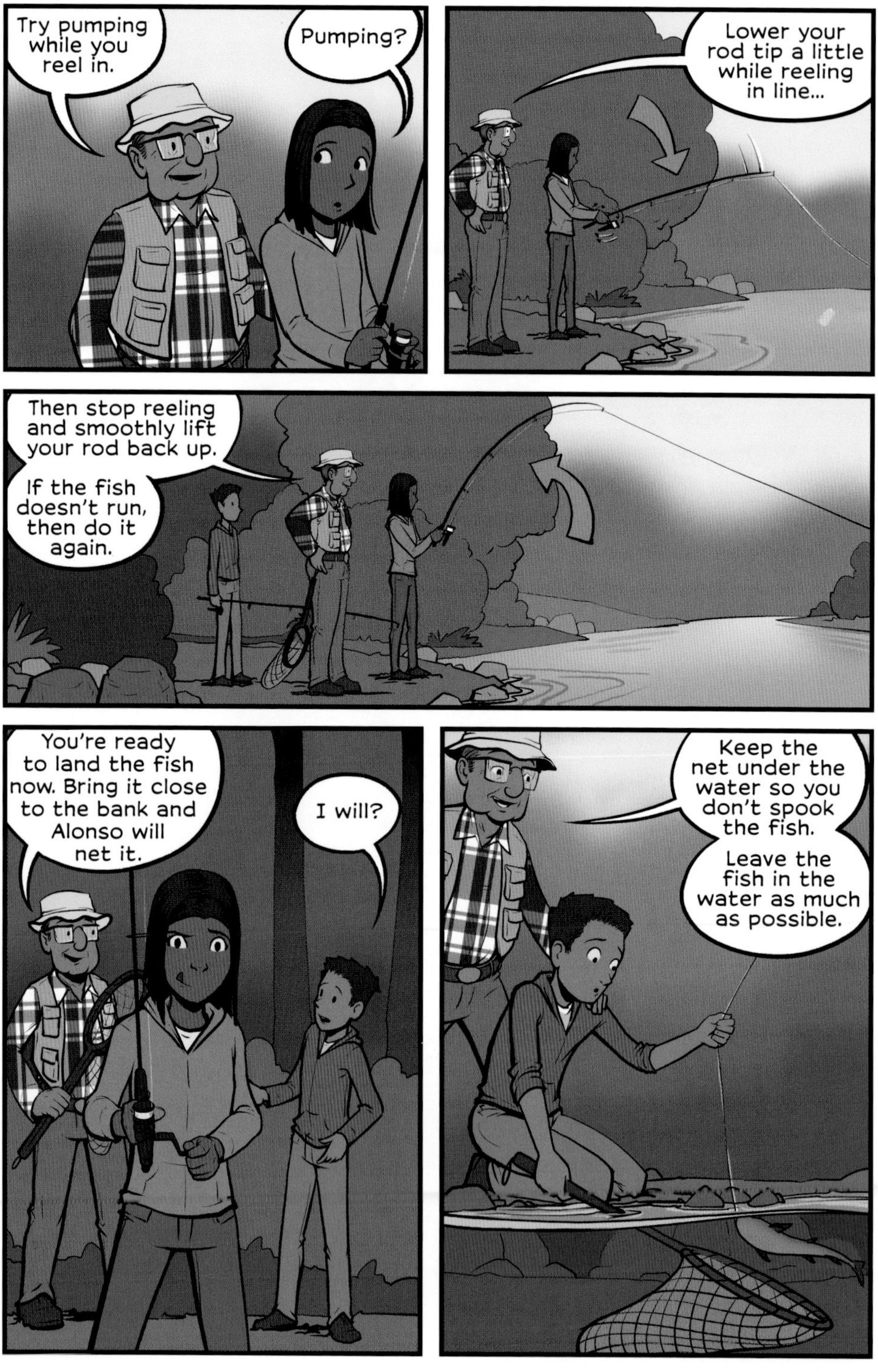
Try pumping while you reel in.
Pumping?
Lower your rod tip a little while reeling in line...
Then stop reeling and smoothly lift your rod back up.
If the fish doesn't run, then do it again.
You're ready to land the fish now. Bring it close to the bank and Alonso will net it.
I will?
Keep the net under the water so you don't spook the fish.
Leave the fish in the water as much as possible.

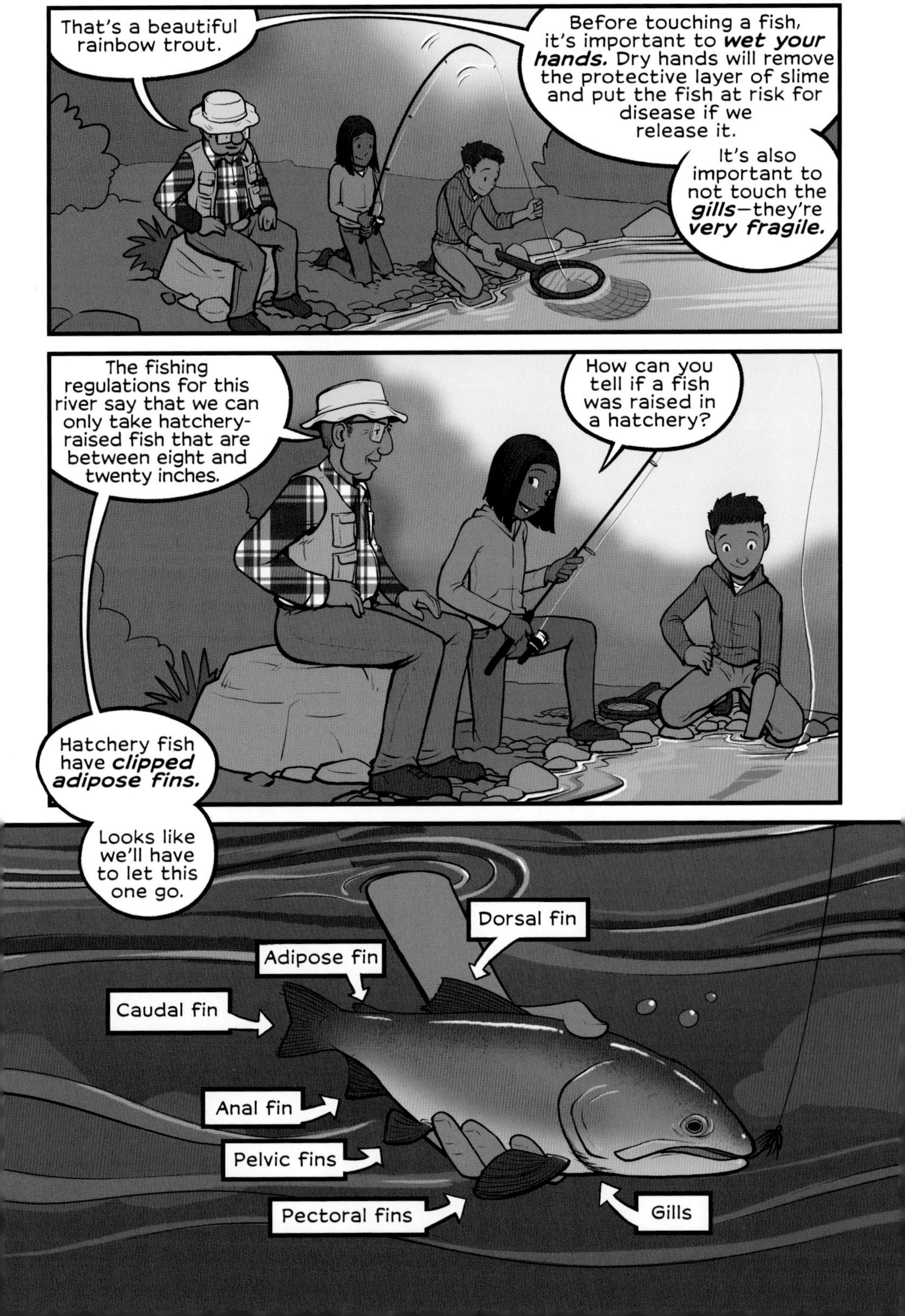
That's a beautiful rainbow trout.
Before touching a fish, it's important to ***wet your hands.*** Dry hands will remove the protective layer of slime and put the fish at risk for disease if we release it.
It's also important to not touch the ***gills***—they're ***very fragile.***
The fishing regulations for this river say that we can only take hatchery-raised fish that are between eight and twenty inches.
How can you tell if a fish was raised in a hatchery?
Hatchery fish have ***clipped adipose fins.***
Looks like we'll have to let this one go.
Dorsal fin
Adipose fin
Caudal fin
Anal fin
Pelvic fins
Pectoral fins
Gills

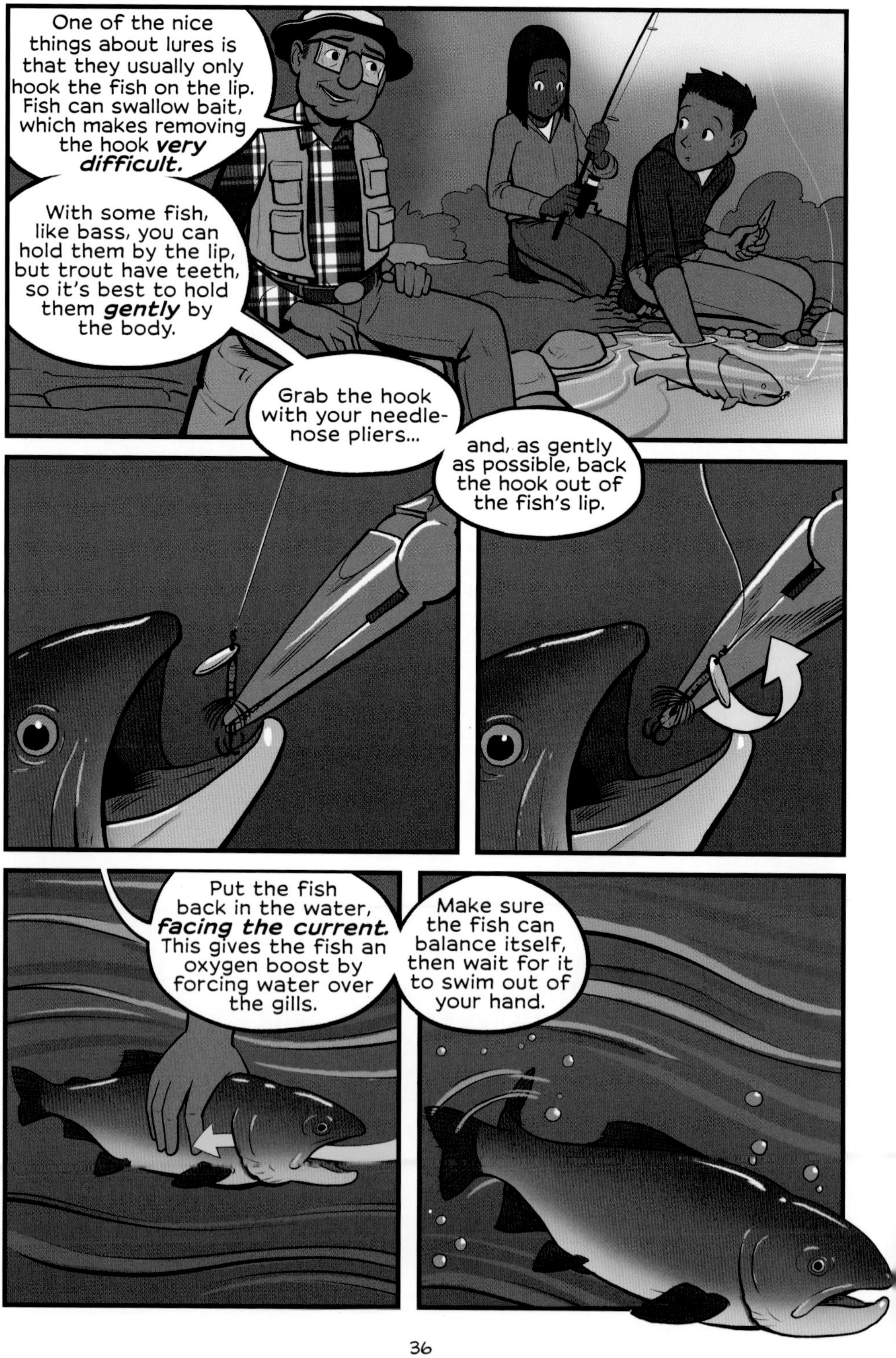
One of the nice things about lures is that they usually only hook the fish on the lip. Fish can swallow bait, which makes removing the hook ***very difficult.***
With some fish, like bass, you can hold them by the lip, but trout have teeth, so it's best to hold them ***gently*** by the body.
Grab the hook with your needle-nose pliers...
and, as gently as possible, back the hook out of the fish's lip.
Put the fish back in the water, ***facing the current.*** This gives the fish an oxygen boost by forcing water over the gills.
Make sure the fish can balance itself, then wait for it to swim out of your hand.

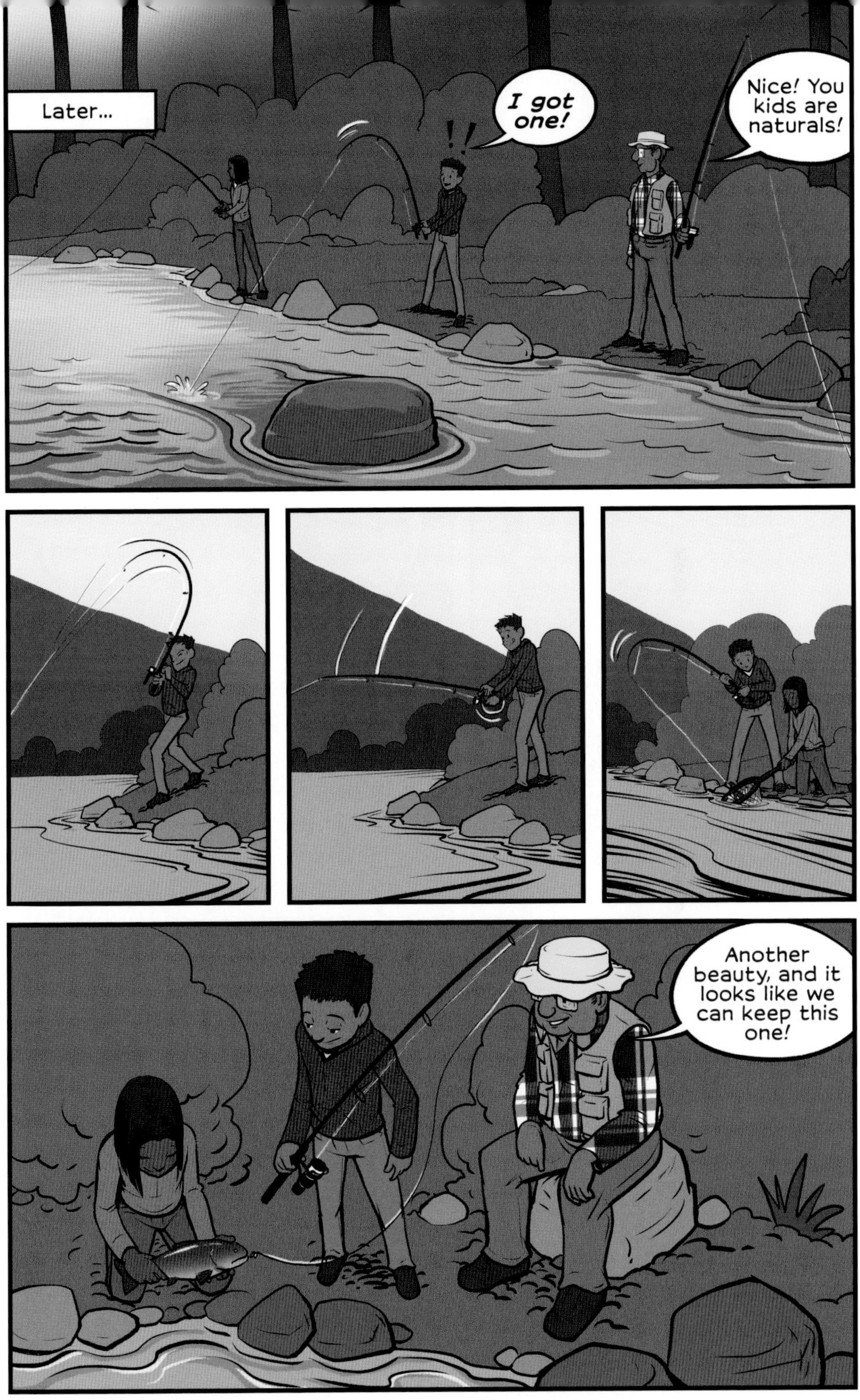
Later...
I got one!
Nice! You kids are naturals!
Another beauty, and it looks like we can keep this one!

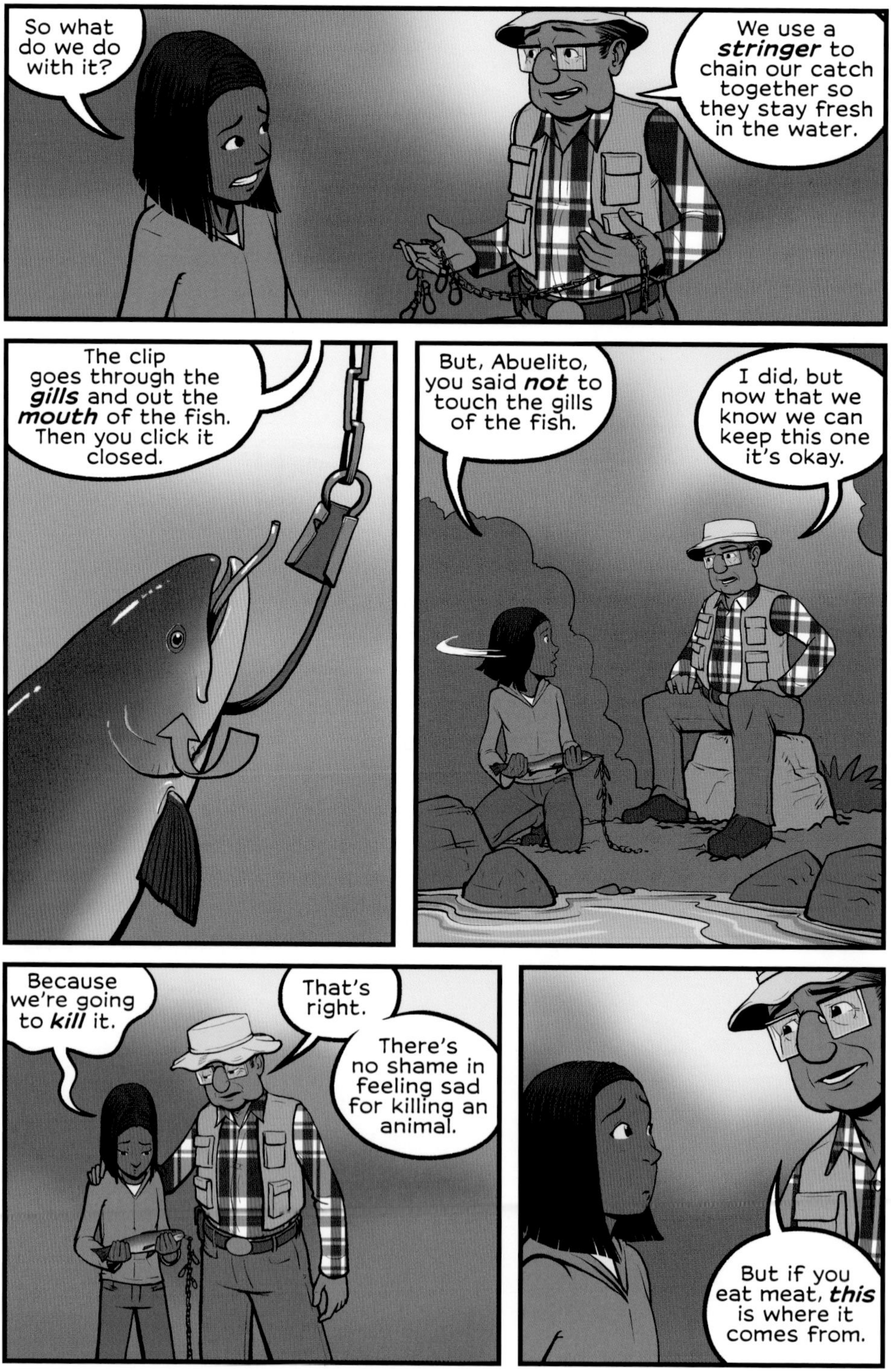
So what do we do with it?
We use a ***stringer*** to chain our catch together so they stay fresh in the water.
The clip goes through the ***gills*** and out the ***mouth*** of the fish. Then you click it closed.
But, Abuelito, you said ***not*** to touch the gills of the fish.
I did, but now that we know we can keep this one it's okay.
Because we're going to ***kill*** it.
That's right.
There's no shame in feeling sad for killing an animal.
But if you eat meat, ***this*** is where it comes from.

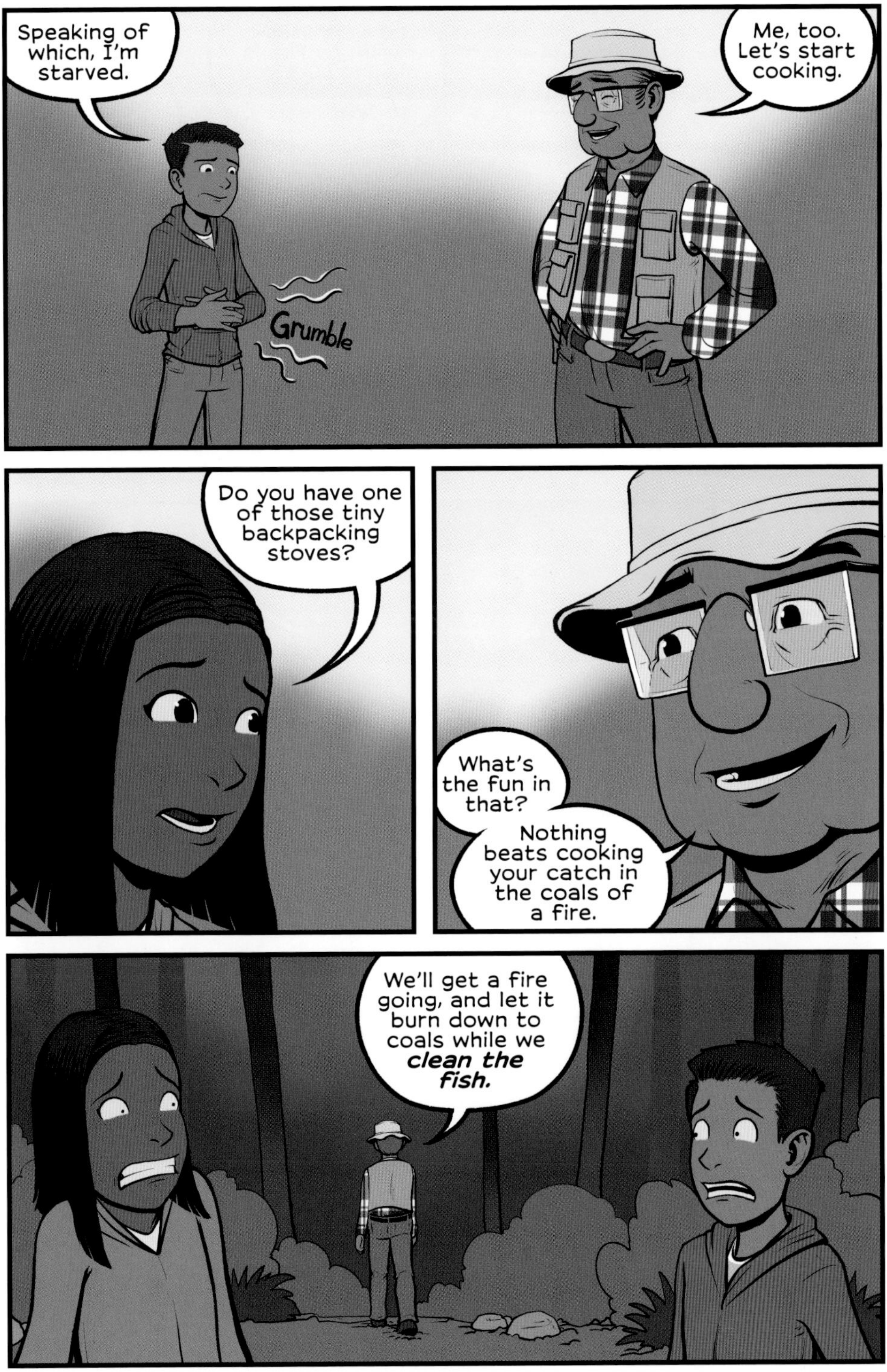
Speaking of which, I'm starved.
Grumble
Me, too. Let's start cooking.
Do you have one of those tiny backpacking stoves?
What's the fun in that?
Nothing beats cooking your catch in the coals of a fire.
We'll get a fire going, and let it burn down to coals while we ***clean the fish.***

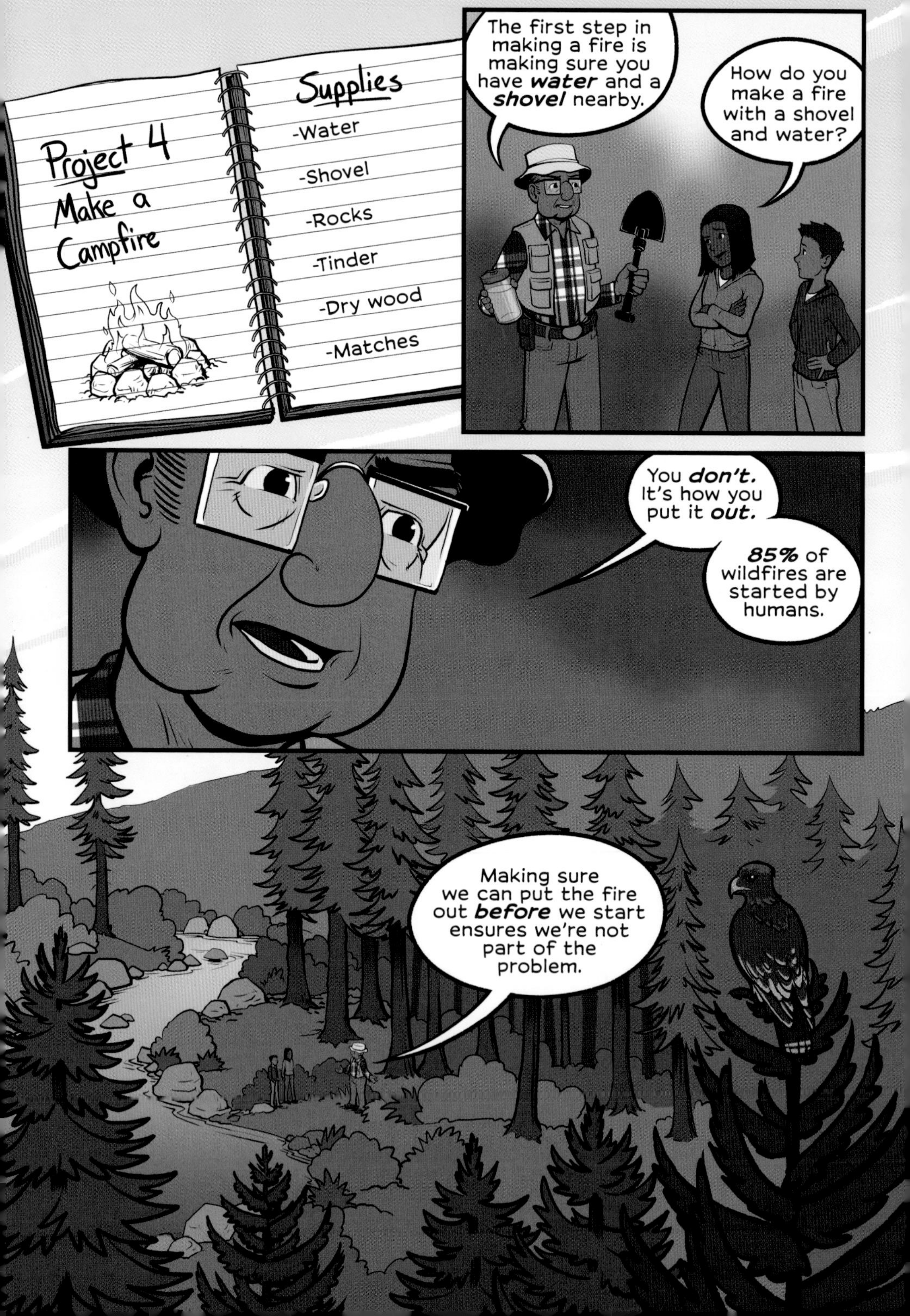
Project 4
Make a Campfire
Supplies
-Water
-Shovel
-Rocks
-Tinder
-Dry wood
-Matches
The first step in making a fire is making sure you have ***water*** and a ***shovel*** nearby.
How do you make a fire with a shovel and water?
You ***don't.*** It's how you put it ***out.***
***85%*** of wildfires are started by humans.
Making sure we can put the fire out ***before*** we start ensures we're not part of the problem.

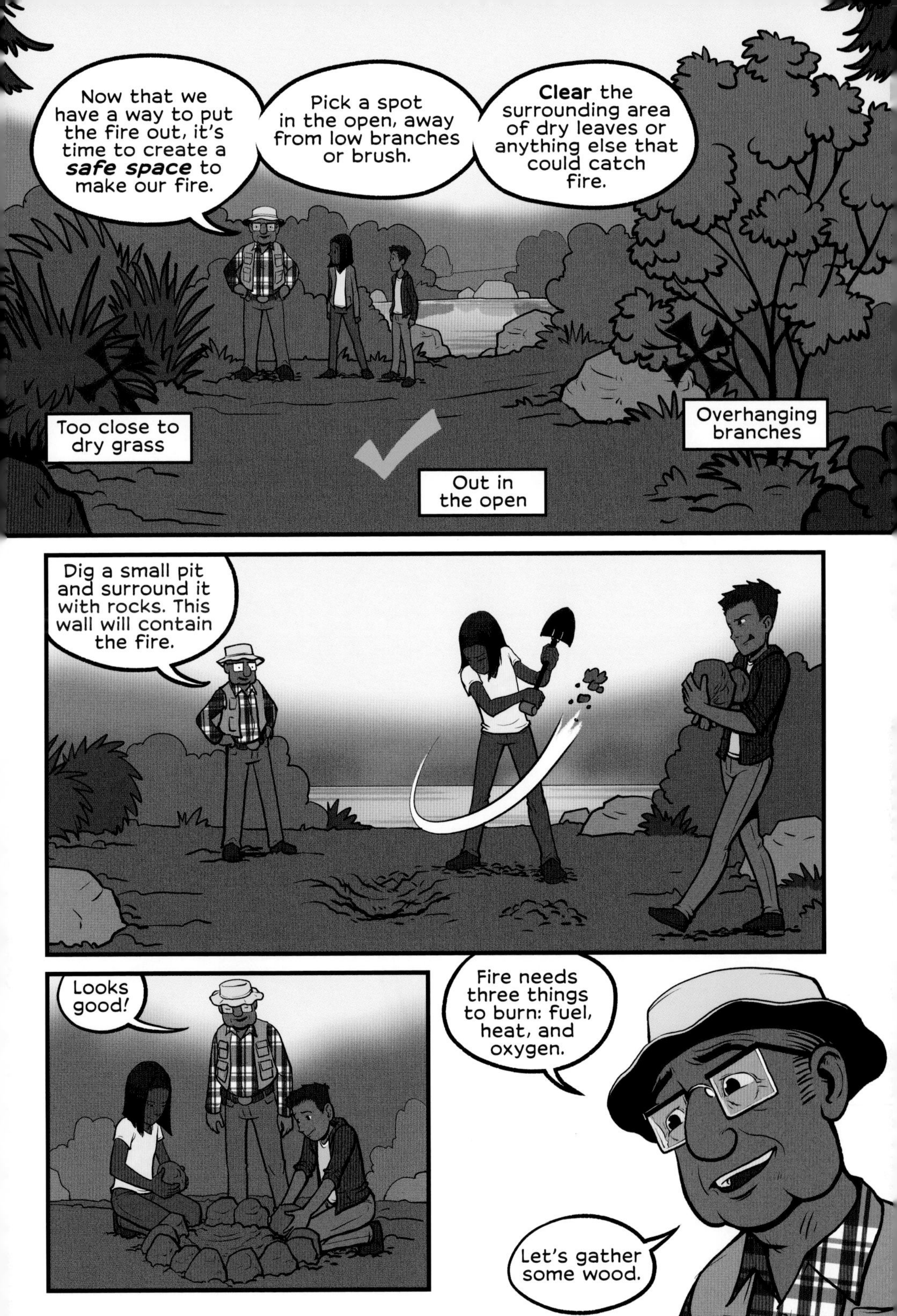
Now that we have a way to put the fire out, it's time to create a ***safe space*** to make our fire.
Pick a spot in the open, away from low branches or brush.
**Clear** the surrounding area of dry leaves or anything else that could catch fire.
Too close to dry grass
Out in the open
Overhanging branches
Dig a small pit and surround it with rocks. This wall will contain the fire.
Looks good!
Fire needs three things to burn: fuel, heat, and oxygen.
Let's gather some wood.

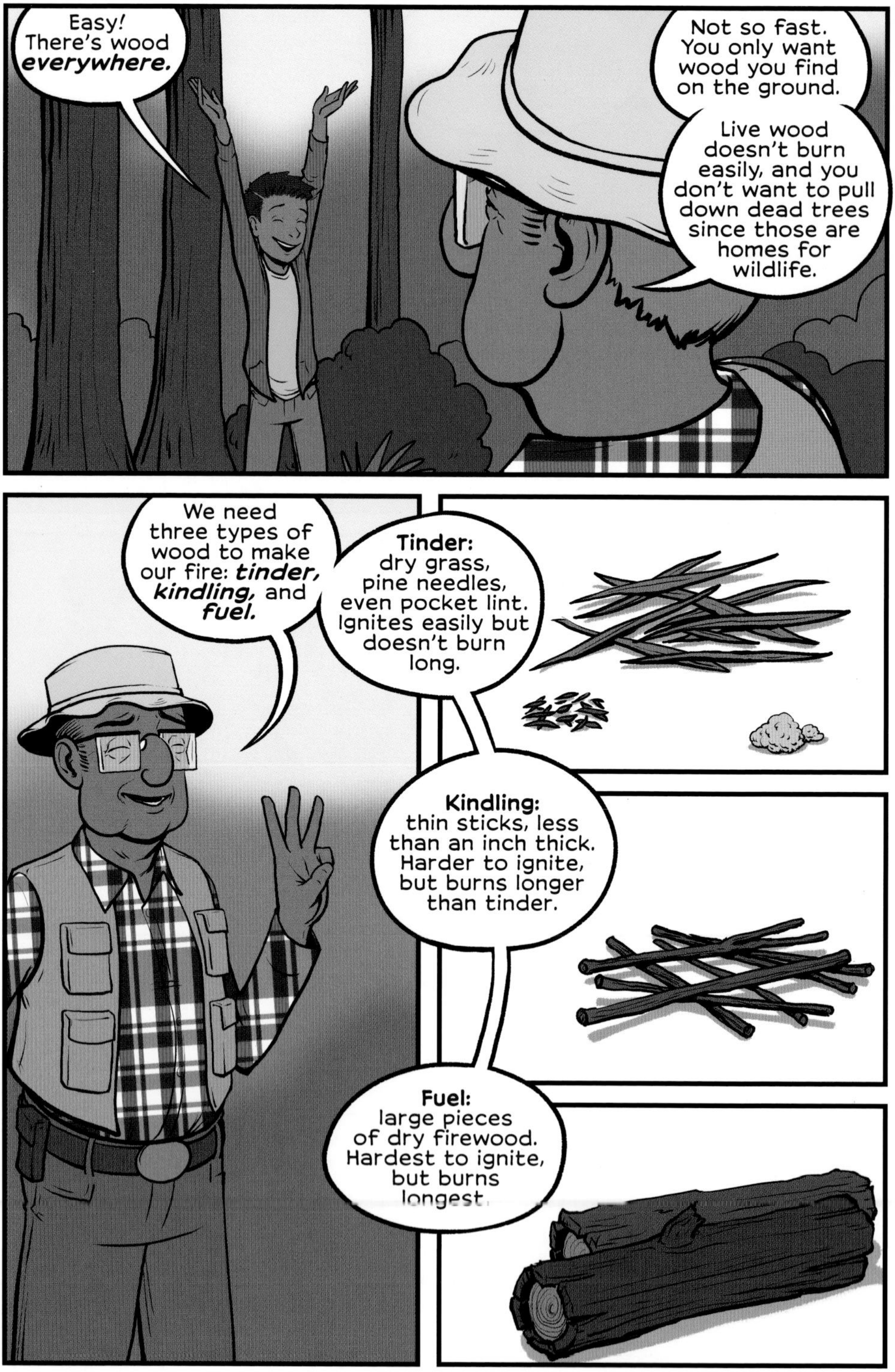
Easy! There's wood *everywhere.*
Not so fast. You only want wood you find on the ground.
Live wood doesn't burn easily, and you don't want to pull down dead trees since those are homes for wildlife.
We need three types of wood to make our fire: *tinder, kindling,* and *fuel.*
**Tinder:** dry grass, pine needles, even pocket lint. Ignites easily but doesn't burn long.
**Kindling:** thin sticks, less than an inch thick. Harder to ignite, but burns longer than tinder.
**Fuel:** large pieces of dry firewood. Hardest to ignite, but burns longest.

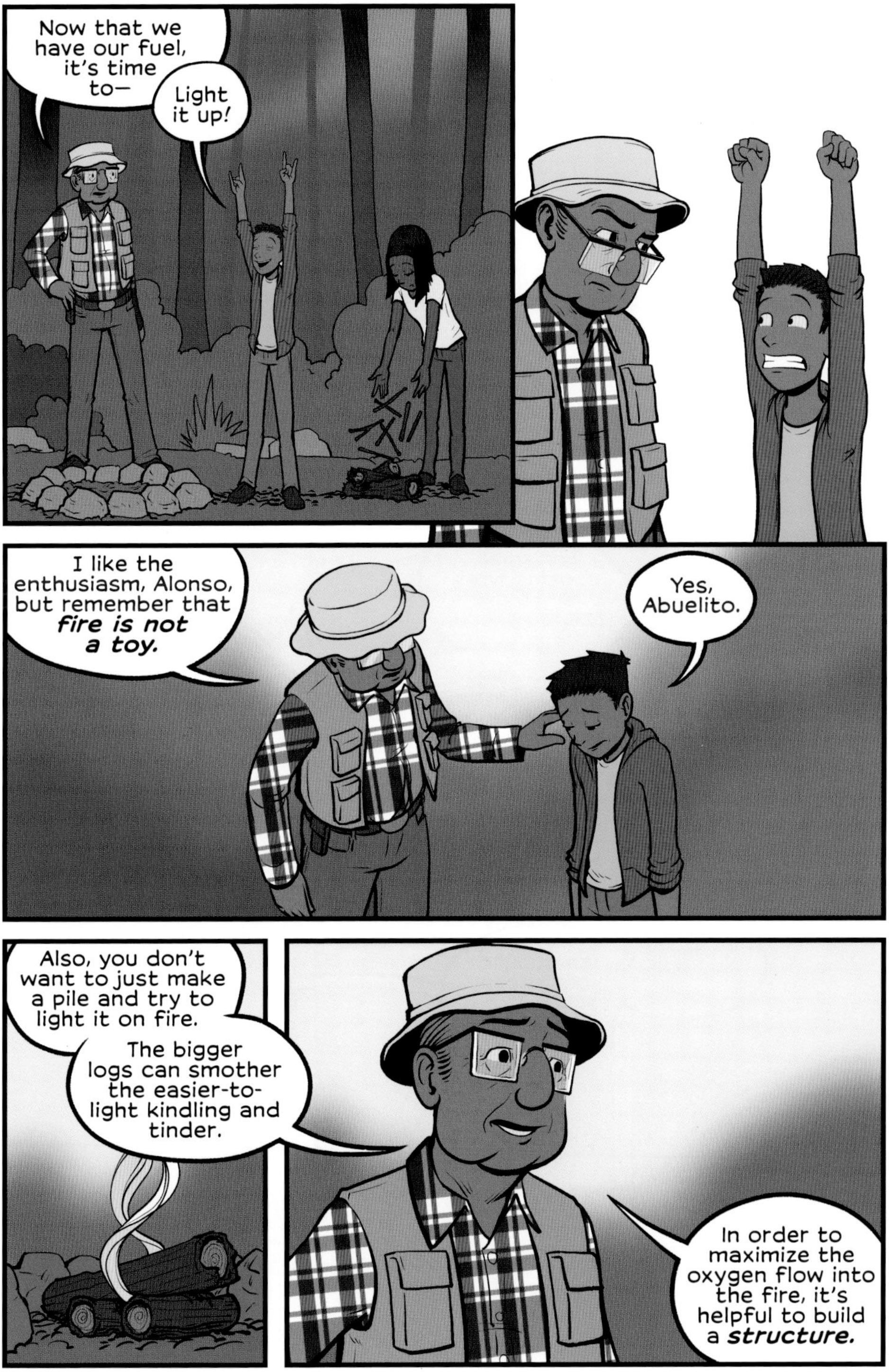
Now that we have our fuel, it's time to—
Light it up!
I like the enthusiasm, Alonso, but remember that ***fire is not a toy.***
Yes, Abuelito.
Also, you don't want to just make a pile and try to light it on fire.
The bigger logs can smother the easier-to-light kindling and tinder.
In order to maximize the oxygen flow into the fire, it's helpful to build a ***structure.***

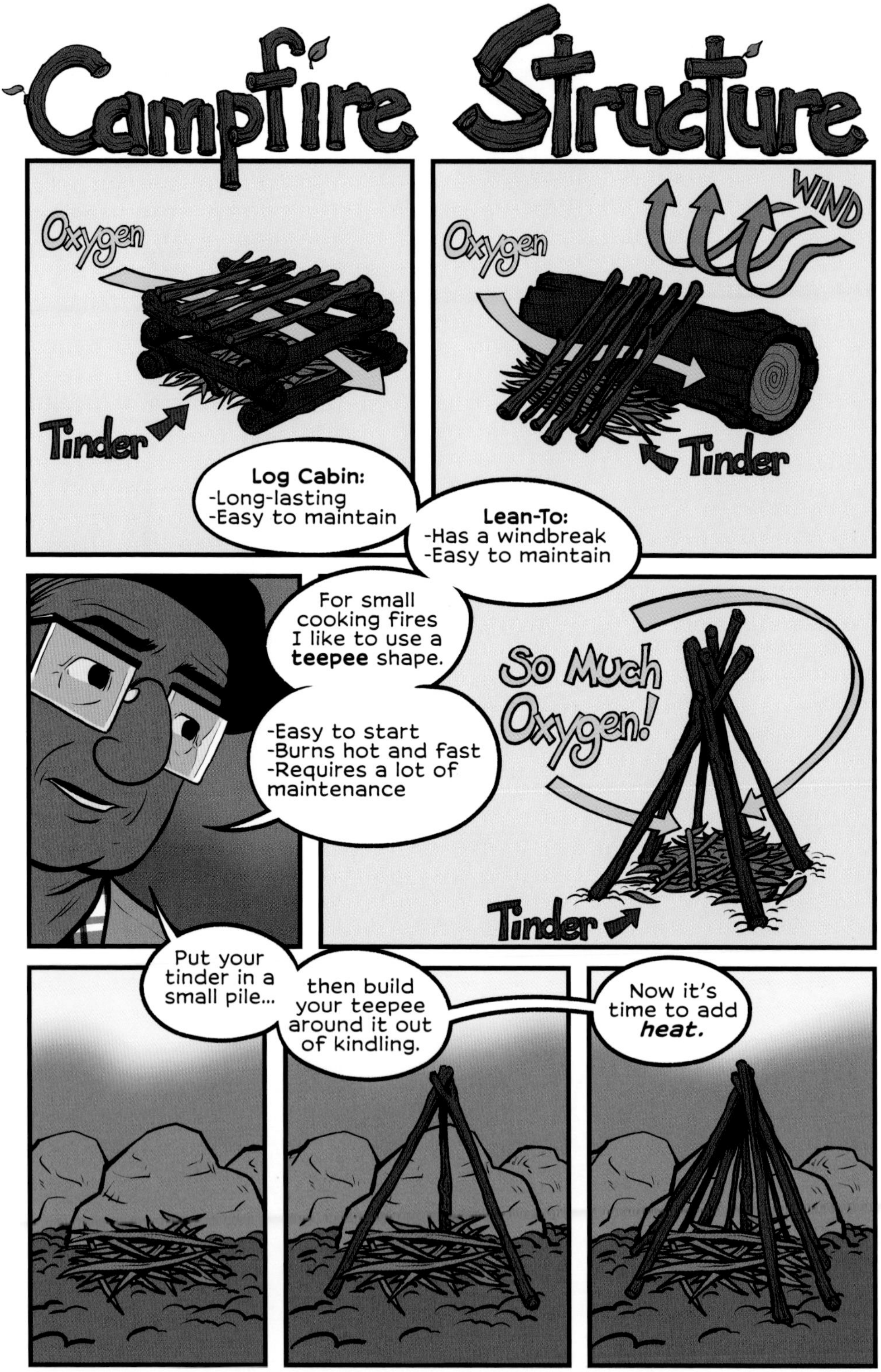
Campfire Structure
Oxygen
Tinder
Oxygen
WIND
Tinder
Log Cabin:
-Long-lasting
-Easy to maintain
Lean-To:
-Has a windbreak
-Easy to maintain
For small cooking fires I like to use a teepee shape.
-Easy to start
-Burns hot and fast
-Requires a lot of maintenance
So Much Oxygen!
Tinder
Put your tinder in a small pile...
then build your teepee around it out of kindling.
Now it's time to add heat.

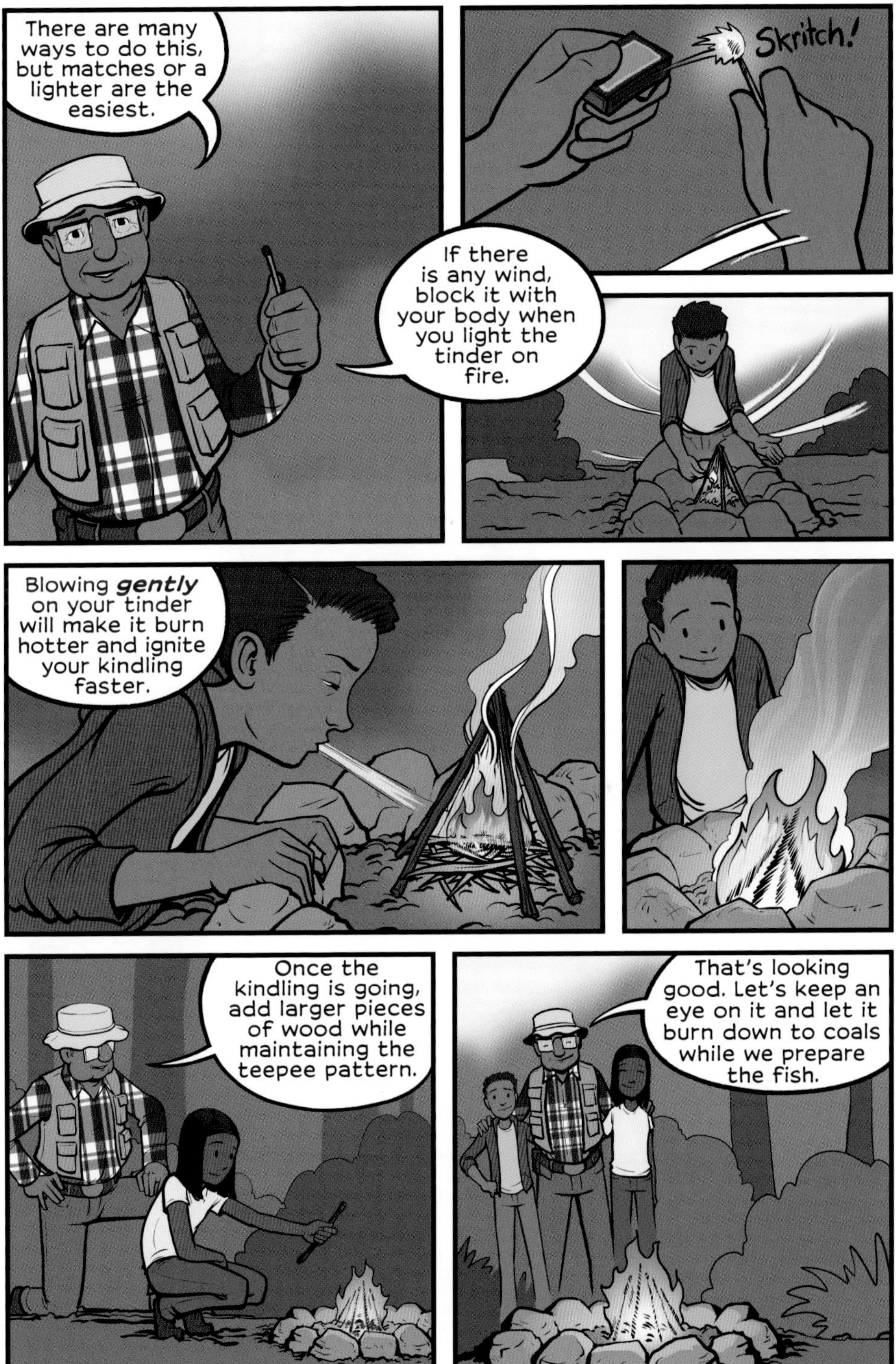
There are many ways to do this, but matches or a lighter are the easiest.
Skritch!
If there is any wind, block it with your body when you light the tinder on fire.
Blowing ***gently*** on your tinder will make it burn hotter and ignite your kindling faster.
Once the kindling is going, add larger pieces of wood while maintaining the teepee pattern.
That's looking good. Let's keep an eye on it and let it burn down to coals while we prepare the fish.

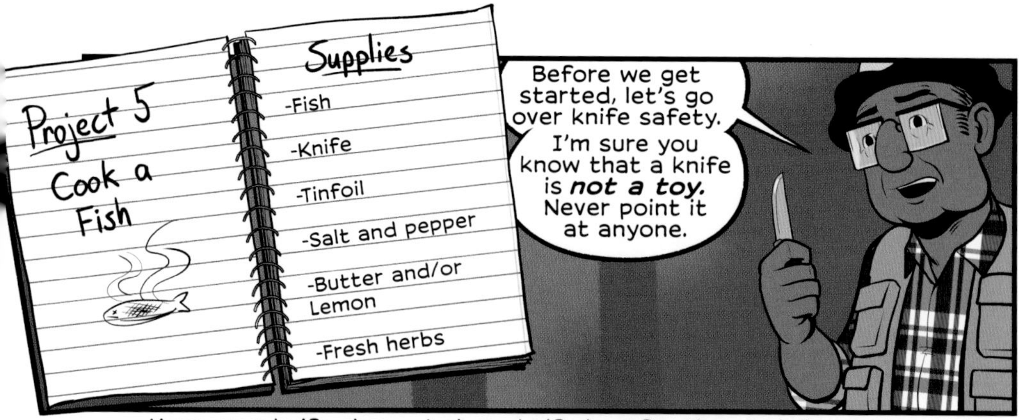
Project 5
Cook a Fish
Supplies
-Fish
-Knife
-Tinfoil
-Salt and pepper
-Butter and/or Lemon
-Fresh herbs
Before we get started, let's go over knife safety.
I'm sure you know that a knife is ***not a toy.*** Never point it at anyone.

Keep your knife sharp. A sharp knife is safer than a dull one since it is less likely to slip off the object you are cutting.

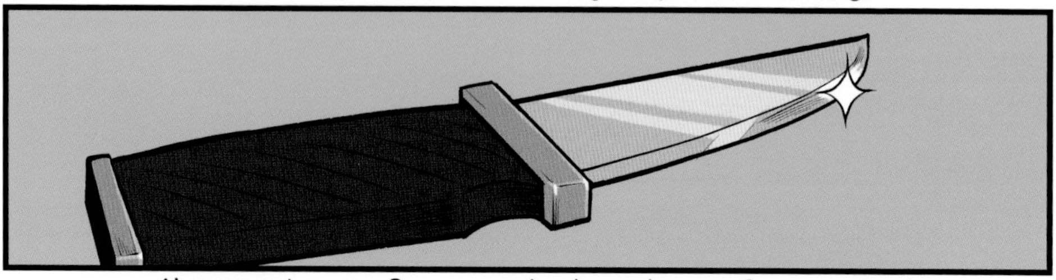

Always cut away from your body and away from anybody around you. Think about where the knife will go if it slips.

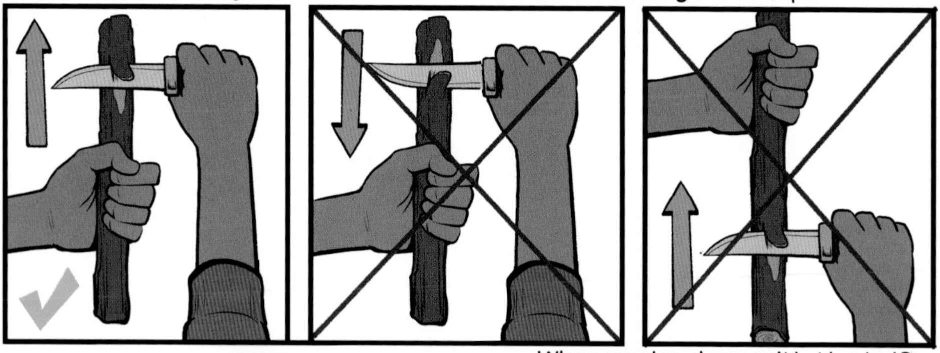

Carving away from your body with your elbows on your knees is a really safe position. It protects the femoral arteries on your inner thighs.

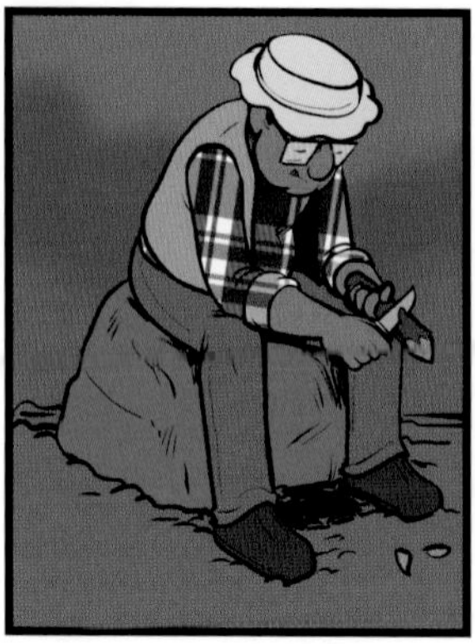

When you're done with the knife, put it back in its sheath or fold it.

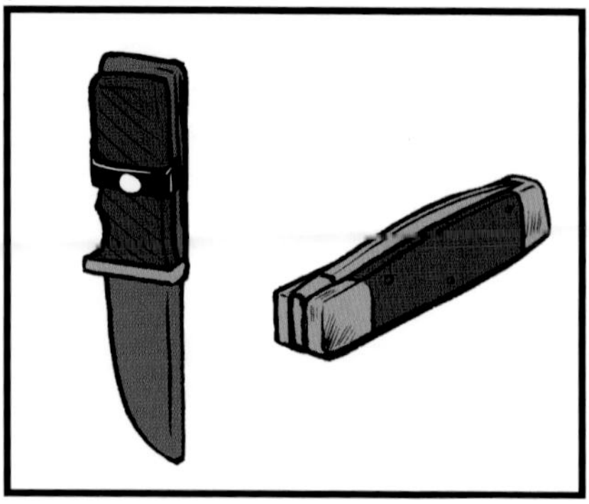

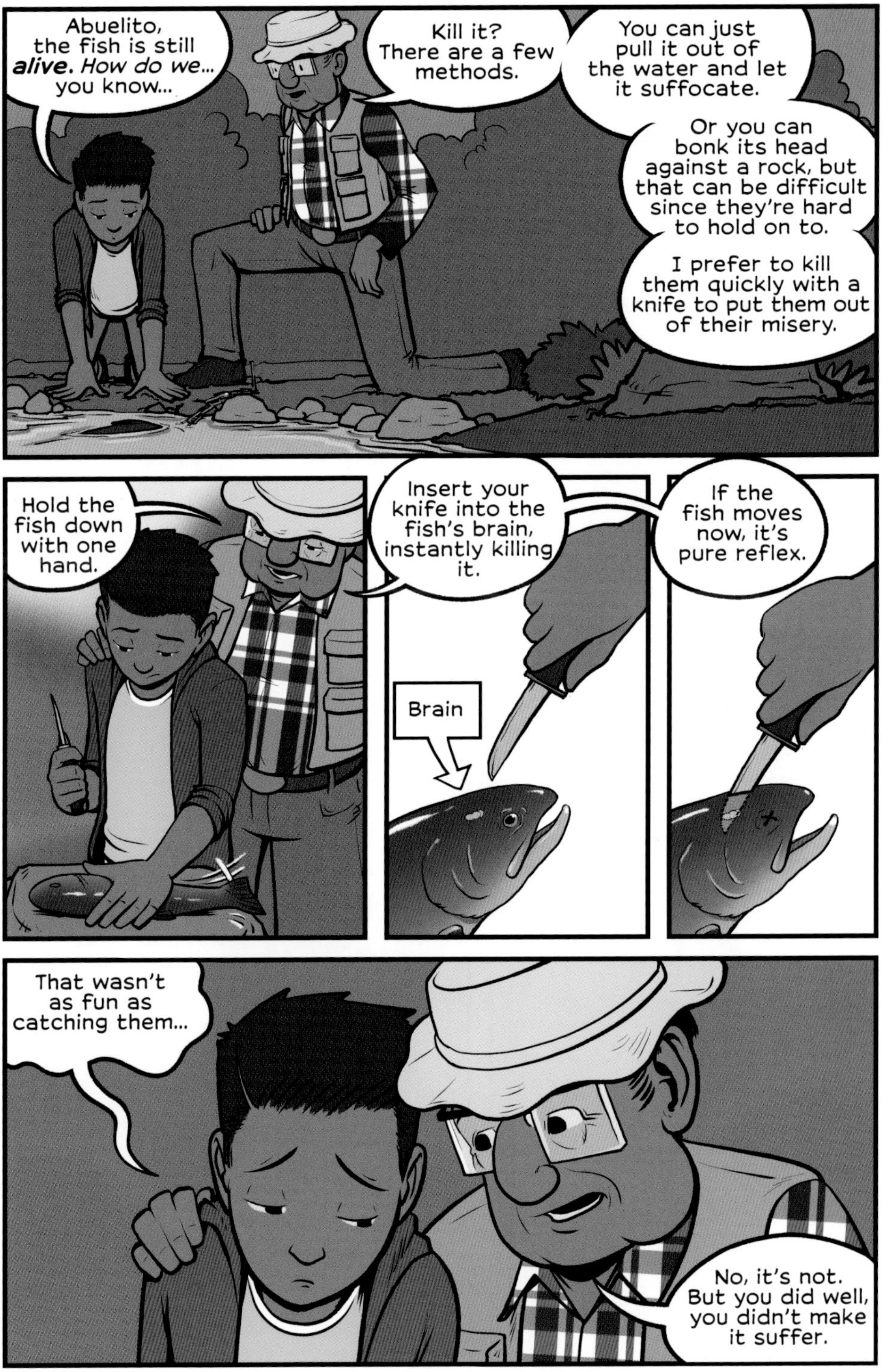
Abuelito, the fish is still ***alive***. *How do we*... you know...
Kill it? There are a few methods.
You can just pull it out of the water and let it suffocate.
Or you can bonk its head against a rock, but that can be difficult since they're hard to hold on to.
I prefer to kill them quickly with a knife to put them out of their misery.
Hold the fish down with one hand.
Insert your knife into the fish's brain, instantly killing it.
Brain
If the fish moves now, it's pure reflex.
That wasn't as fun as catching them...
No, it's not. But you did well, you didn't make it suffer.

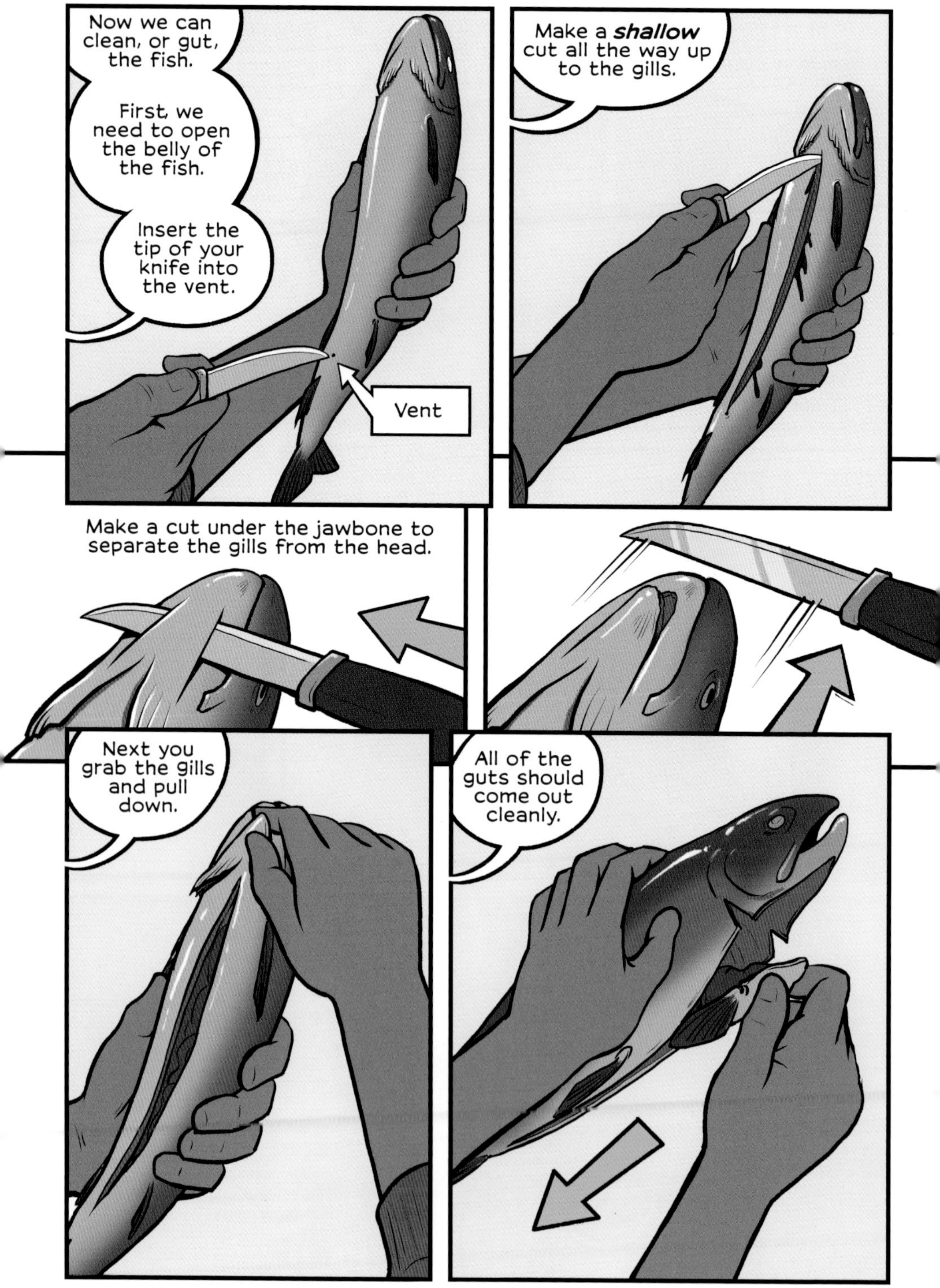
Now we can clean, or gut, the fish.
First, we need to open the belly of the fish.
Insert the tip of your knife into the vent.
Vent
Make a ***shallow*** cut all the way up to the gills.
Make a cut under the jawbone to separate the gills from the head.
Next you grab the gills and pull down.
All of the guts should come out cleanly.

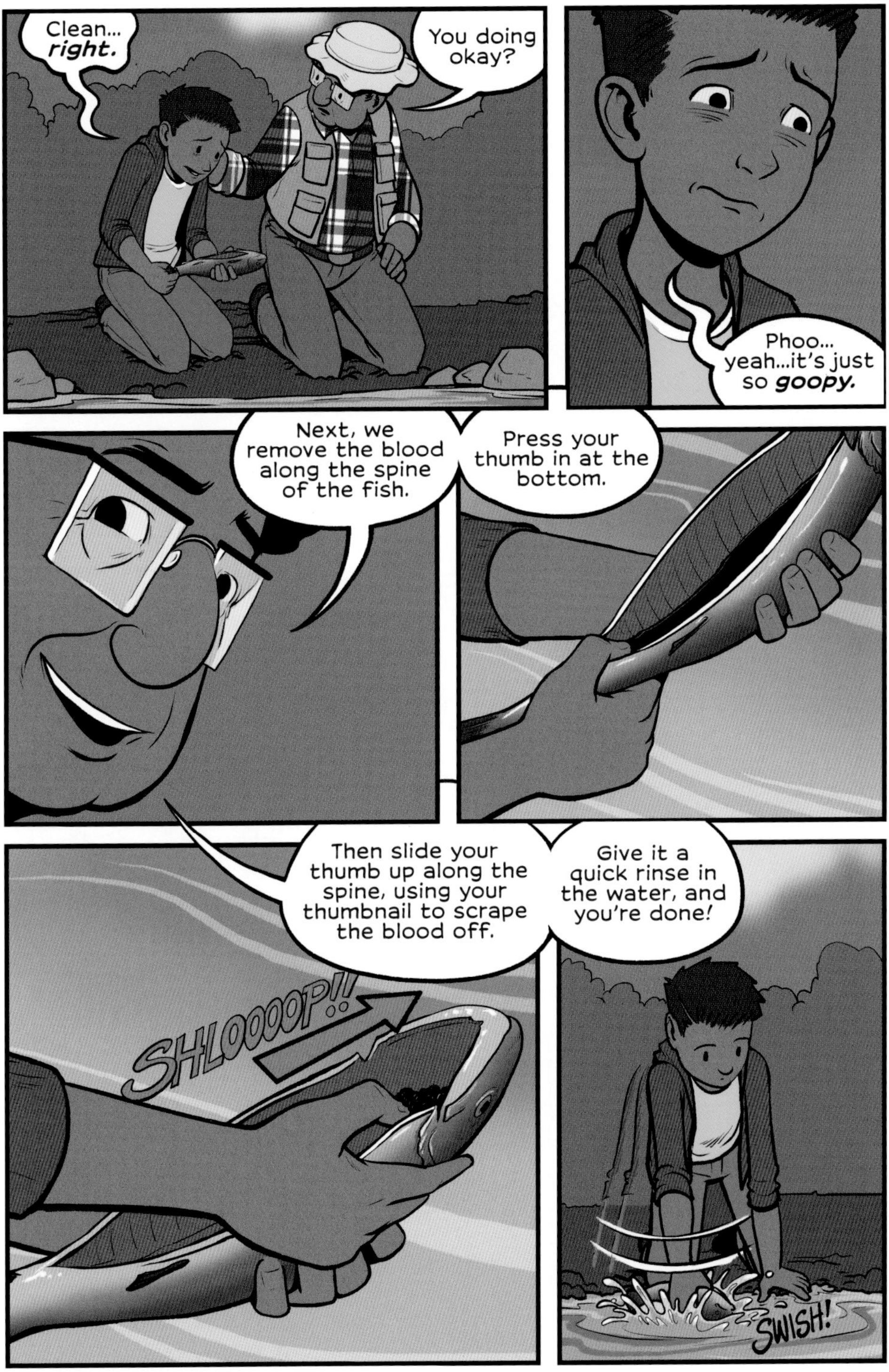
Clean... **right.**
You doing okay?
Phoo... yeah...it's just so **goopy.**
Next, we remove the blood along the spine of the fish.
Press your thumb in at the bottom.
Then slide your thumb up along the spine, using your thumbnail to scrape the blood off.
SHLOOOOP!!
Give it a quick rinse in the water, and you're done!
SWISH!

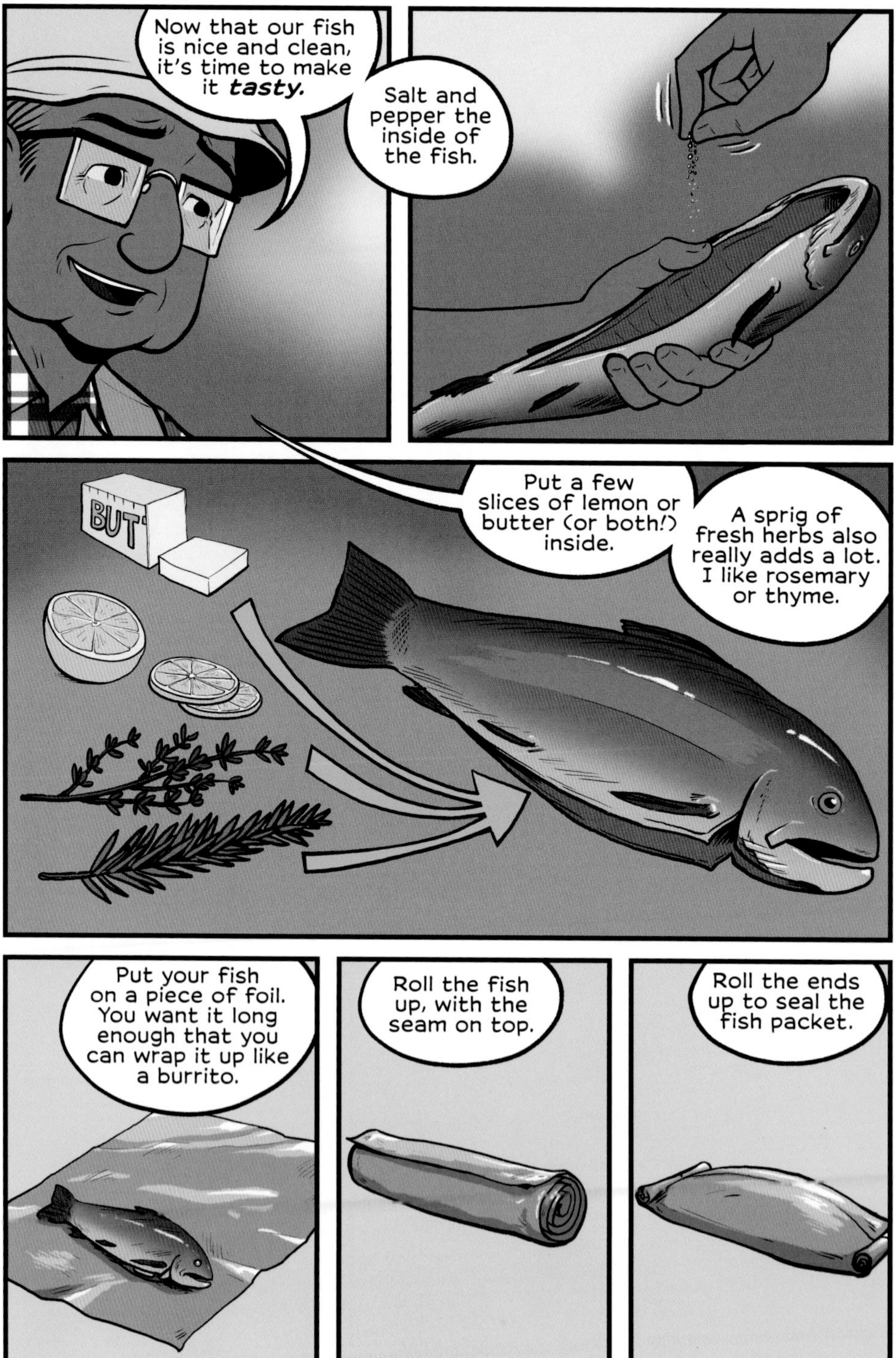
Now that our fish is nice and clean, it's time to make it ***tasty.***
Salt and pepper the inside of the fish.
BUT
Put a few slices of lemon or butter (or both!) inside.
A sprig of fresh herbs also really adds a lot. I like rosemary or thyme.
Put your fish on a piece of foil. You want it long enough that you can wrap it up like a burrito.
Roll the fish up, with the seam on top.
Roll the ends up to seal the fish packet.

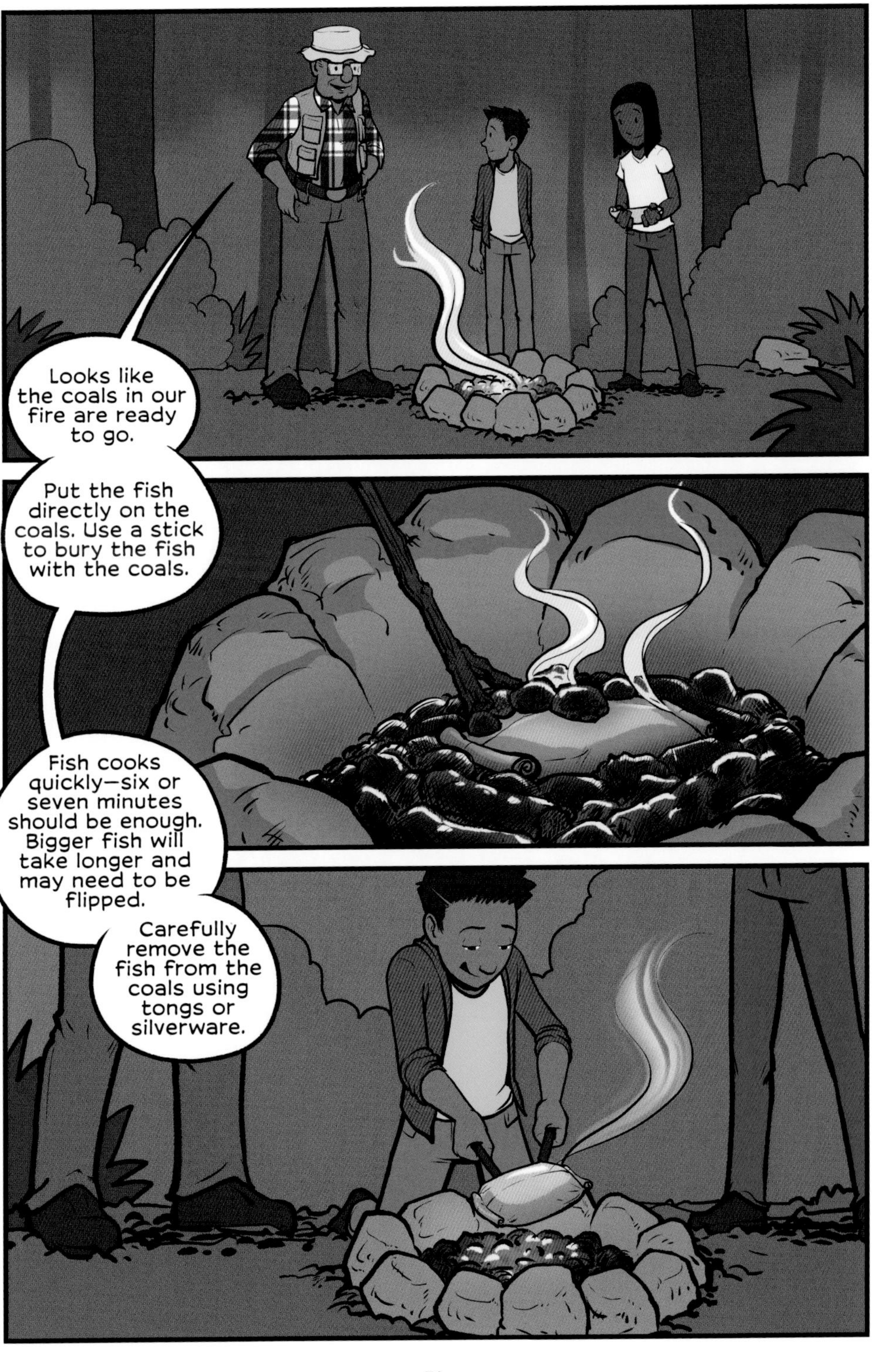
Looks like the coals in our fire are ready to go.
Put the fish directly on the coals. Use a stick to bury the fish with the coals.
Fish cooks quickly—six or seven minutes should be enough. Bigger fish will take longer and may need to be flipped.
Carefully remove the fish from the coals using tongs or silverware.

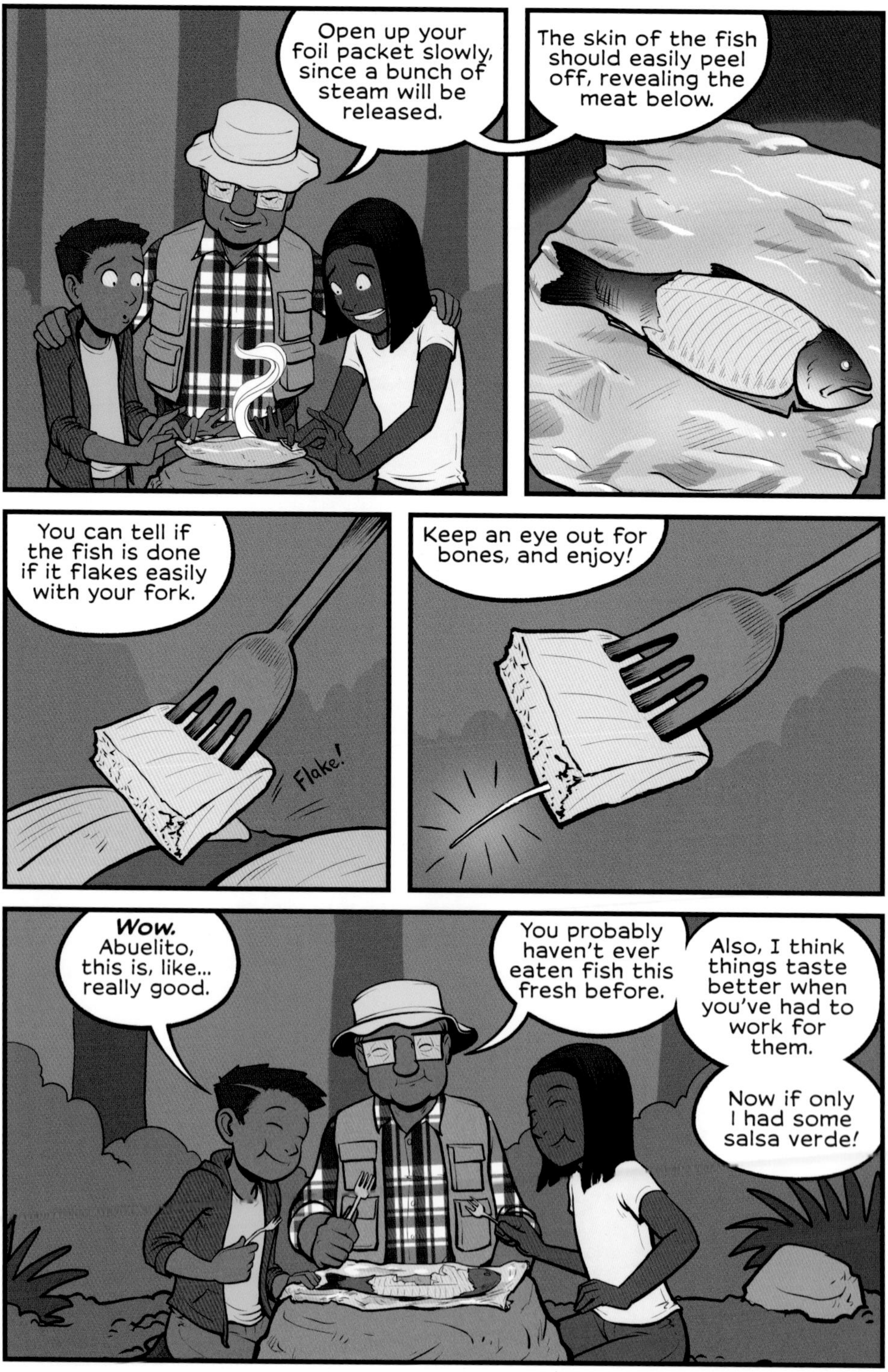

Open up your foil packet slowly, since a bunch of steam will be released.
The skin of the fish should easily peel off, revealing the meat below.
You can tell if the fish is done if it flakes easily with your fork.
Flake!
Keep an eye out for bones, and enjoy!
**Wow.** Abuelito, this is, like... really good.
You probably haven't ever eaten fish this fresh before.
Also, I think things taste better when you've had to work for them.
Now if only I had some salsa verde!

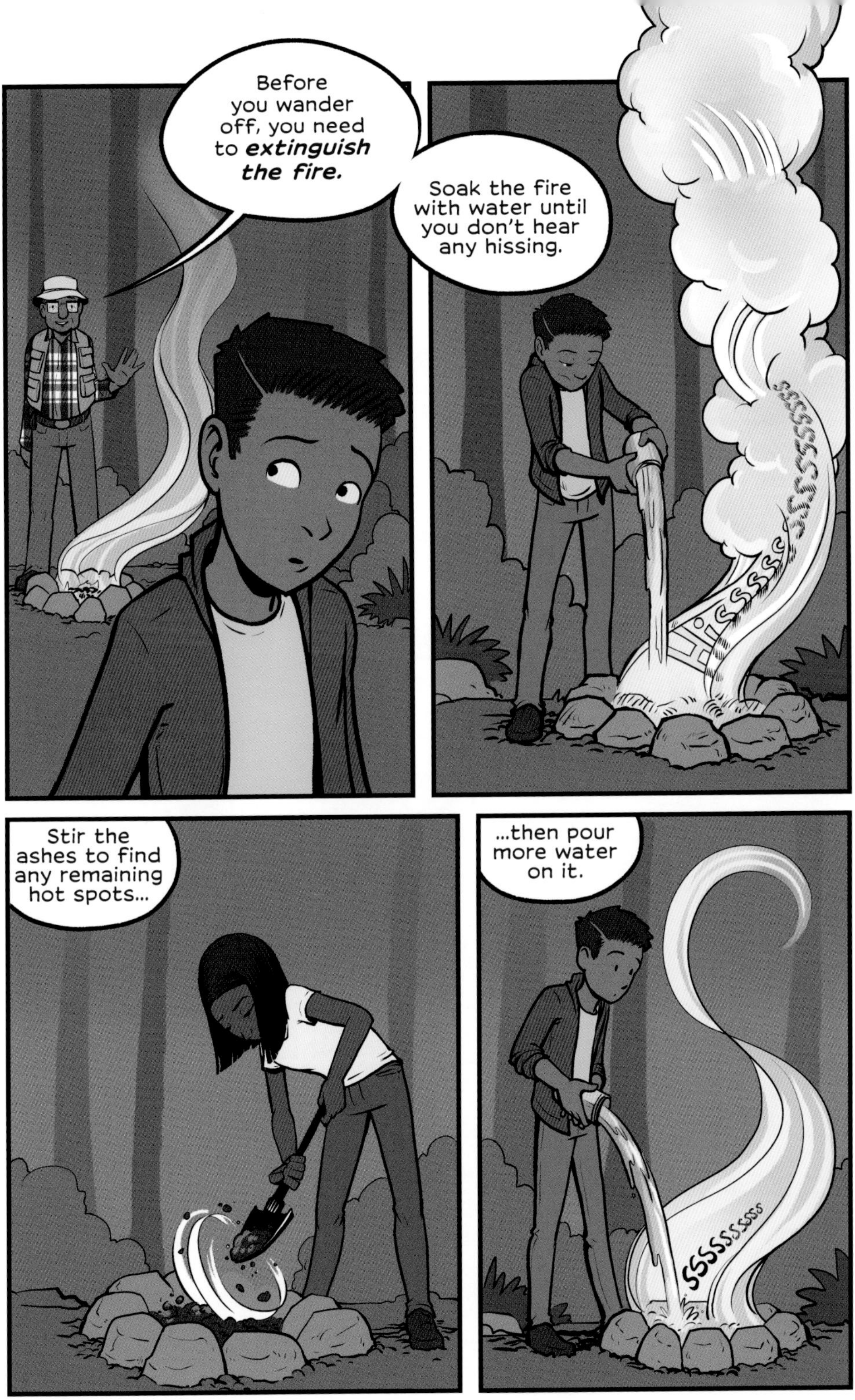
Before you wander off, you need to ***extinguish the fire.***
Soak the fire with water until you don't hear any hissing.
SSSSSSSSSSSS
Stir the ashes to find any remaining hot spots...
...then pour more water on it.
SSSSSSSSSS

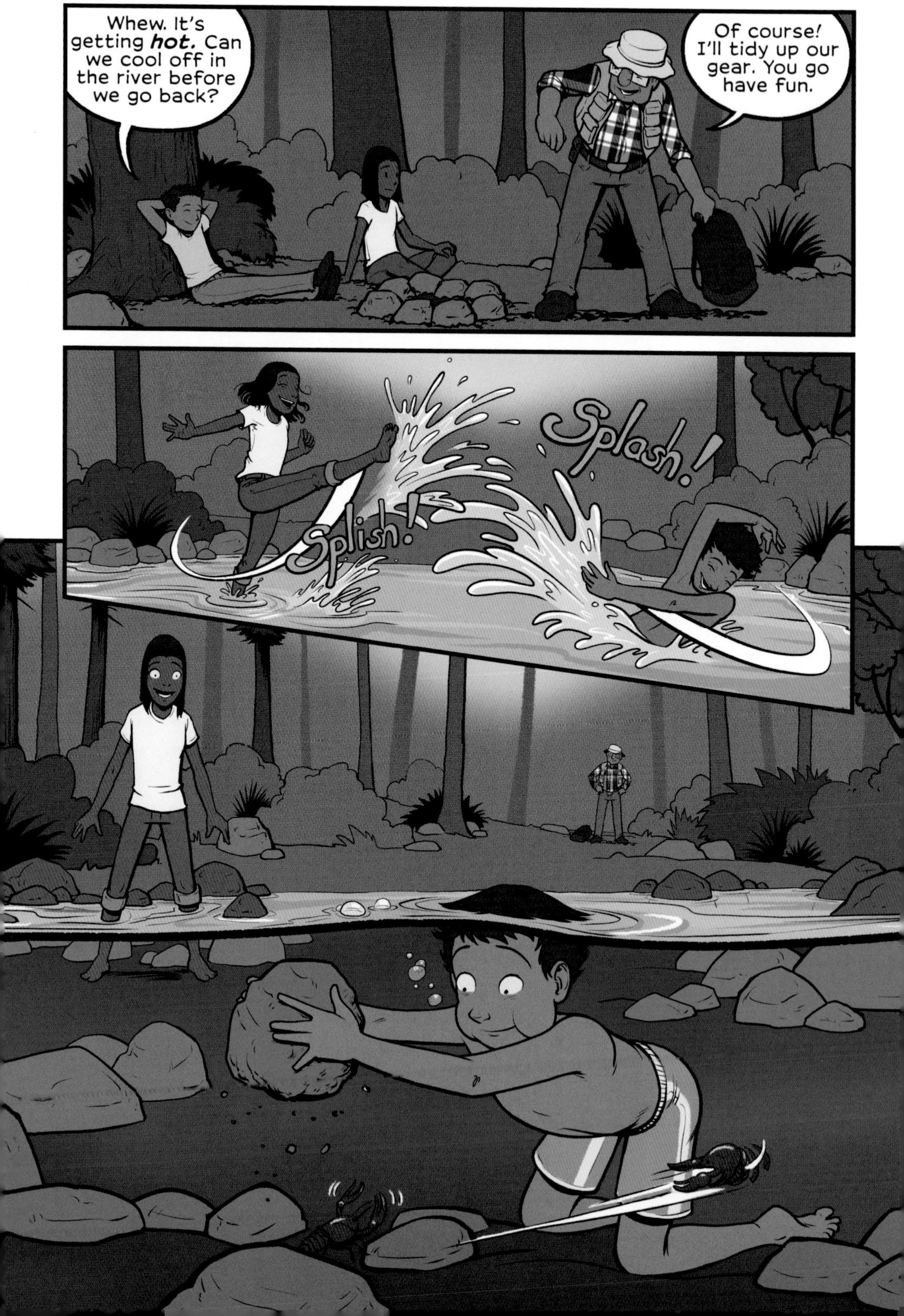
Whew. It's getting **hot.** Can we cool off in the river before we go back?
Of course! I'll tidy up our gear. You go have fun.
Splash!
Splish!

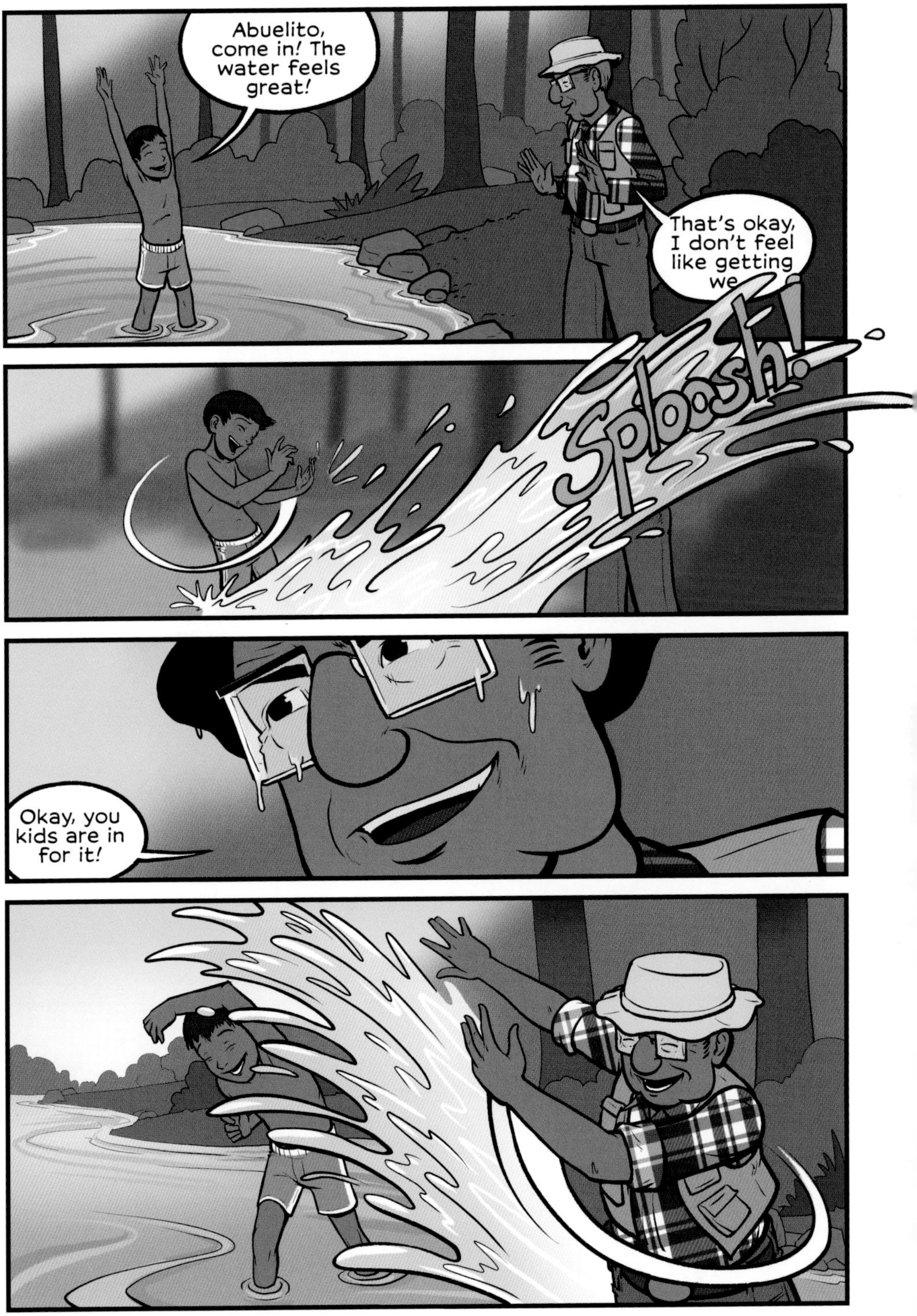
Abuelito, come in! The water feels great!
That's okay, I don't feel like getting we—
Sploosh!
Okay, you kids are in for it!

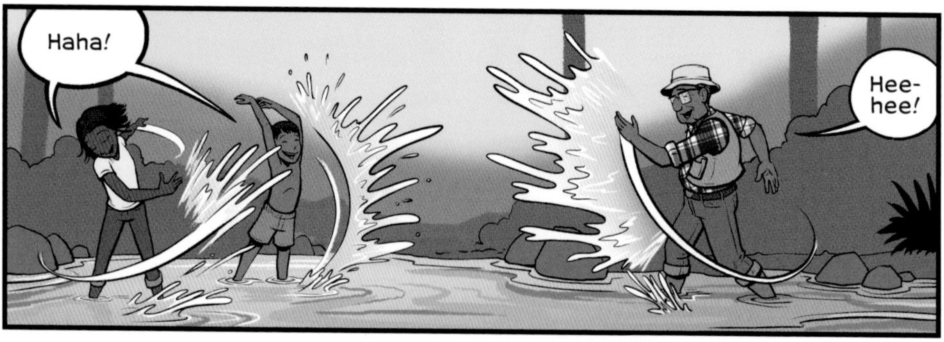
Haha!
Hee-hee!

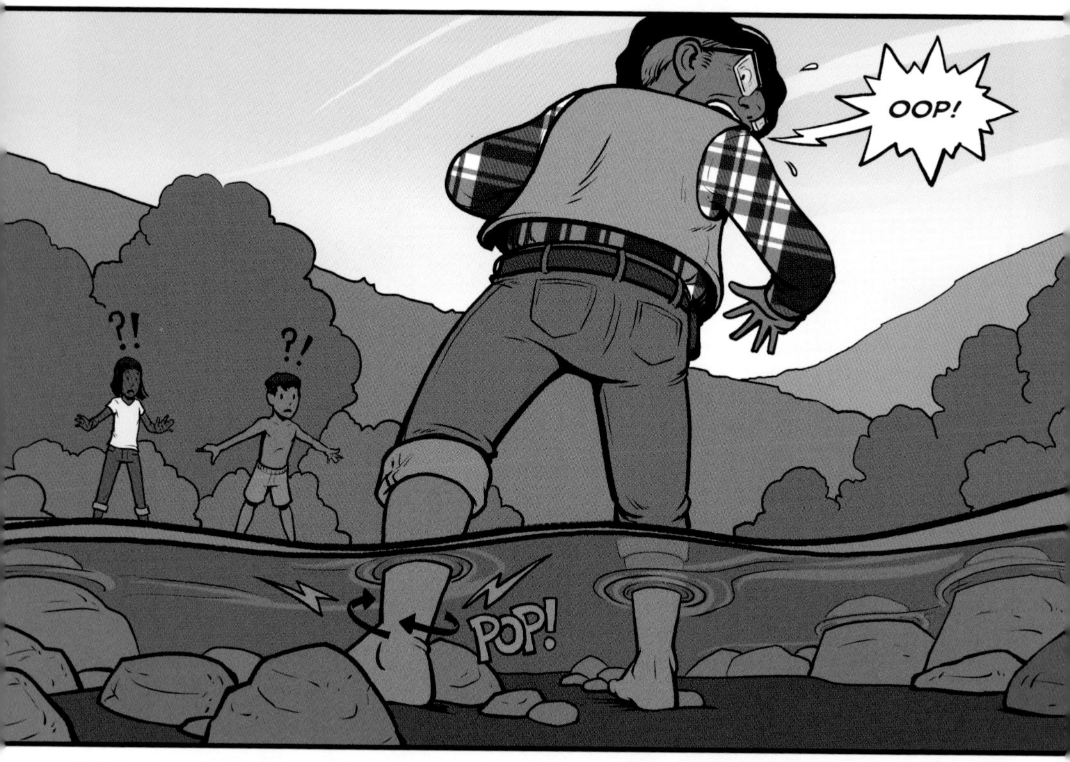
OOP!
?!
?!
POP!

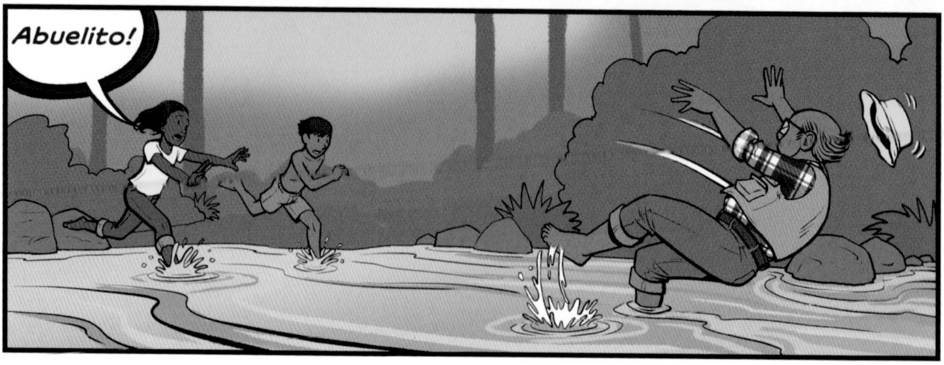
Abuelito!

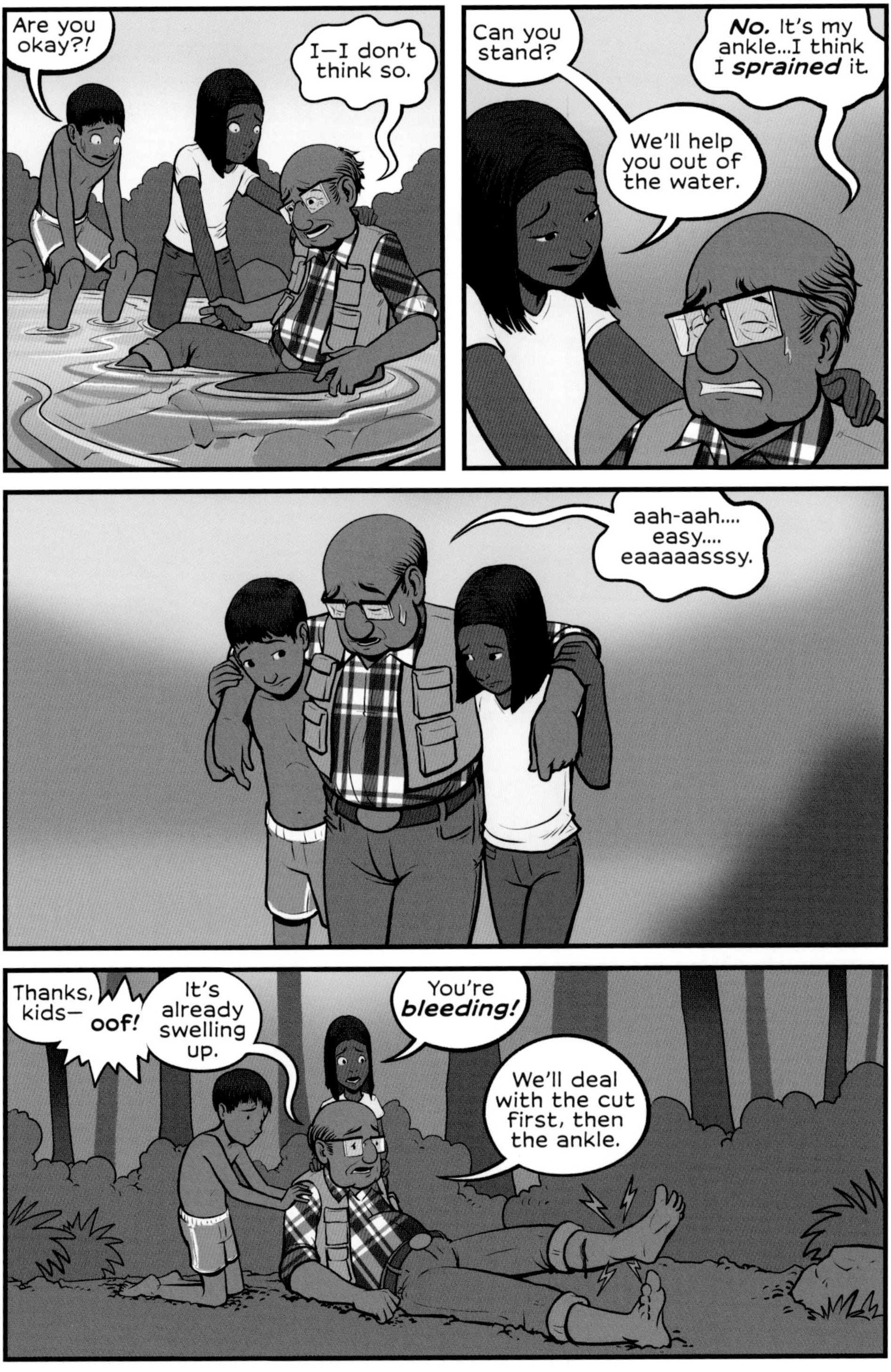
Are you okay?!
I—I don't think so.
Can you stand?
**No.** It's my ankle...I think I ***sprained*** it.
We'll help you out of the water.
aah-aah.... easy.... eaaaaasssy.
Thanks, kids—
**oof!**
It's already swelling up.
You're ***bleeding!***
We'll deal with the cut first, then the ankle.

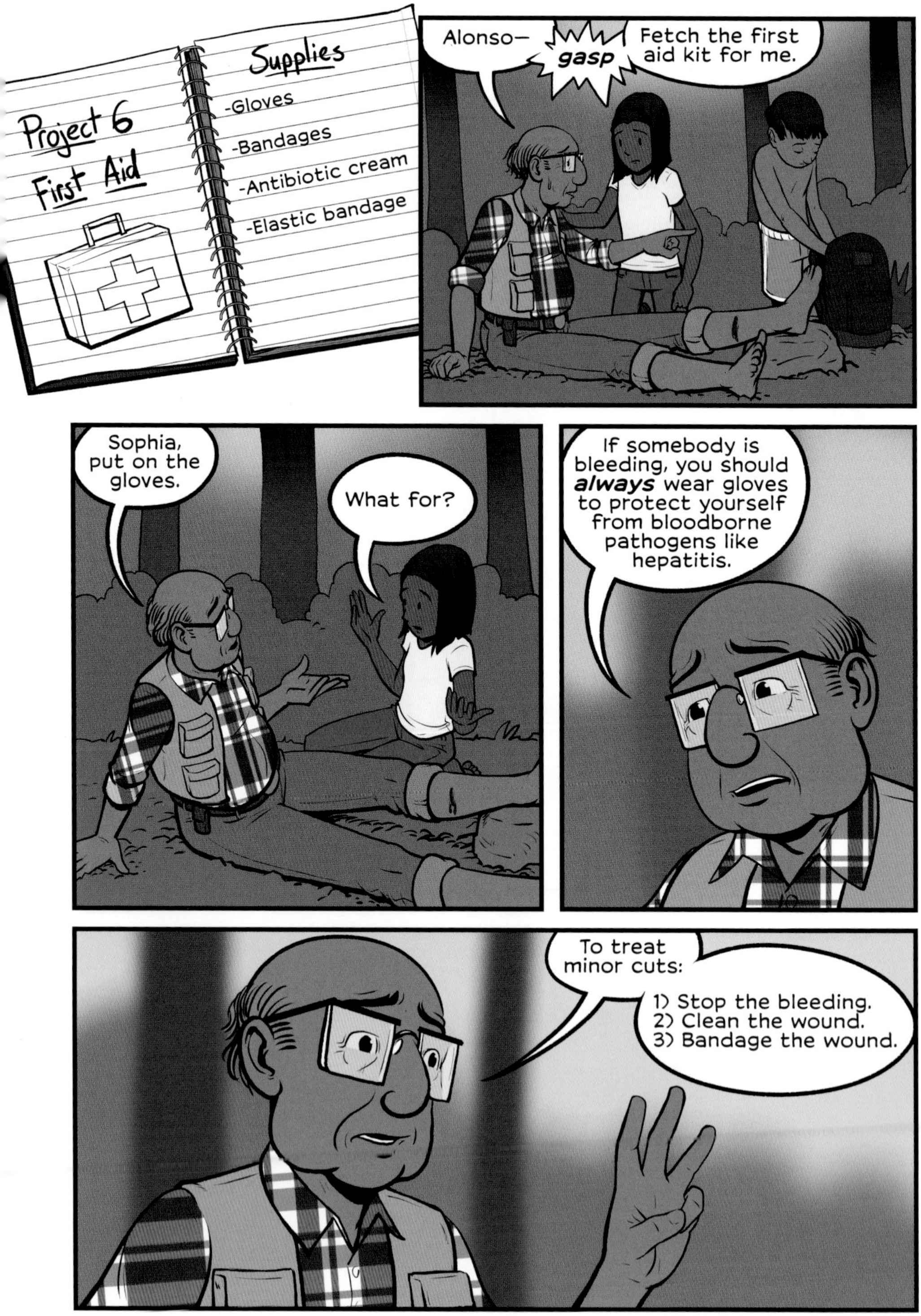
Project 6
First Aid
Supplies
-Gloves
-Bandages
-Antibiotic cream
-Elastic bandage
Alonso—
gasp
Fetch the first aid kit for me.
Sophia, put on the gloves.
What for?
If somebody is bleeding, you should *always* wear gloves to protect yourself from bloodborne pathogens like hepatitis.
To treat minor cuts:
1) Stop the bleeding.
2) Clean the wound.
3) Bandage the wound.

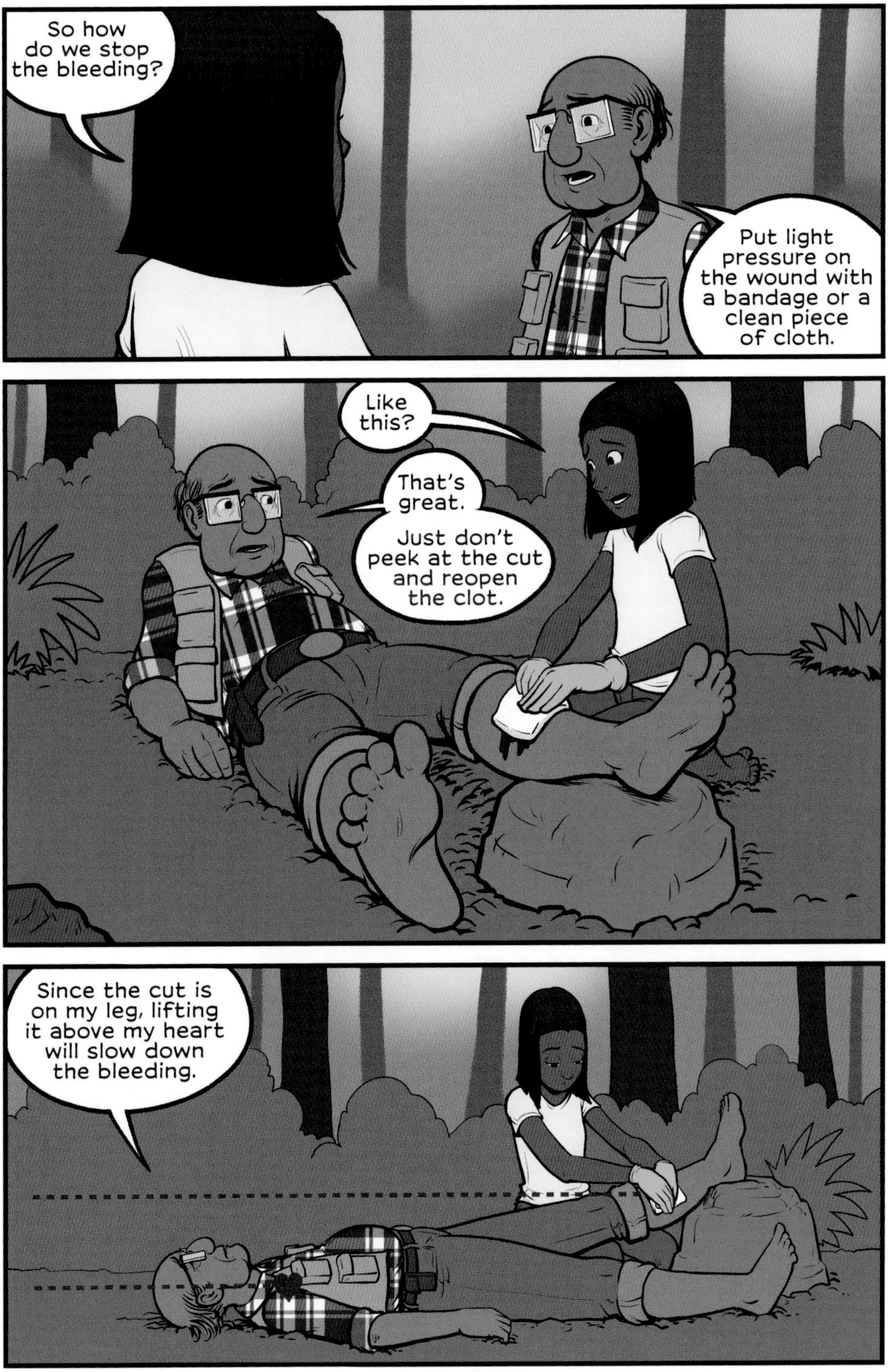
So how do we stop the bleeding?
Put light pressure on the wound with a bandage or a clean piece of cloth.
Like this?
That's great.
Just don't peek at the cut and reopen the clot.
Since the cut is on my leg, lifting it above my heart will slow down the bleeding.

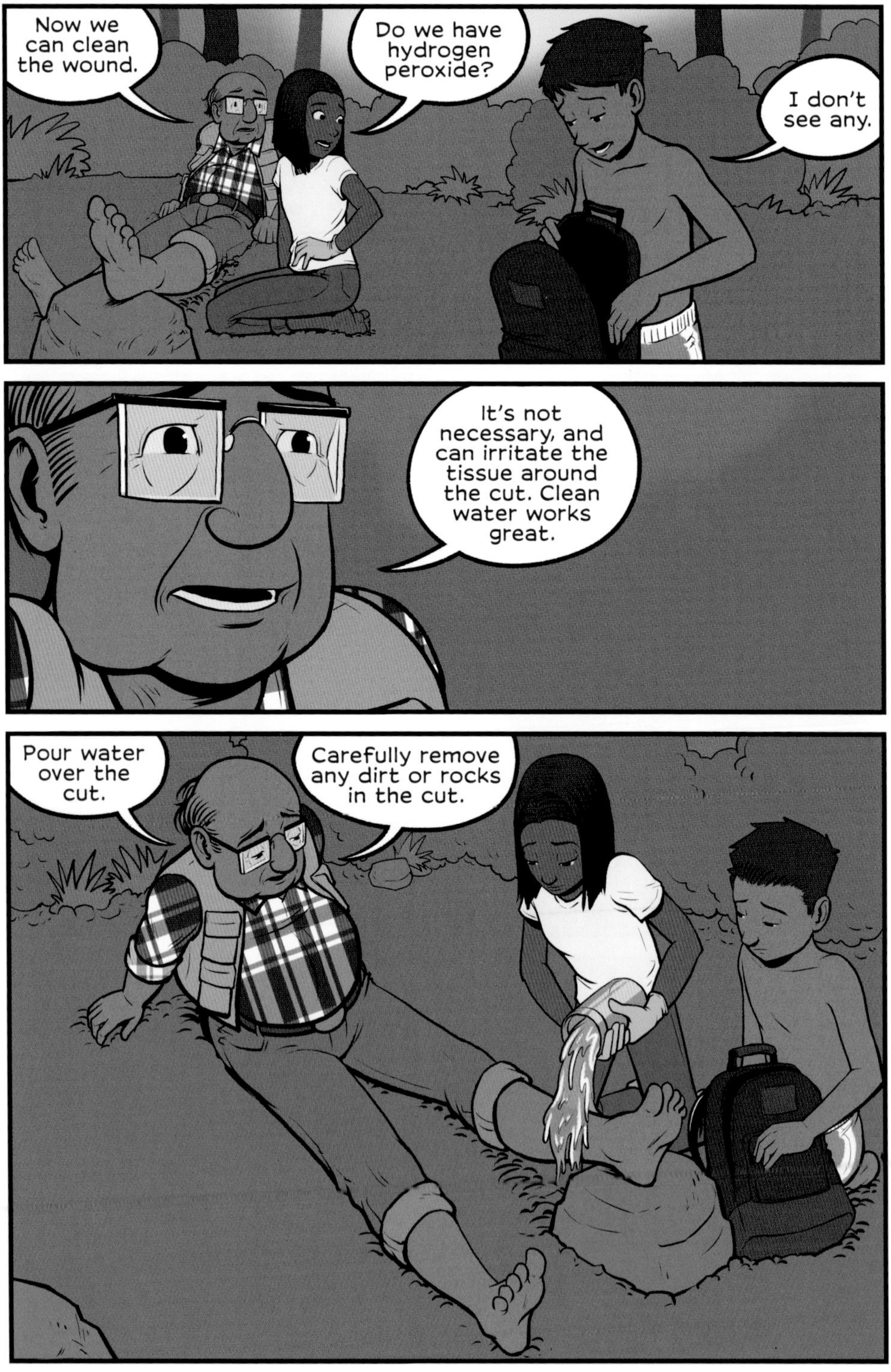
Now we can clean the wound.
Do we have hydrogen peroxide?
I don't see any.
It's not necessary, and can irritate the tissue around the cut. Clean water works great.
Pour water over the cut.
Carefully remove any dirt or rocks in the cut.

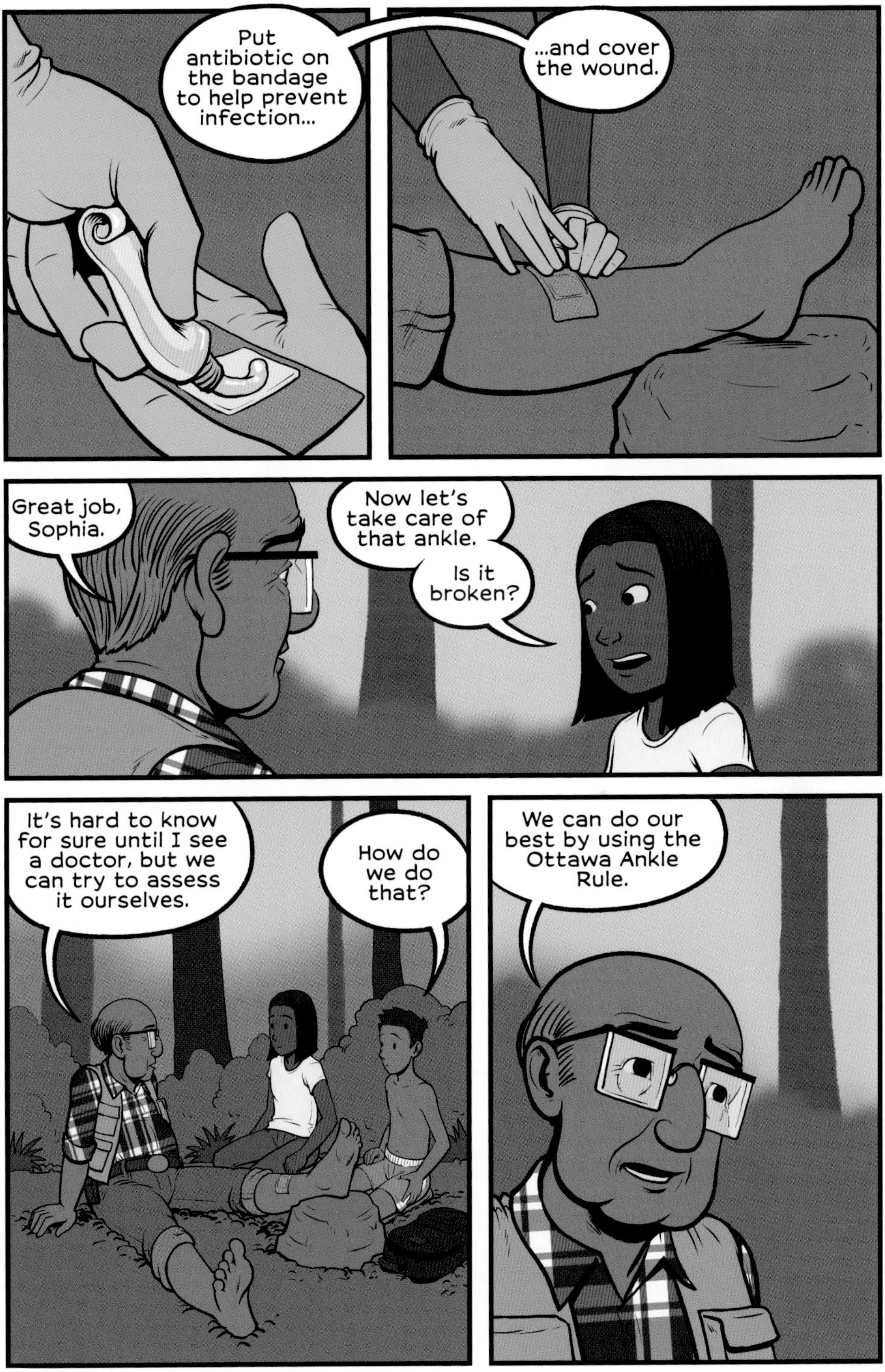
Put antibiotic on the bandage to help prevent infection...
...and cover the wound.
Great job, Sophia.
Now let's take care of that ankle.
Is it broken?
It's hard to know for sure until I see a doctor, but we can try to assess it ourselves.
How do we do that?
We can do our best by using the Ottawa Ankle Rule.

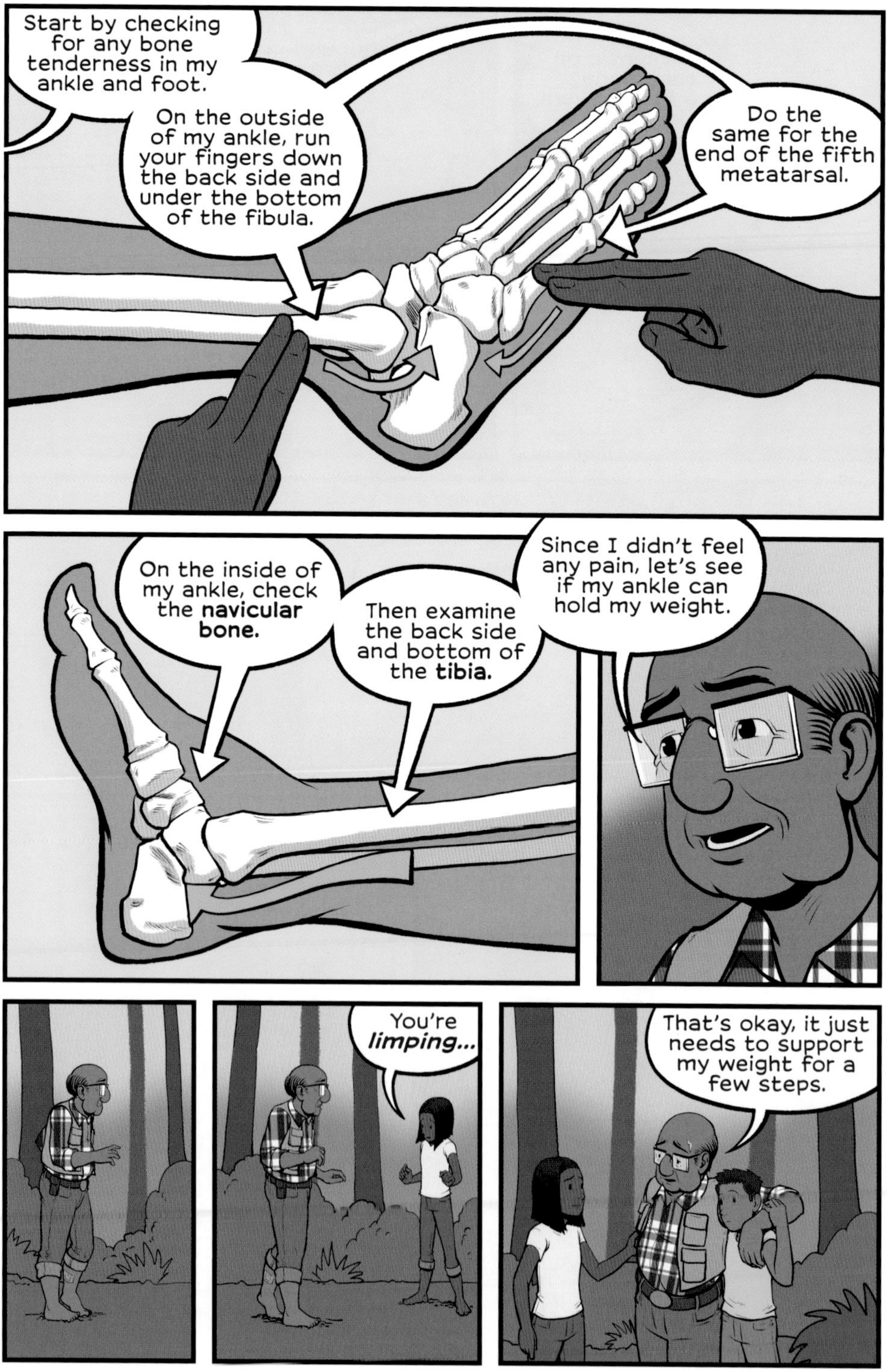
Start by checking for any bone tenderness in my ankle and foot.
On the outside of my ankle, run your fingers down the back side and under the bottom of the fibula.
Do the same for the end of the fifth metatarsal.
On the inside of my ankle, check the **navicular bone.**
Then examine the back side and bottom of the **tibia.**
Since I didn't feel any pain, let's see if my ankle can hold my weight.
You're *limping...*
That's okay, it just needs to support my weight for a few steps.

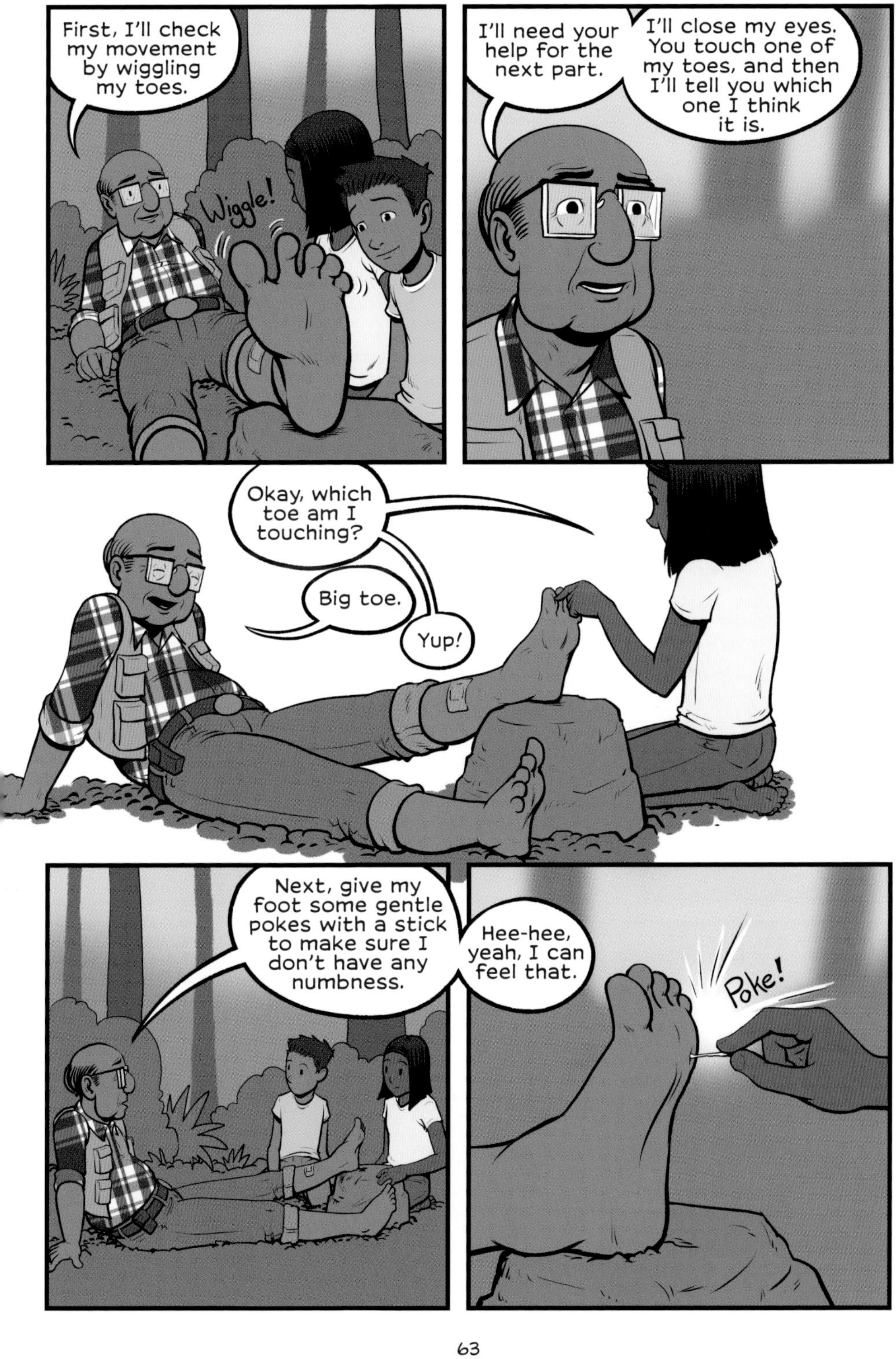
First, I'll check my movement by wiggling my toes.
Wiggle!
I'll need your help for the next part.
I'll close my eyes. You touch one of my toes, and then I'll tell you which one I think it is.
Okay, which toe am I touching?
Big toe.
Yup!
Next, give my foot some gentle pokes with a stick to make sure I don't have any numbness.
Hee-hee, yeah, I can feel that.
Poke!

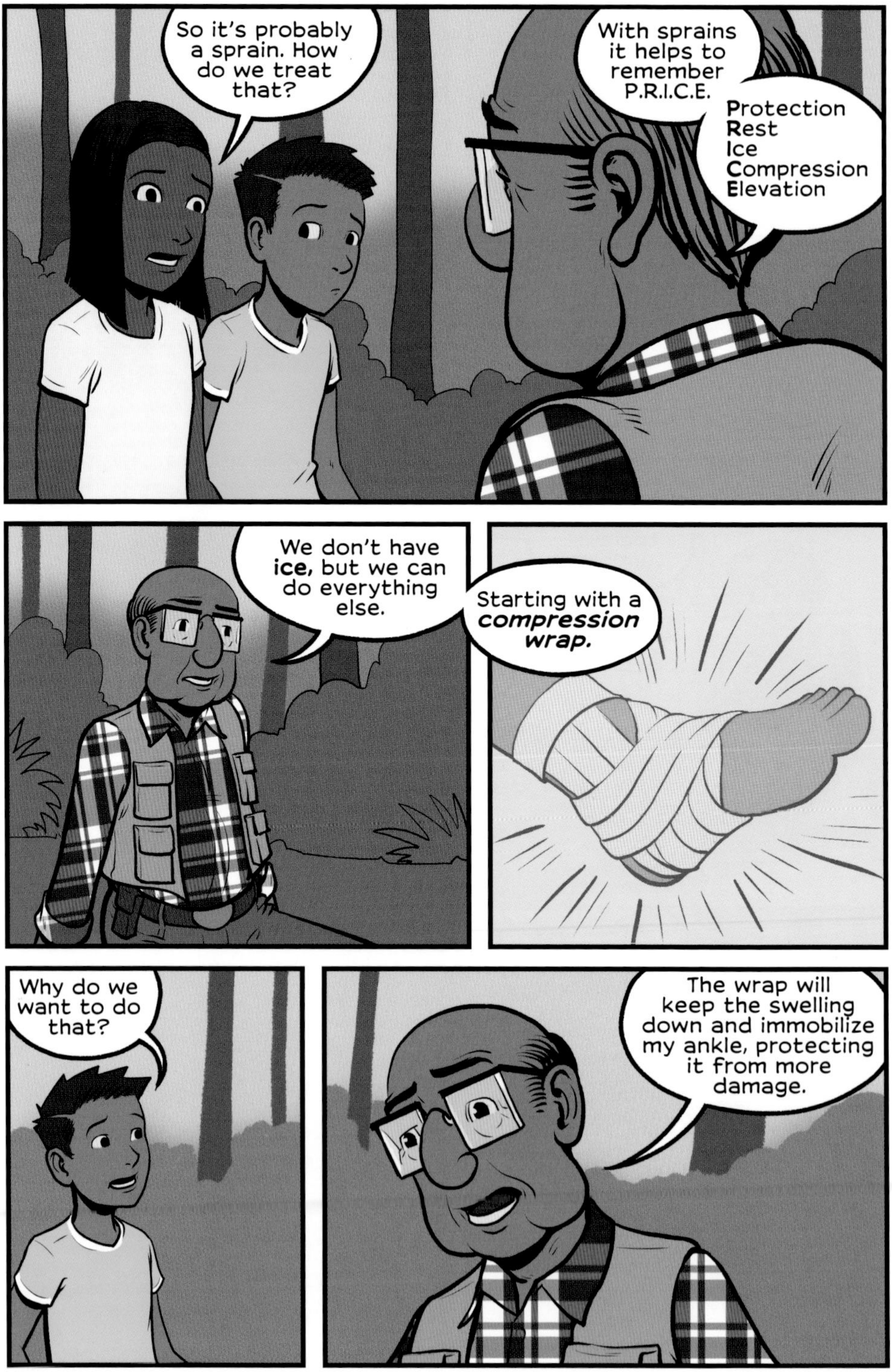
So it's probably a sprain. How do we treat that?
With sprains it helps to remember P.R.I.C.E.
Protection
Rest
Ice
Compression
Elevation
We don't have **ice**, but we can do everything else.
Starting with a ***compression wrap.***
Why do we want to do that?
The wrap will keep the swelling down and immobilize my ankle, protecting it from more damage.

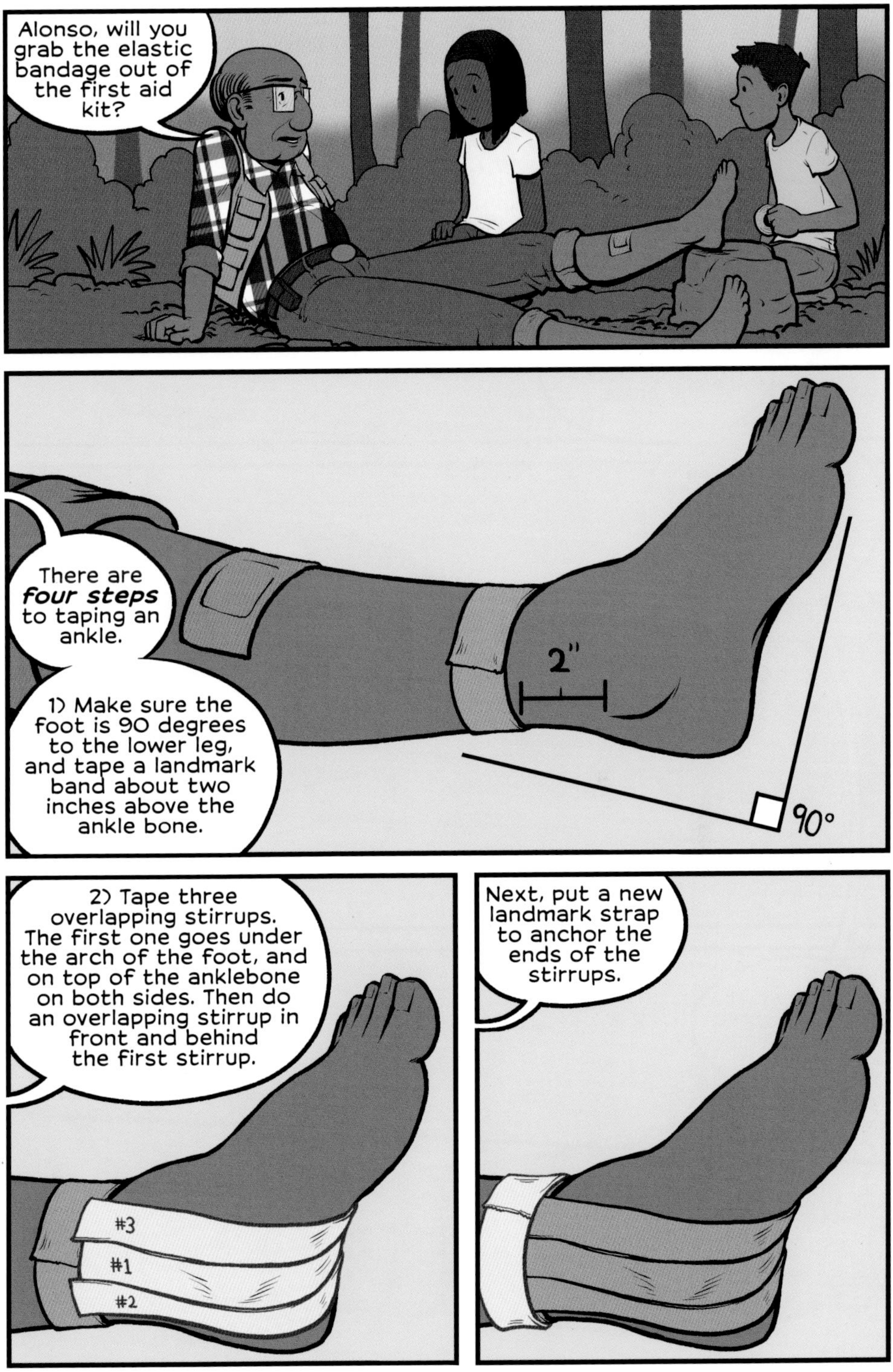
Alonso, will you grab the elastic bandage out of the first aid kit?
There are **four steps** to taping an ankle.
1) Make sure the foot is 90 degrees to the lower leg, and tape a landmark band about two inches above the ankle bone.
2"
90°
2) Tape three overlapping stirrups. The first one goes under the arch of the foot, and on top of the anklebone on both sides. Then do an overlapping stirrup in front and behind the first stirrup.
#3
#1
#2
Next, put a new landmark strap to anchor the ends of the stirrups.

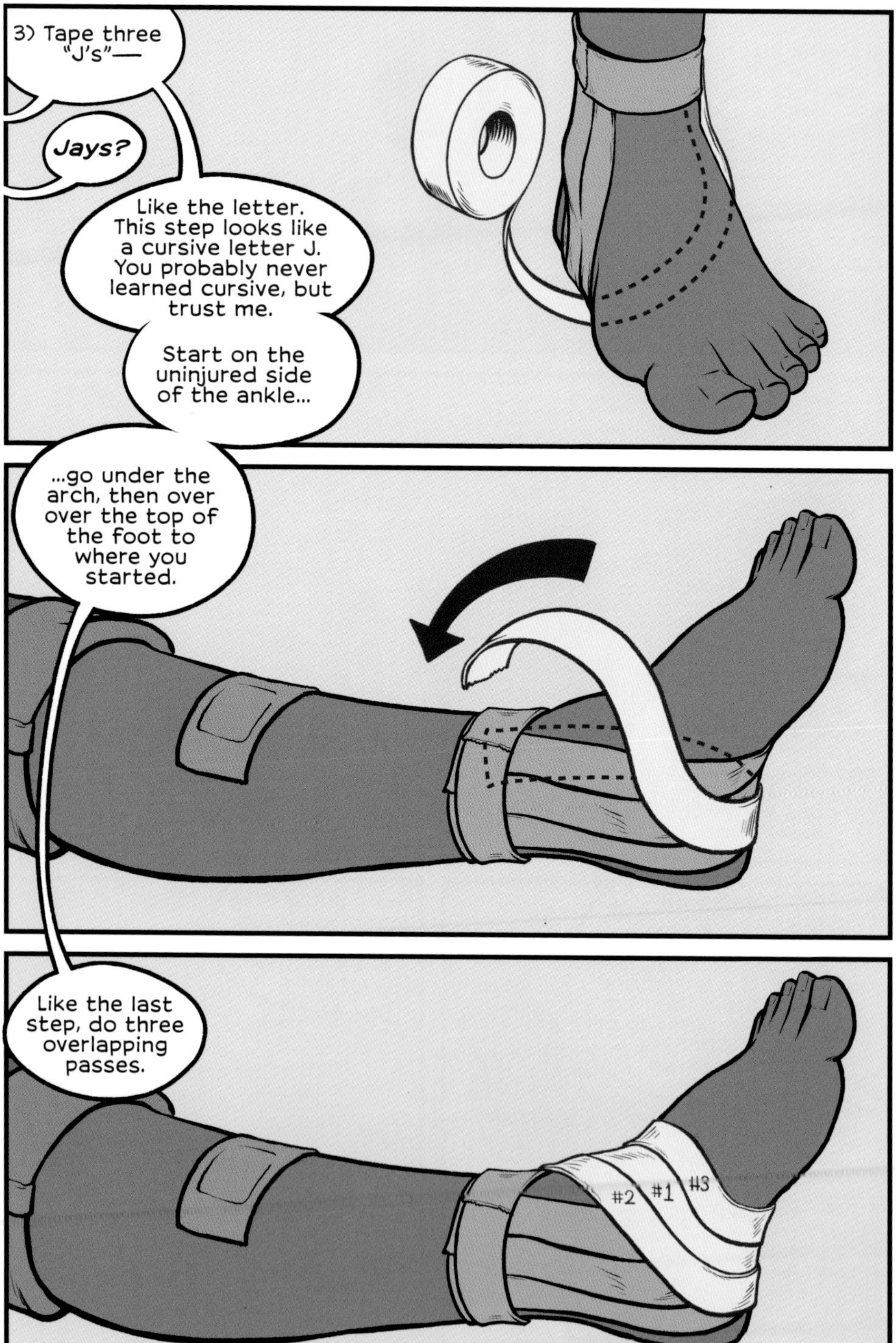
3) Tape three "J's"—
Jays?
Like the letter. This step looks like a cursive letter J. You probably never learned cursive, but trust me.
Start on the uninjured side of the ankle...
...go under the arch, then over over the top of the foot to where you started.
Like the last step, do three overlapping passes.
#2
#1
#3

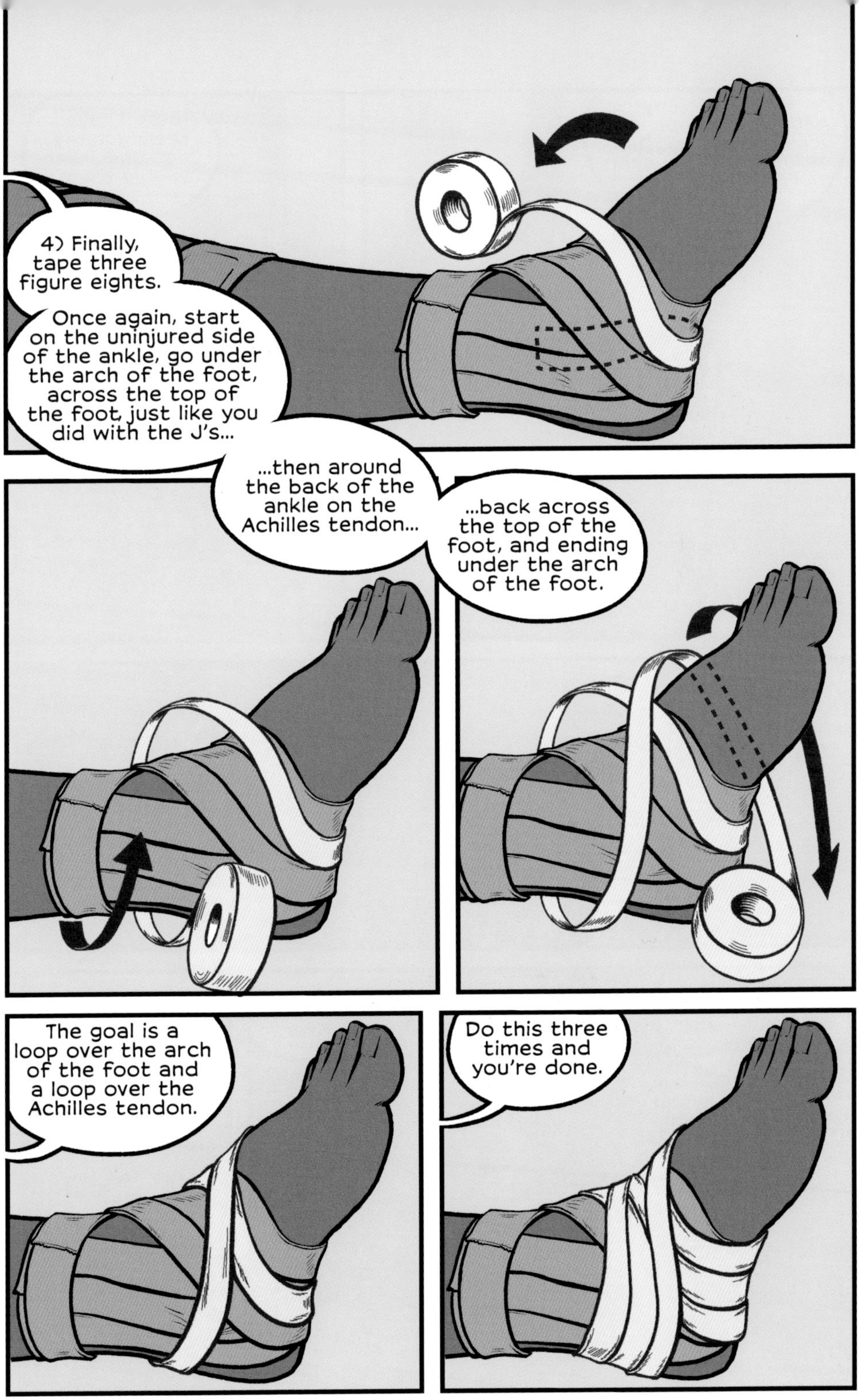
4) Finally, tape three figure eights.
Once again, start on the uninjured side of the ankle, go under the arch of the foot, across the top of the foot, just like you did with the J's...
...then around the back of the ankle on the Achilles tendon...
...back across the top of the foot, and ending under the arch of the foot.
The goal is a loop over the arch of the foot and a loop over the Achilles tendon.
Do this three times and you're done.

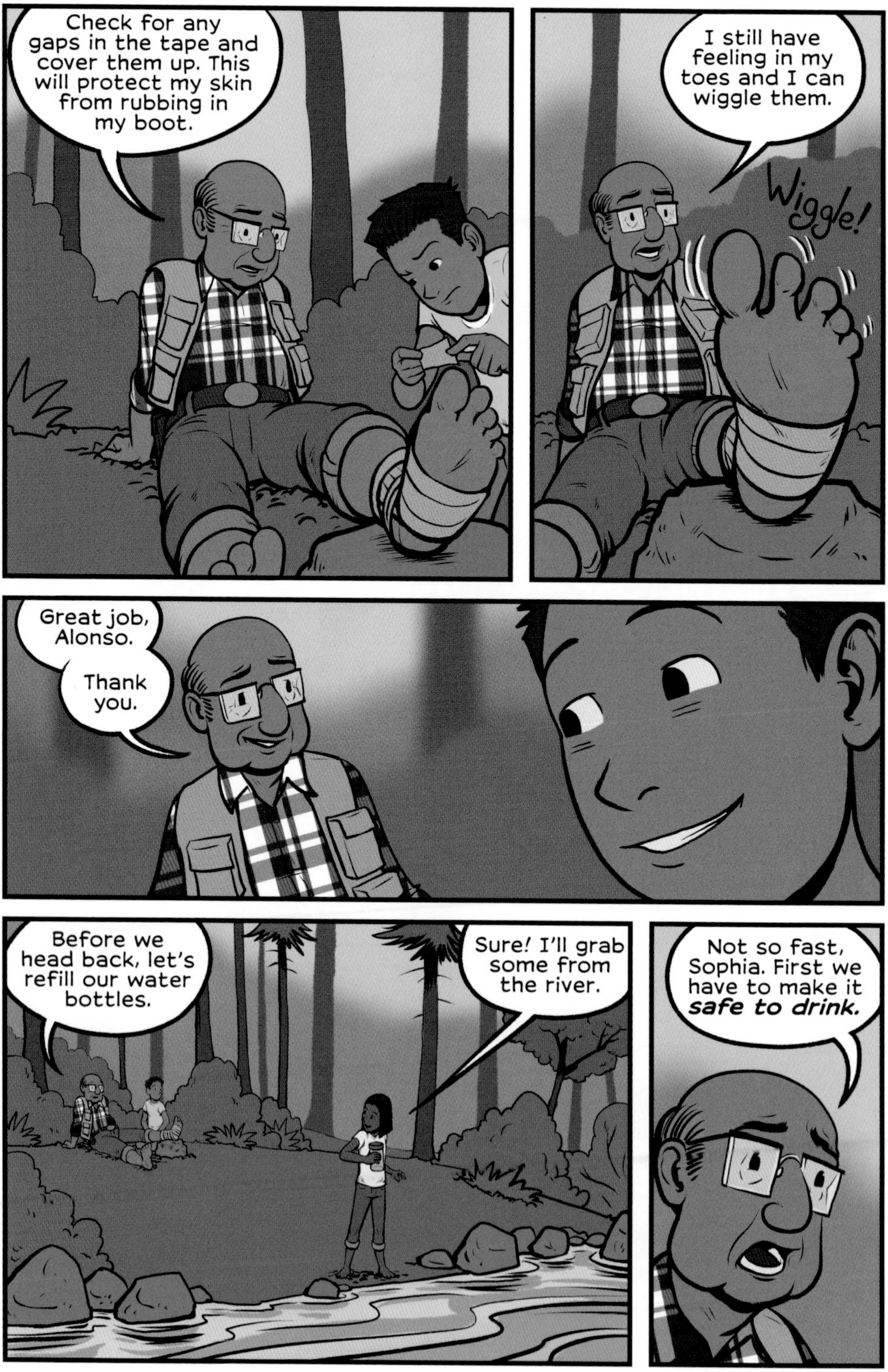
Check for any gaps in the tape and cover them up. This will protect my skin from rubbing in my boot.
I still have feeling in my toes and I can wiggle them.
Wiggle!
Great job, Alonso.
Thank you.
Before we head back, let's refill our water bottles.
Sure! I'll grab some from the river.
Not so fast, Sophia. First we have to make it ***safe to drink.***

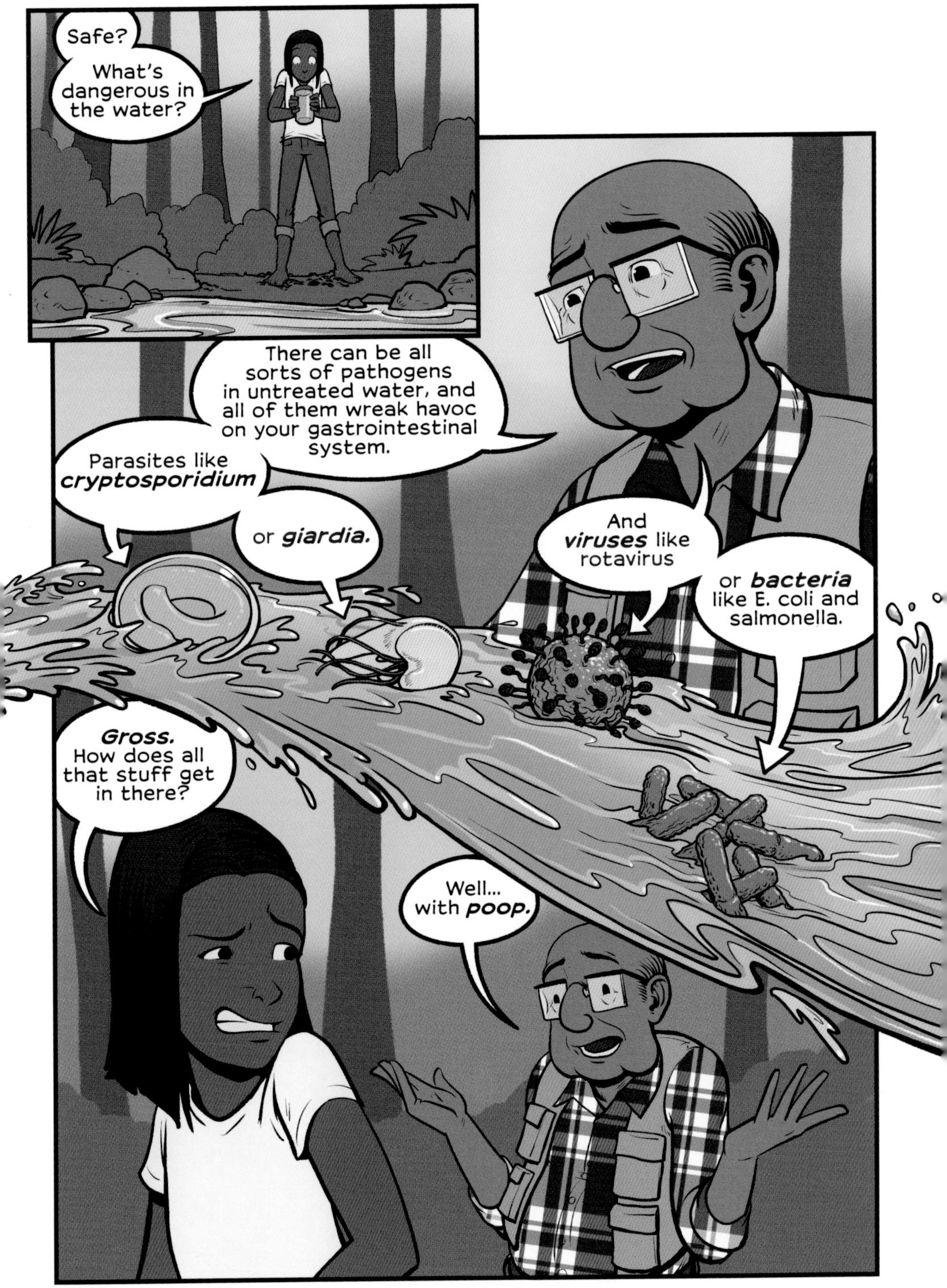

Safe?
What's dangerous in the water?
There can be all sorts of pathogens in untreated water, and all of them wreak havoc on your gastrointestinal system.
Parasites like *cryptosporidium*
or *giardia.*
And *viruses* like rotavirus
or *bacteria* like E. coli and salmonella.
*Gross.* How does all that stuff get in there?
Well... with *poop.*

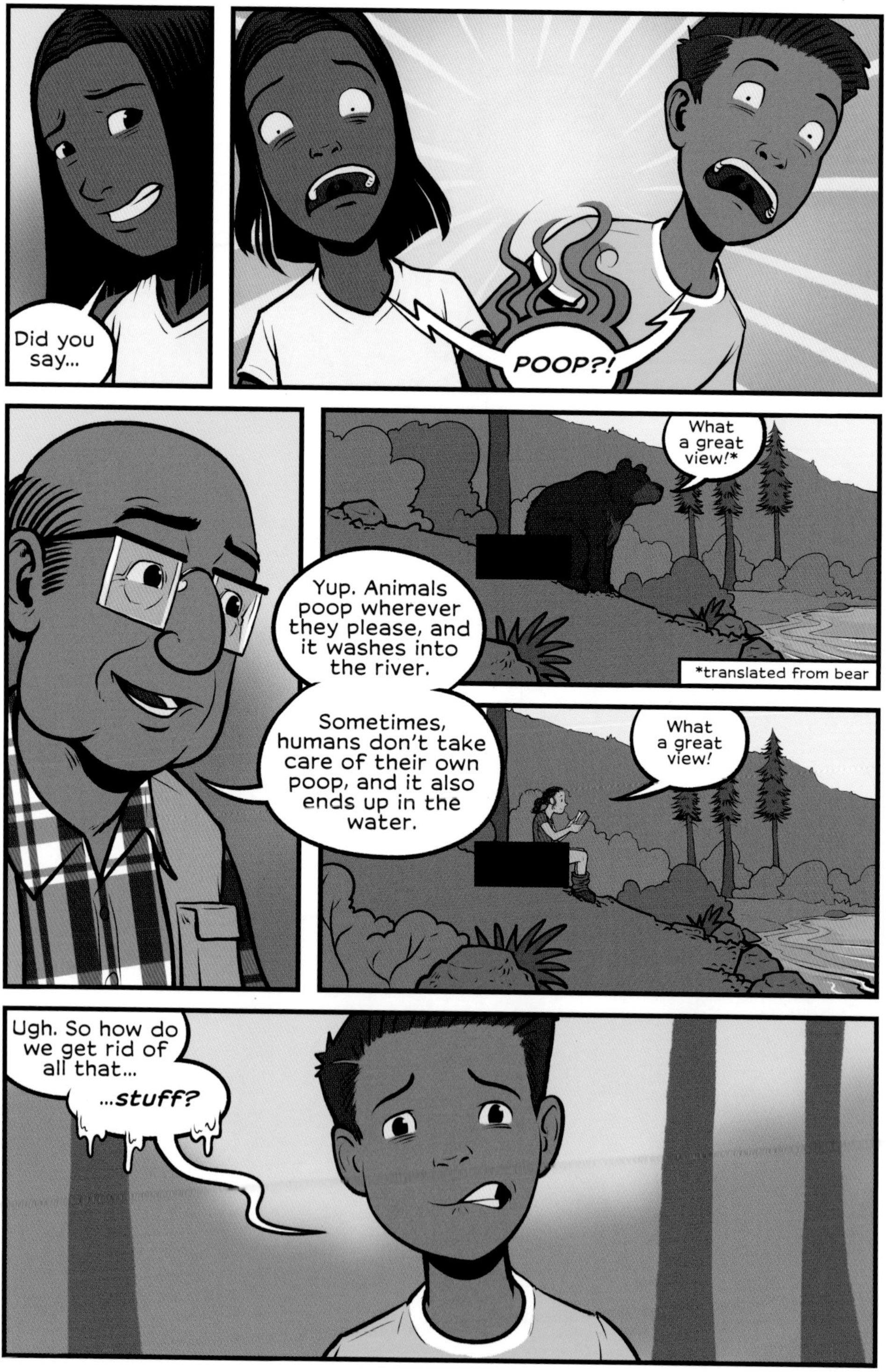
Did you say...
POOP?!
Yup. Animals poop wherever they please, and it washes into the river.
What a great view!*
*translated from bear
Sometimes, humans don't take care of their own poop, and it also ends up in the water.
What a great view!
Ugh. So how do we get rid of all that...
...stuff?

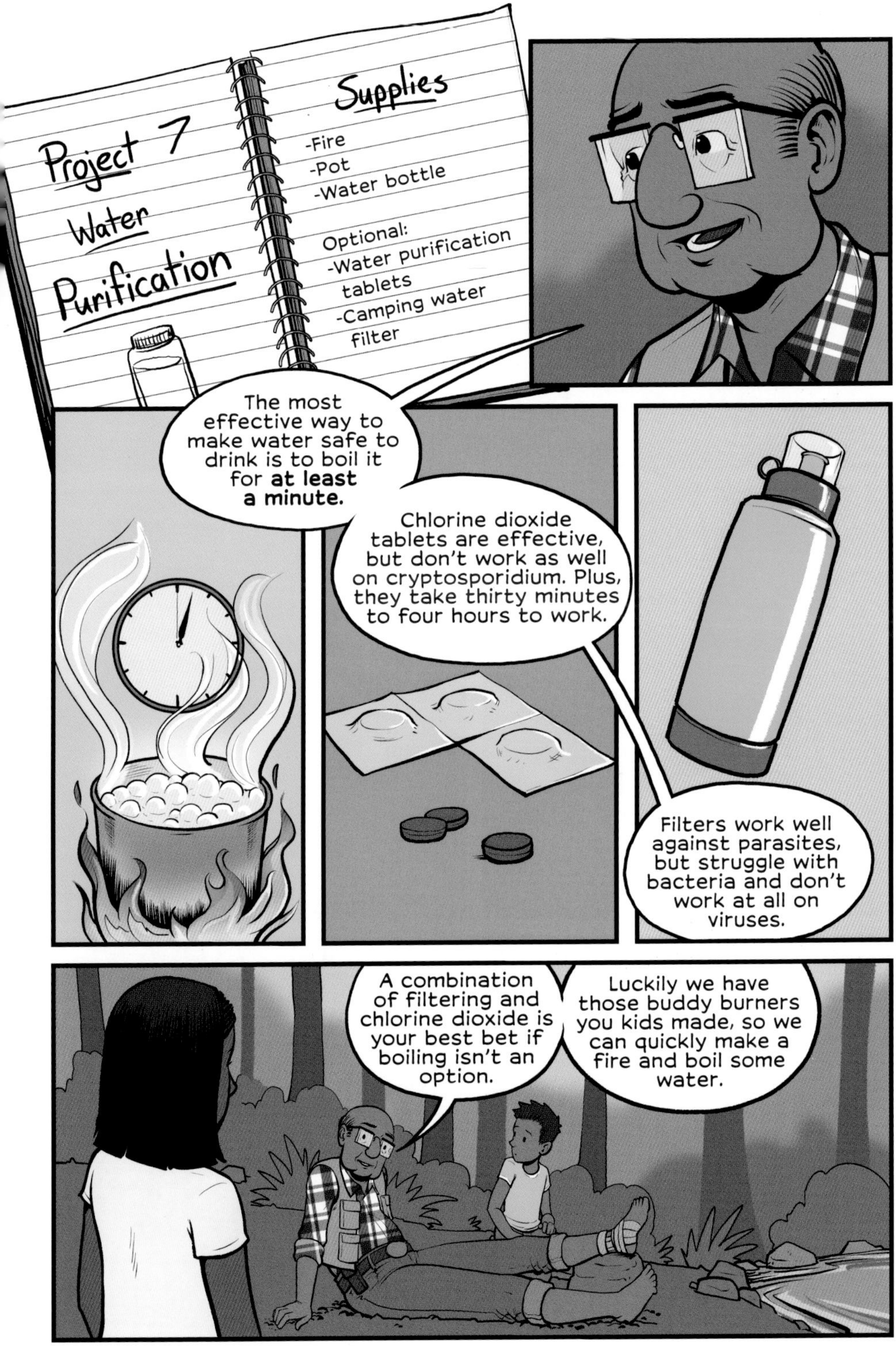
Project 7
Water
Purification
Supplies
-Fire
-Pot
-Water bottle
Optional:
-Water purification
tablets
-Camping water
filter
The most effective way to make water safe to drink is to boil it for **at least a minute.**
Chlorine dioxide tablets are effective, but don't work as well on cryptosporidium. Plus, they take thirty minutes to four hours to work.
Filters work well against parasites, but struggle with bacteria and don't work at all on viruses.
A combination of filtering and chlorine dioxide is your best bet if boiling isn't an option.
Luckily we have those buddy burners you kids made, so we can quickly make a fire and boil some water.

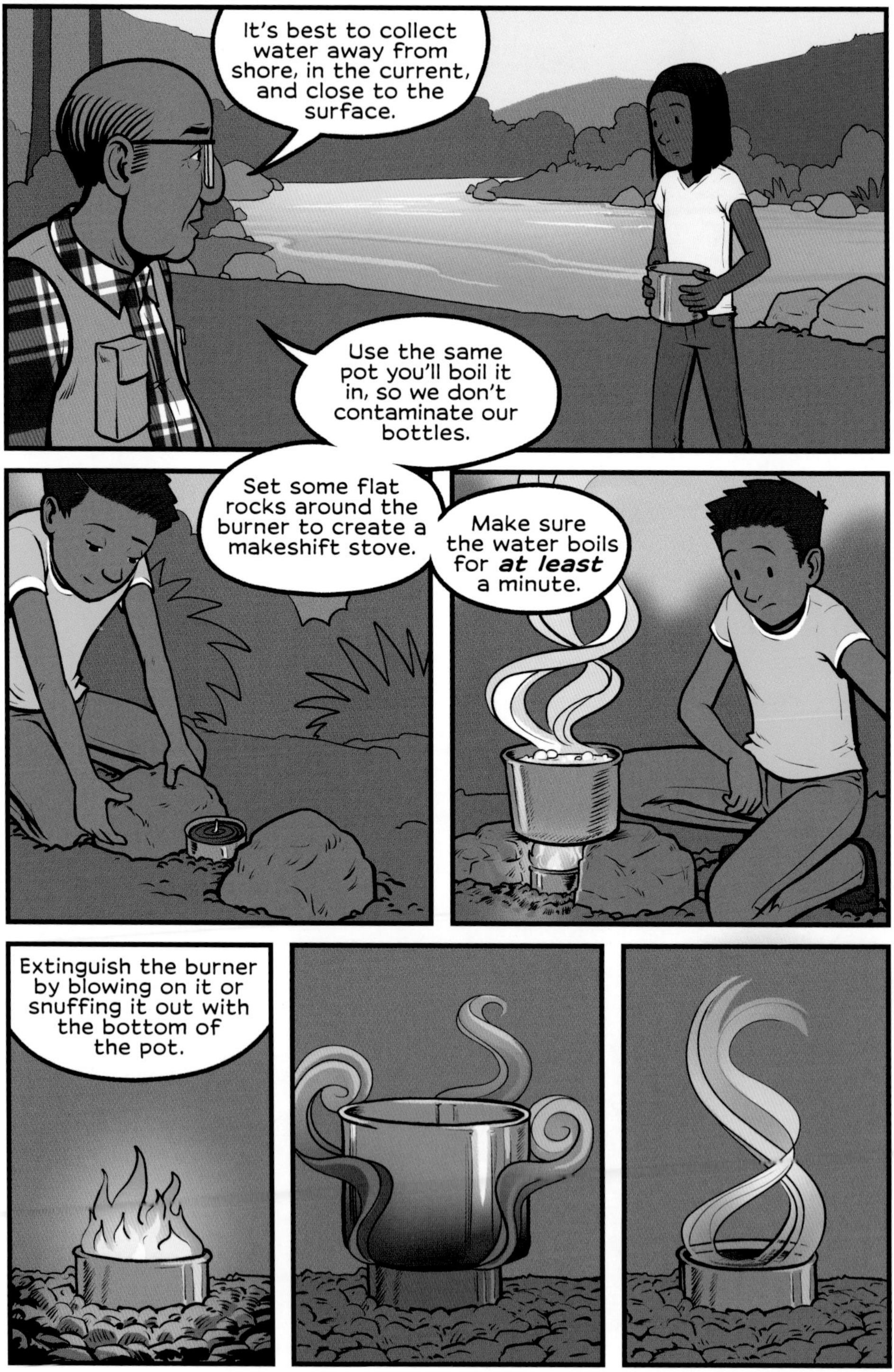
It's best to collect water away from shore, in the current, and close to the surface.
Use the same pot you'll boil it in, so we don't contaminate our bottles.
Set some flat rocks around the burner to create a makeshift stove.
Make sure the water boils for ***at least*** a minute.
Extinguish the burner by blowing on it or snuffing it out with the bottom of the pot.

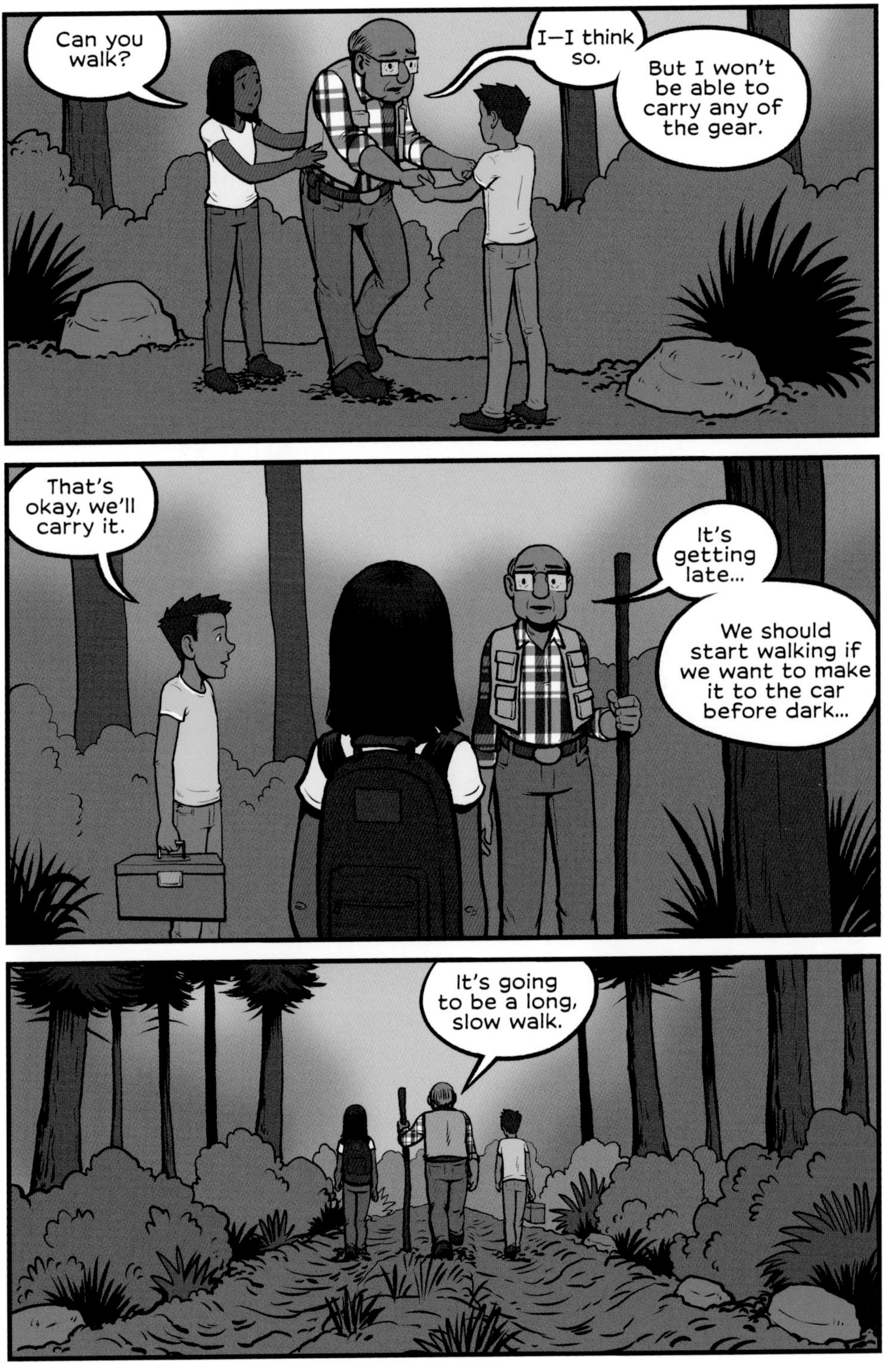

Can you walk?
I—I think so.
But I won't be able to carry any of the gear.
That's okay, we'll carry it.
It's getting late...
We should start walking if we want to make it to the car before dark...
It's going to be a long, slow walk.

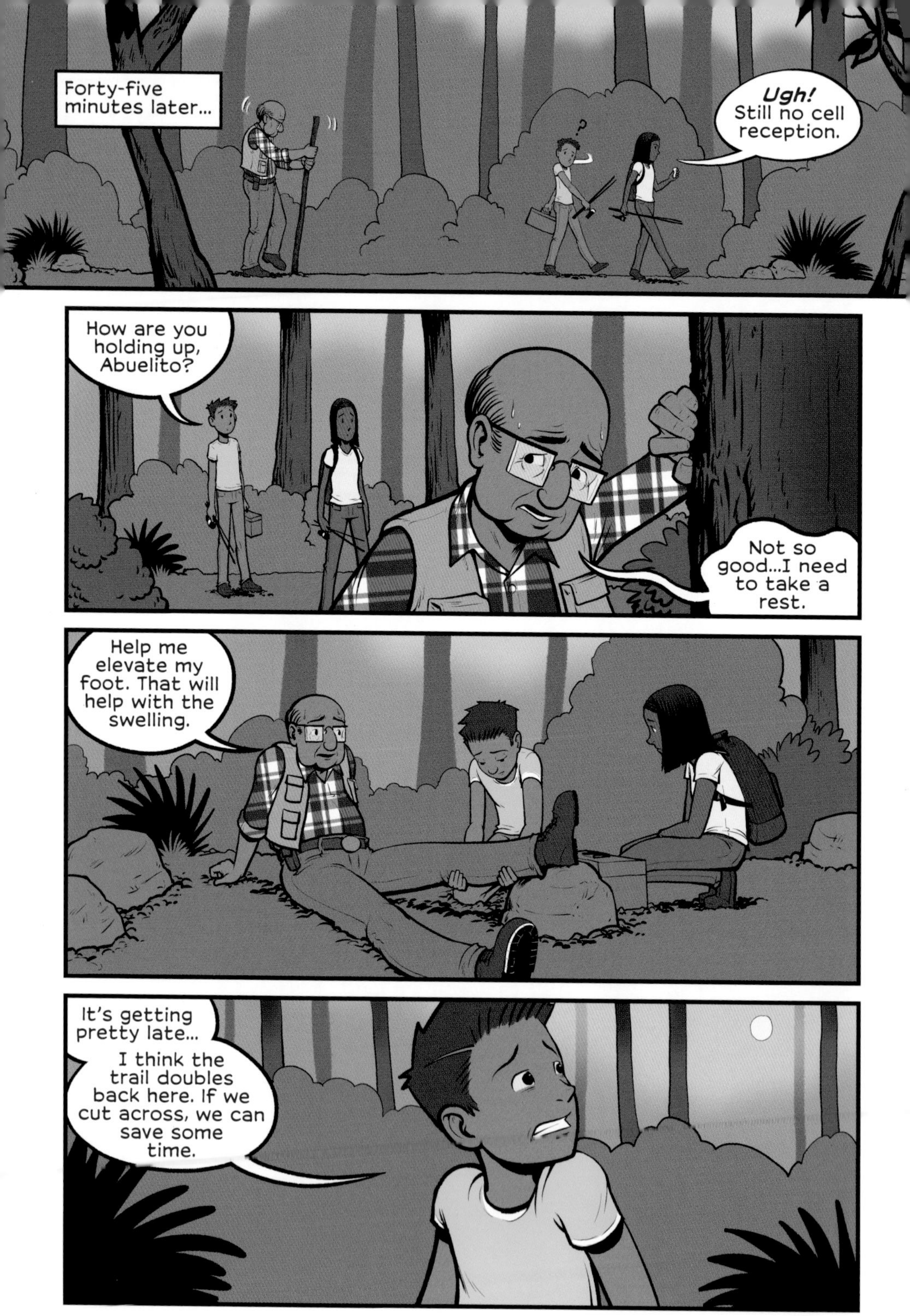
Forty-five minutes later...
Ugh! Still no cell reception.
?
How are you holding up, Abuelito?
Not so good...I need to take a rest.
Help me elevate my foot. That will help with the swelling.
It's getting pretty late...
I think the trail doubles back here. If we cut across, we can save some time.

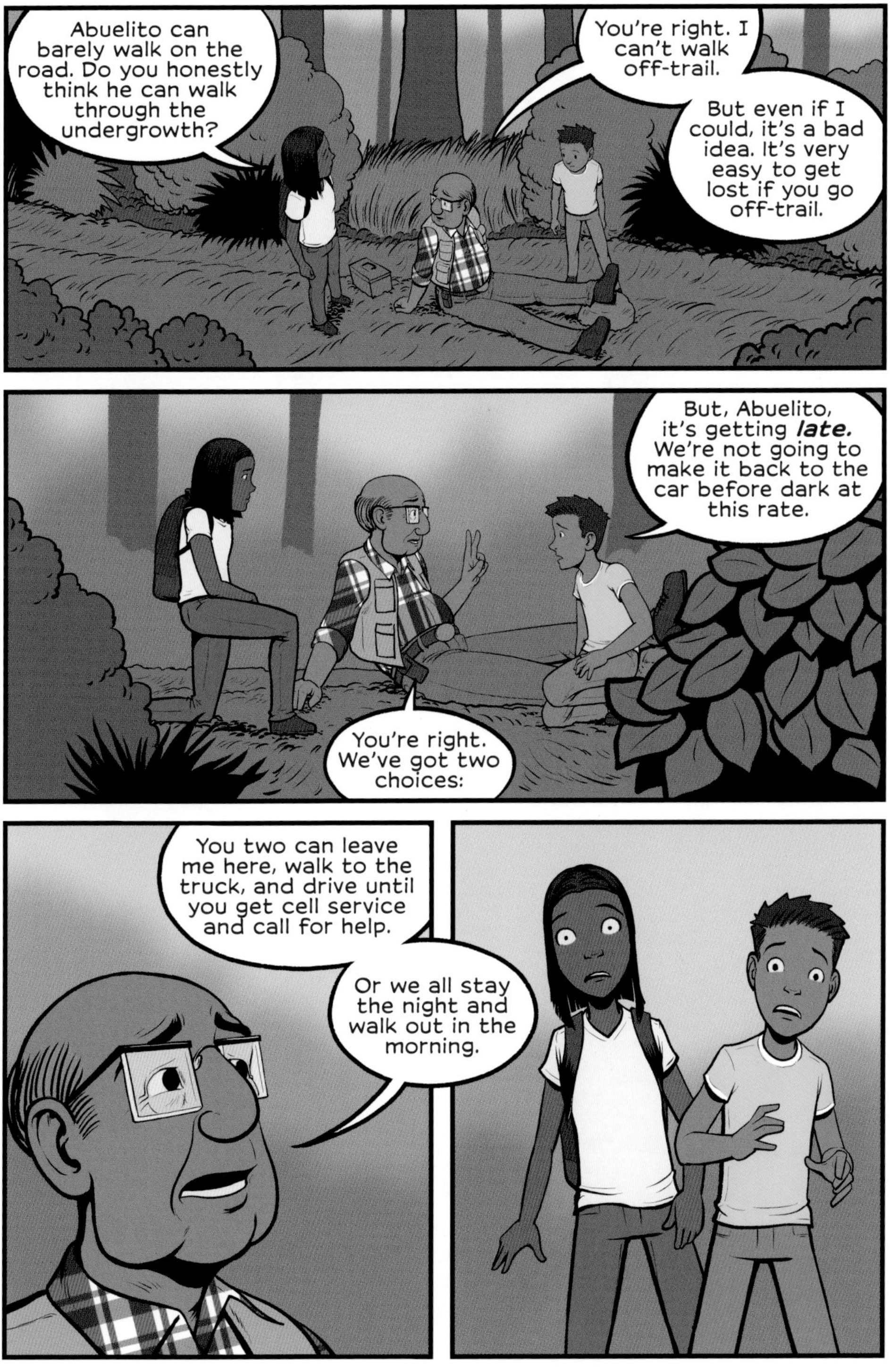
Abuelito can barely walk on the road. Do you honestly think he can walk through the undergrowth?
You're right. I can't walk off-trail.
But even if I could, it's a bad idea. It's very easy to get lost if you go off-trail.
But, Abuelito, it's getting *late.* We're not going to make it back to the car before dark at this rate.
You're right. We've got two choices:
You two can leave me here, walk to the truck, and drive until you get cell service and call for help.
Or we all stay the night and walk out in the morning.

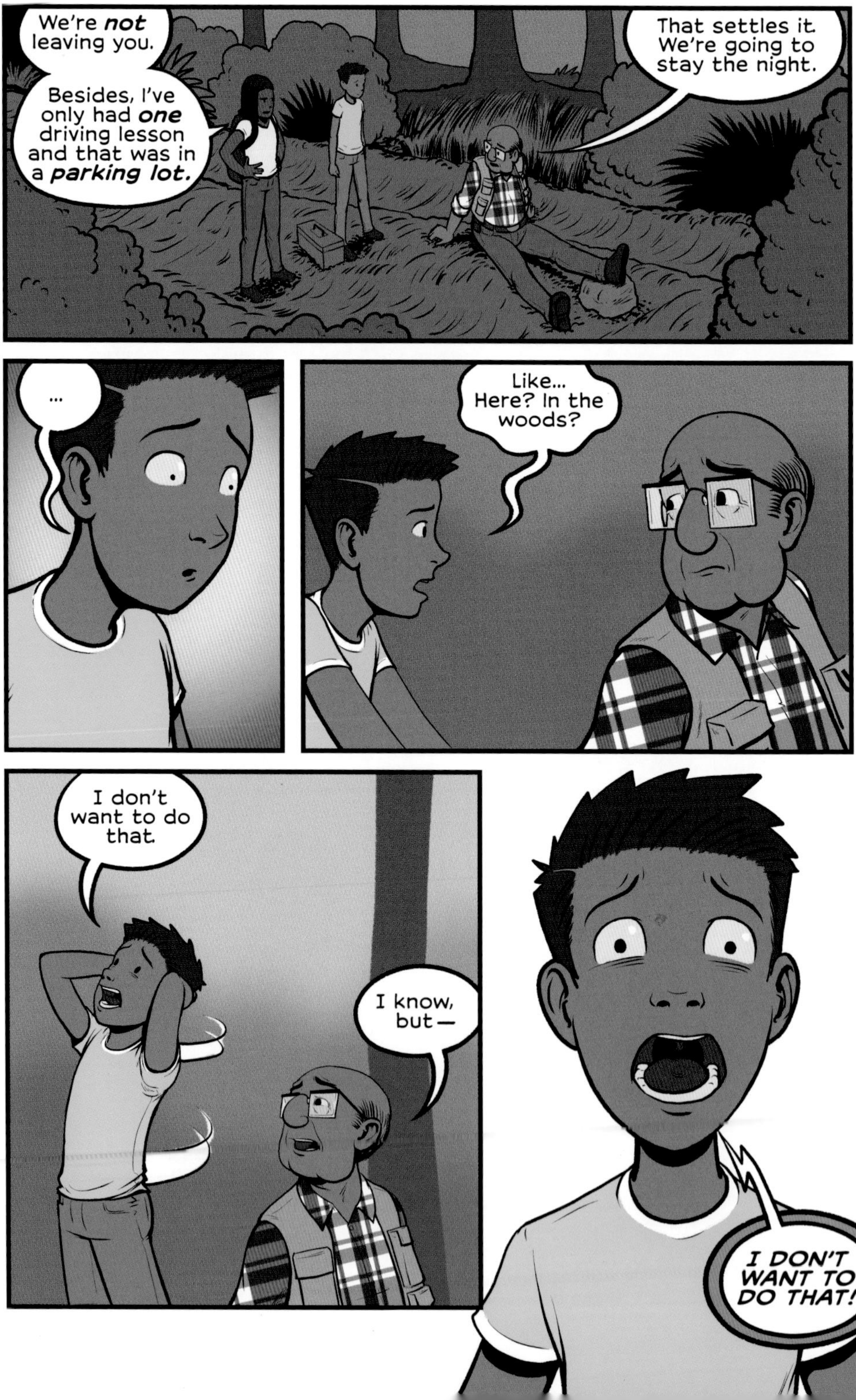

We're *not* leaving you.
Besides, I've only had *one* driving lesson and that was in a *parking lot.*
That settles it. We're going to stay the night.
...
Like... Here? In the woods?
I don't want to do that.
I know, but—
*I DON'T WANT TO DO THAT!*

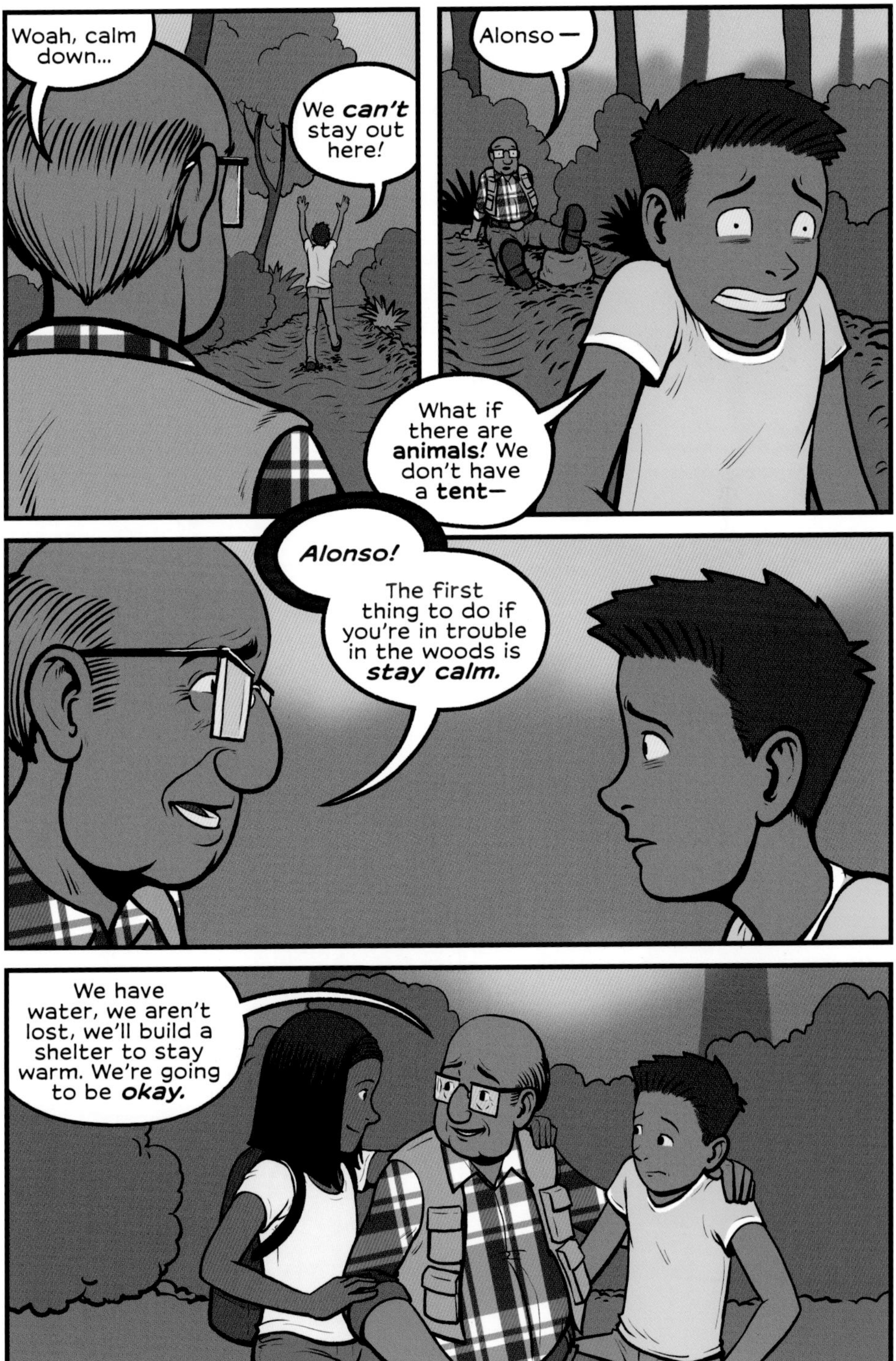
Woah, calm down...
We *can't* stay out here!
Alonso—
What if there are **animals!** We don't have a **tent**—
***Alonso!***
The first thing to do if you're in trouble in the woods is ***stay calm.***
We have water, we aren't lost, we'll build a shelter to stay warm. We're going to be ***okay.***

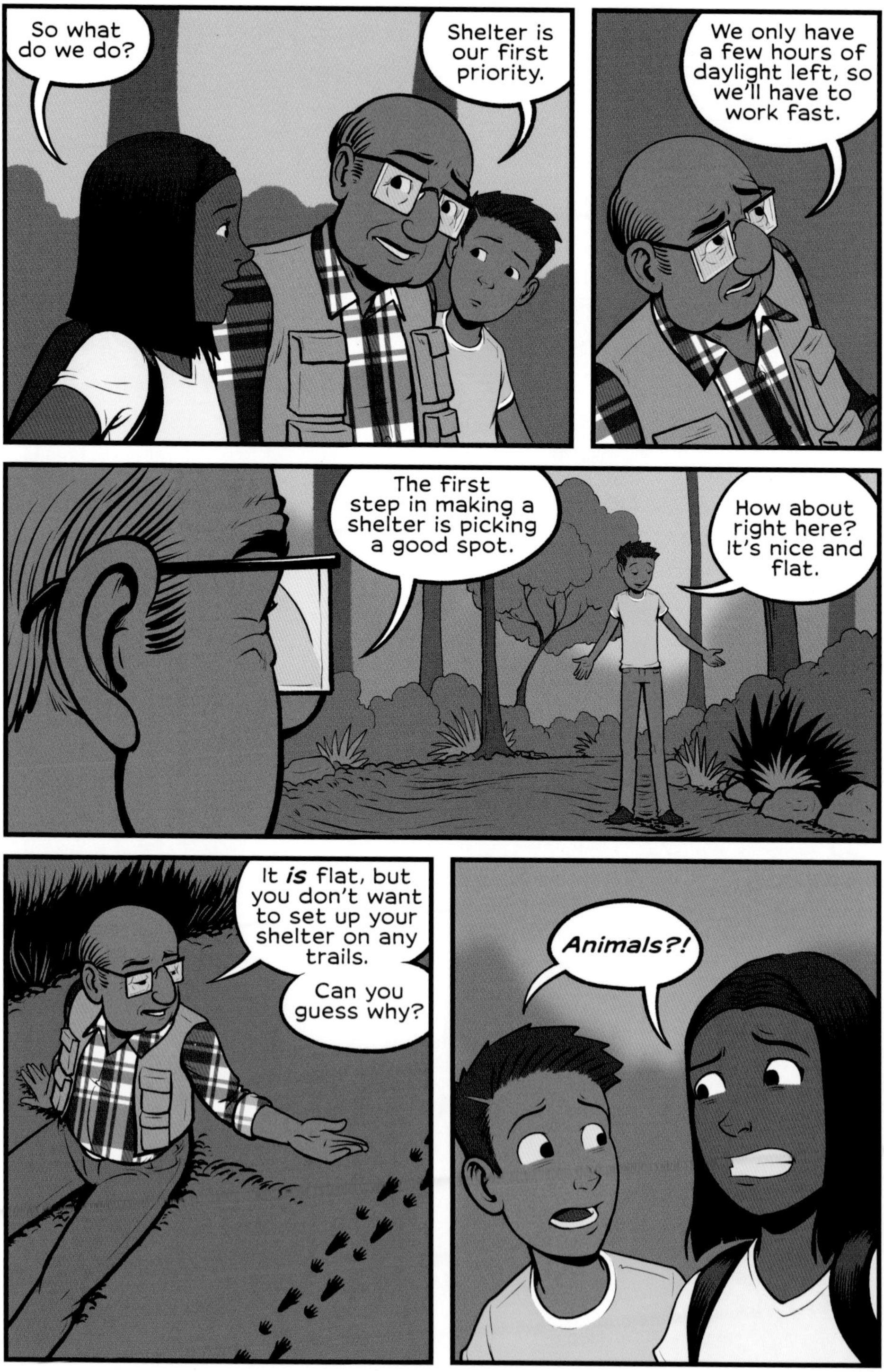

So what do we do?
Shelter is our first priority.
We only have a few hours of daylight left, so we'll have to work fast.
The first step in making a shelter is picking a good spot.
How about right here? It's nice and flat.
It *is* flat, but you don't want to set up your shelter on any trails.
Can you guess why?
*Animals?!*

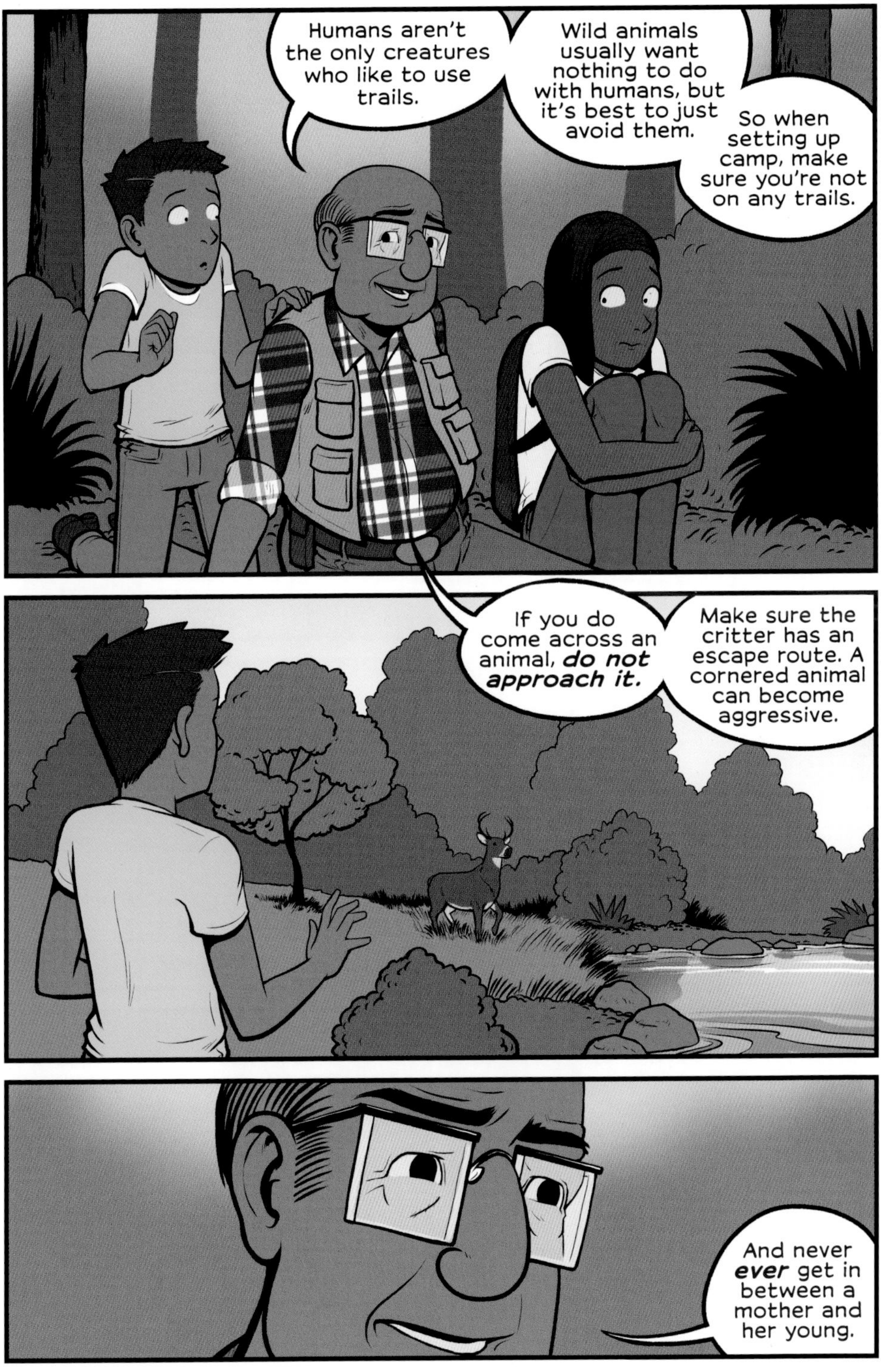
Humans aren't the only creatures who like to use trails.
Wild animals usually want nothing to do with humans, but it's best to just avoid them.
So when setting up camp, make sure you're not on any trails.
If you do come across an animal, ***do not approach it.***
Make sure the critter has an escape route. A cornered animal can become aggressive.
And never ***ever*** get in between a mother and her young.

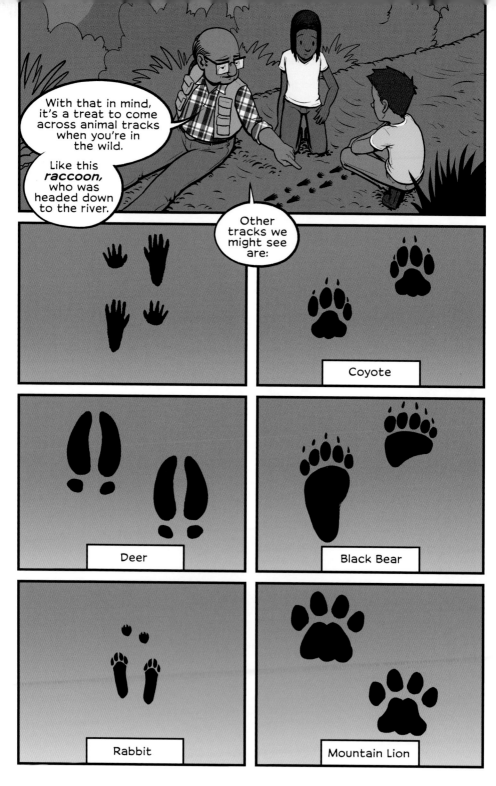

With that in mind, it's a treat to come across animal tracks when you're in the wild.

Like this *raccoon,* who was headed down to the river.

Other tracks we might see are:

Coyote

Deer

Black Bear

Rabbit

Mountain Lion

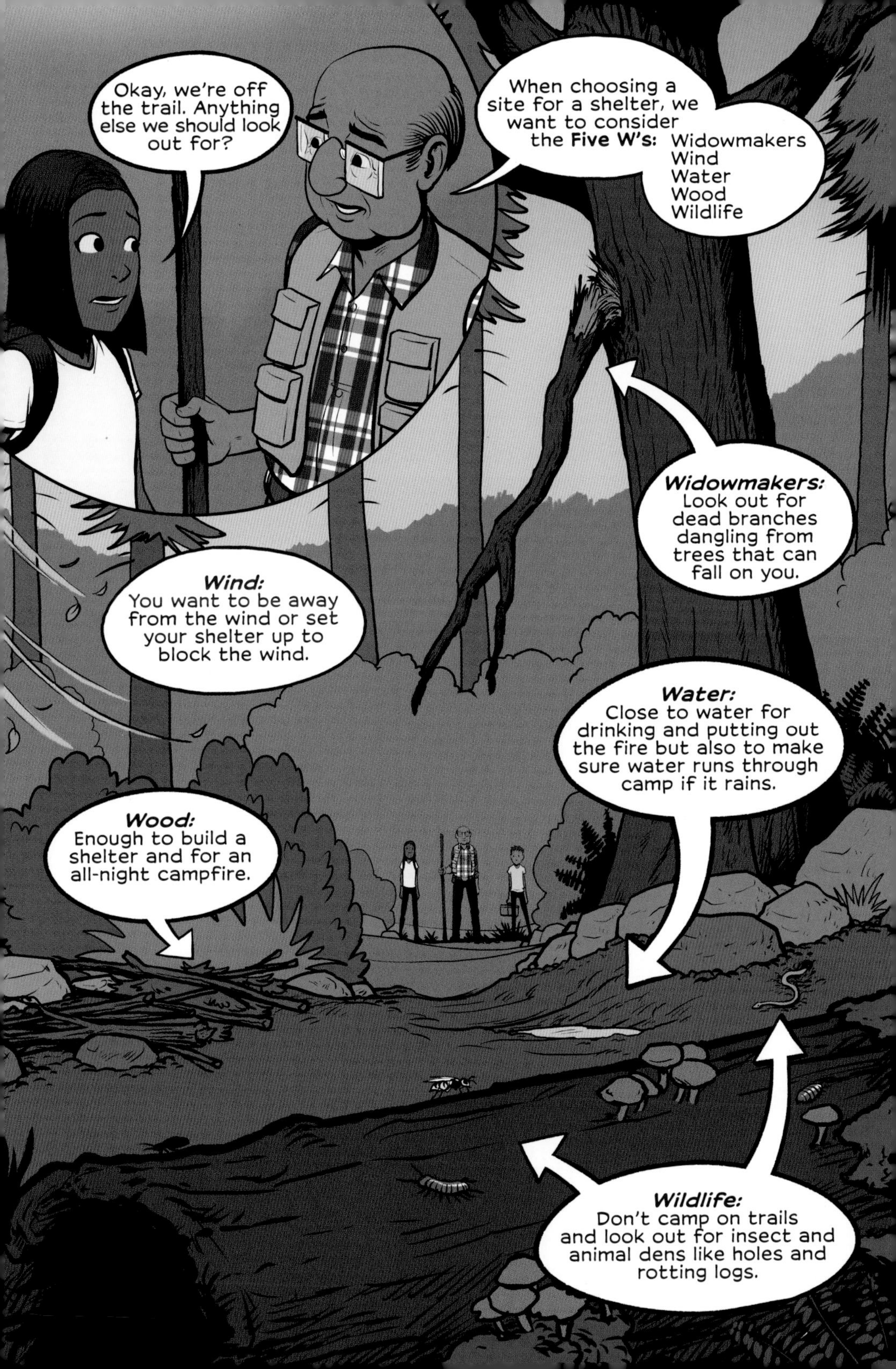

Okay, we're off the trail. Anything else we should look out for?
When choosing a site for a shelter, we want to consider the **Five W's:** Widowmakers Wind Water Wood Wildlife
***Widowmakers:*** Look out for dead branches dangling from trees that can fall on you.
***Wind:*** You want to be away from the wind or set your shelter up to block the wind.
***Water:*** Close to water for drinking and putting out the fire but also to make sure water runs through camp if it rains.
***Wood:*** Enough to build a shelter and for an all-night campfire.
***Wildlife:*** Don't camp on trails and look out for insect and animal dens like holes and rotting logs.

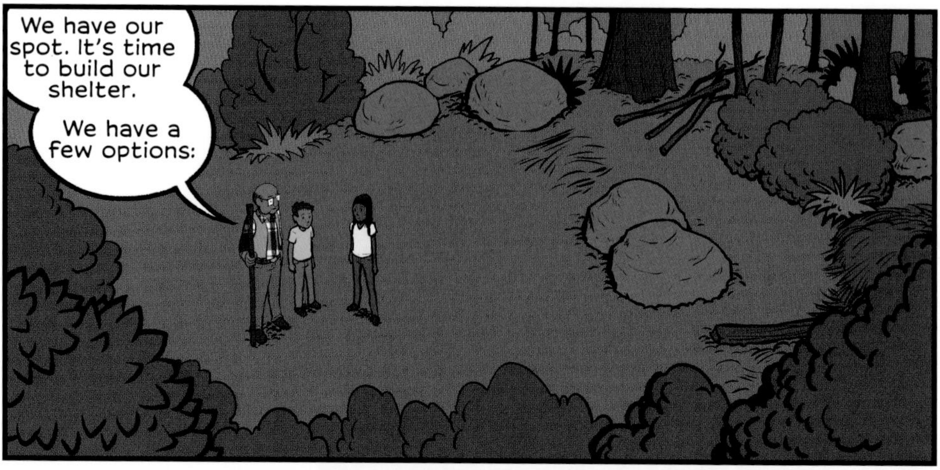
We have our spot. It's time to build our shelter.
We have a few options:

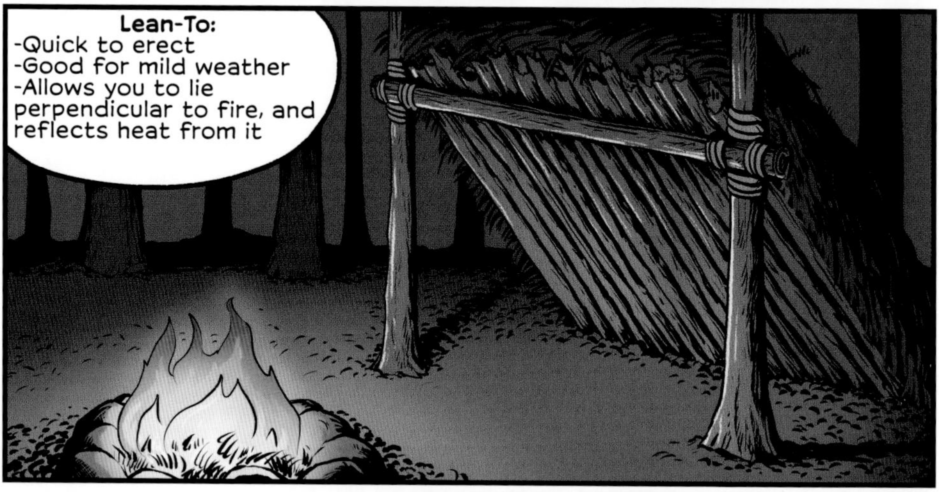
**Lean-To:**
-Quick to erect
-Good for mild weather
-Allows you to lie perpendicular to fire, and reflects heat from it

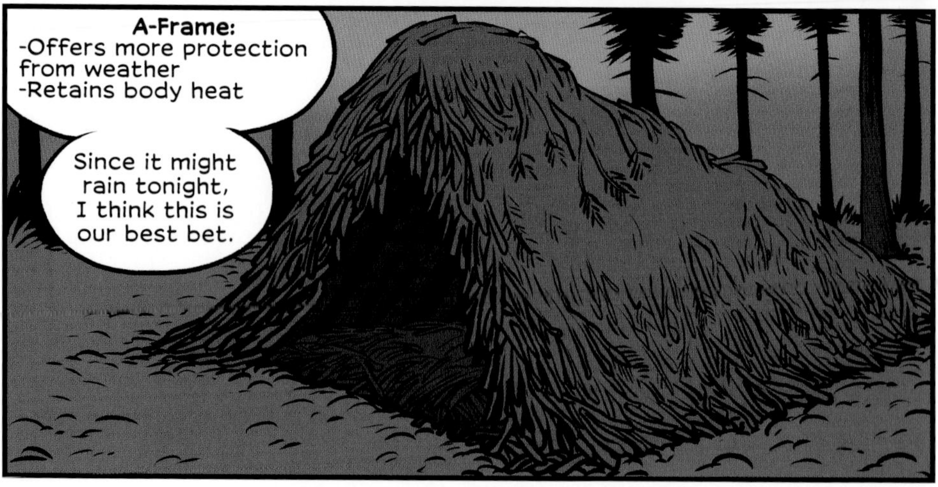
**A-Frame:**
-Offers more protection from weather
-Retains body heat
Since it might rain tonight, I think this is our best bet.

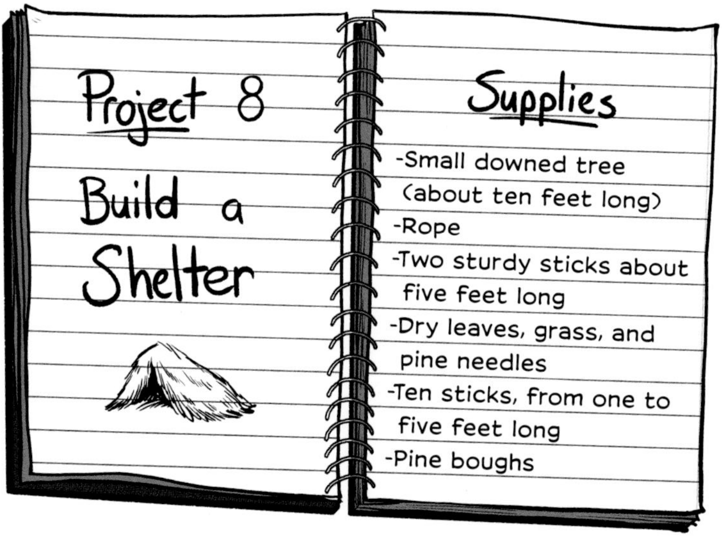
Project 8
Build a Shelter
Supplies
-Small downed tree (about ten feet long)
-Rope
-Two sturdy sticks about five feet long
-Dry leaves, grass, and pine needles
-Ten sticks, from one to five feet long
-Pine boughs

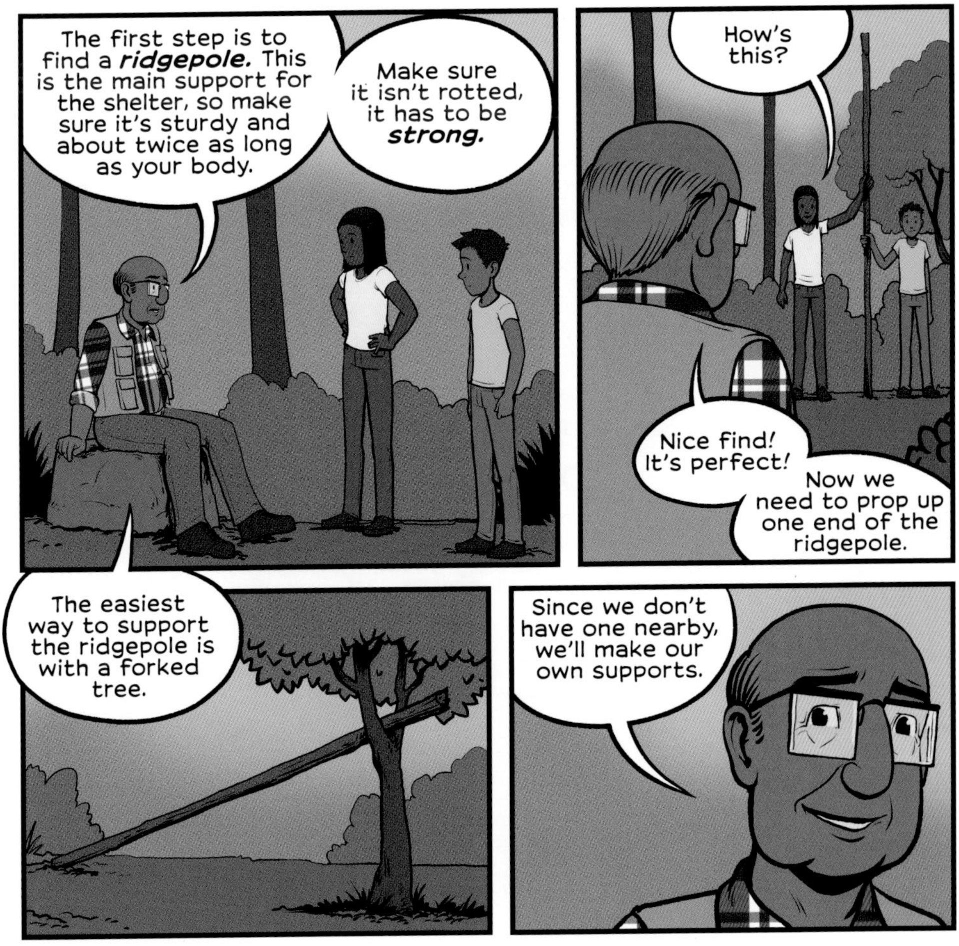
The first step is to find a ridgepole. This is the main support for the shelter, so make sure it's sturdy and about twice as long as your body.
Make sure it isn't rotted, it has to be strong.
How's this?
Nice find! It's perfect!
Now we need to prop up one end of the ridgepole.
The easiest way to support the ridgepole is with a forked tree.
Since we don't have one nearby, we'll make our own supports.

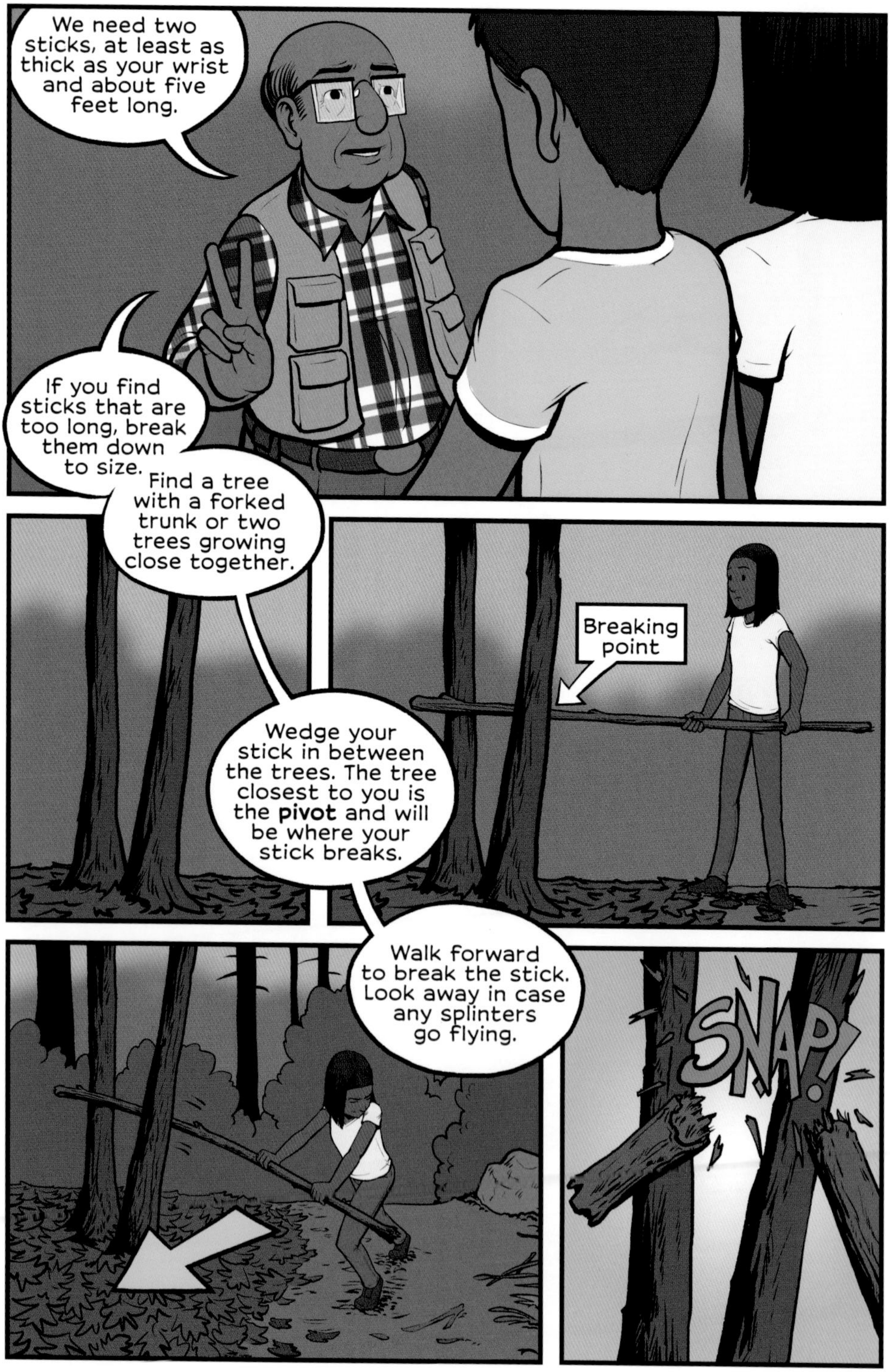

We need two sticks, at least as thick as your wrist and about five feet long.
If you find sticks that are too long, break them down to size.
Find a tree with a forked trunk or two trees growing close together.
Breaking point
Wedge your stick in between the trees. The tree closest to you is the **pivot** and will be where your stick breaks.
Walk forward to break the stick. Look away in case any splinters go flying.
SNAP!

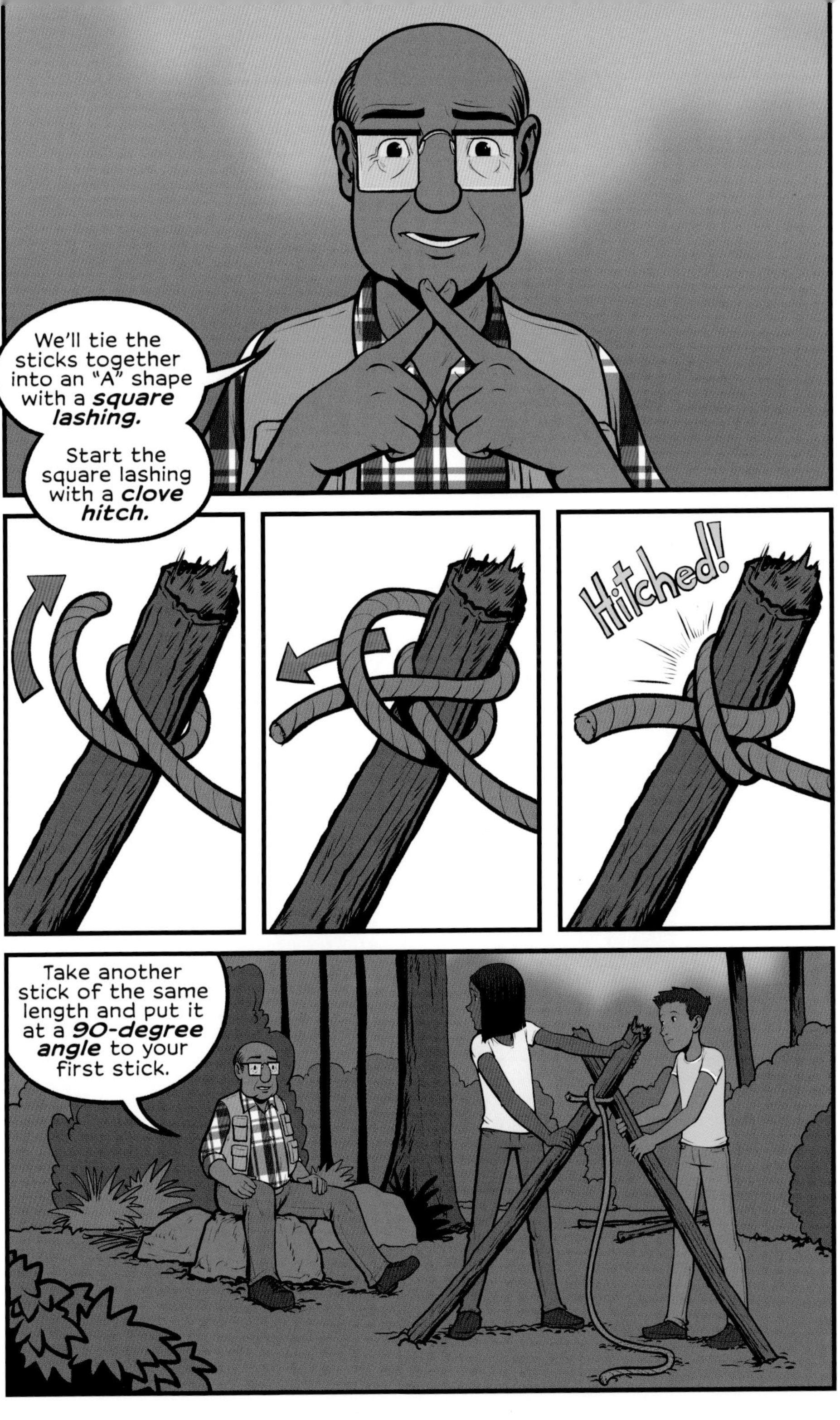
We'll tie the sticks together into an "A" shape with a ***square lashing.***
Start the square lashing with a ***clove hitch.***
Hitched!
Take another stick of the same length and put it at a ***90-degree angle*** to your first stick.

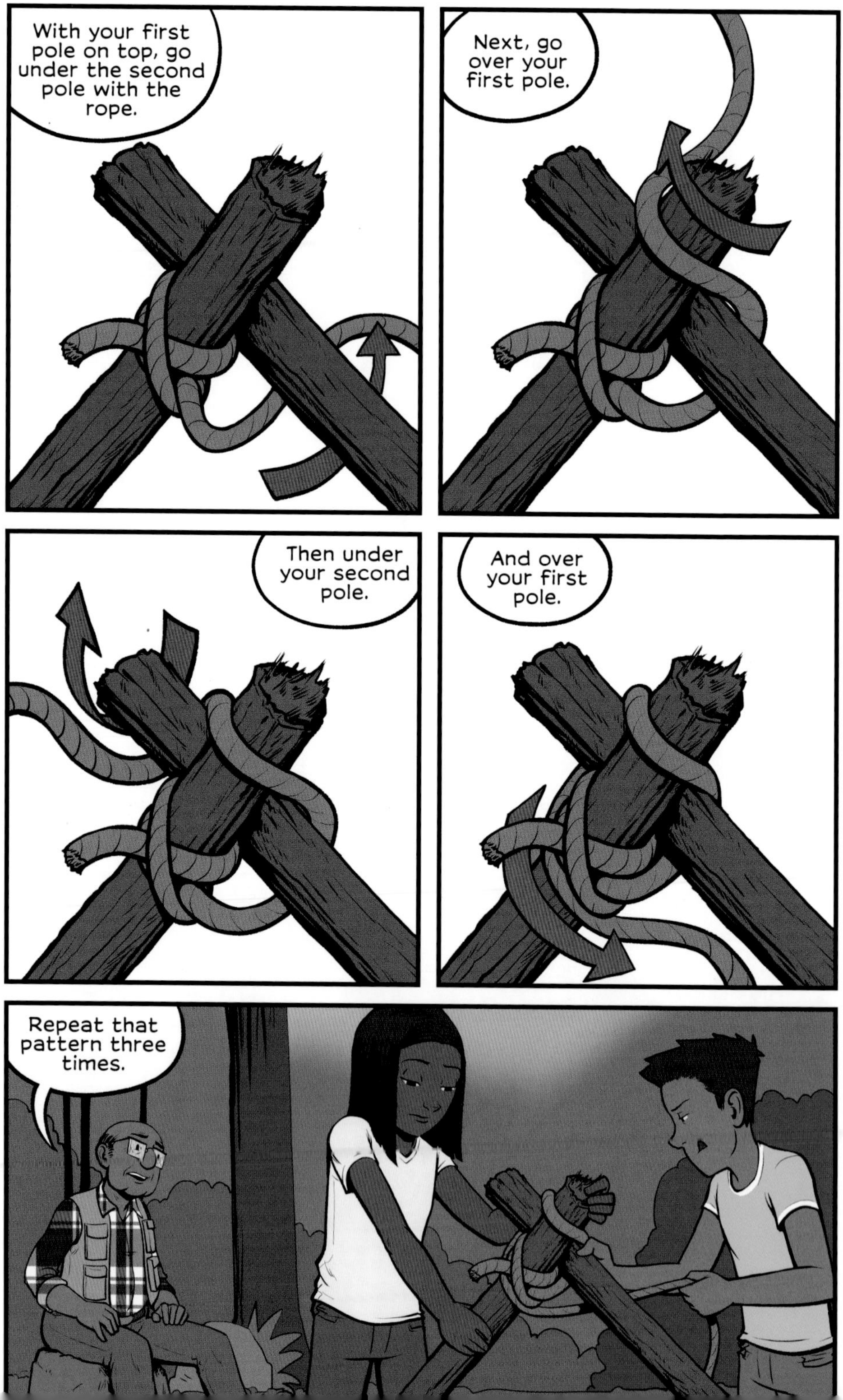
With your first pole on top, go under the second pole with the rope.
Next, go over your first pole.
Then under your second pole.
And over your first pole.
Repeat that pattern three times.

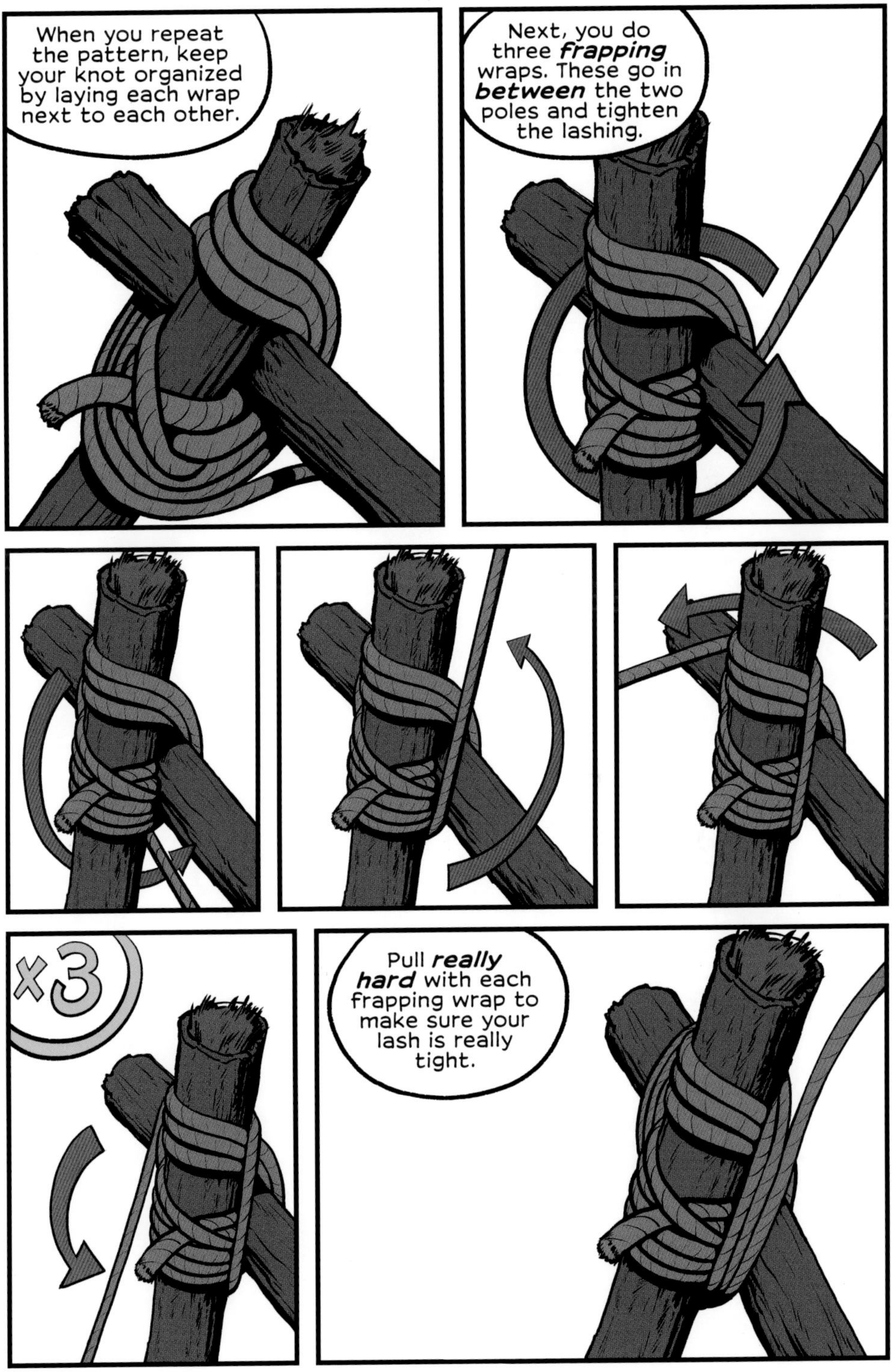
When you repeat the pattern, keep your knot organized by laying each wrap next to each other.
Next, you do three ***frapping*** wraps. These go in ***between*** the two poles and tighten the lashing.
x3
Pull ***really hard*** with each frapping wrap to make sure your lash is really tight.

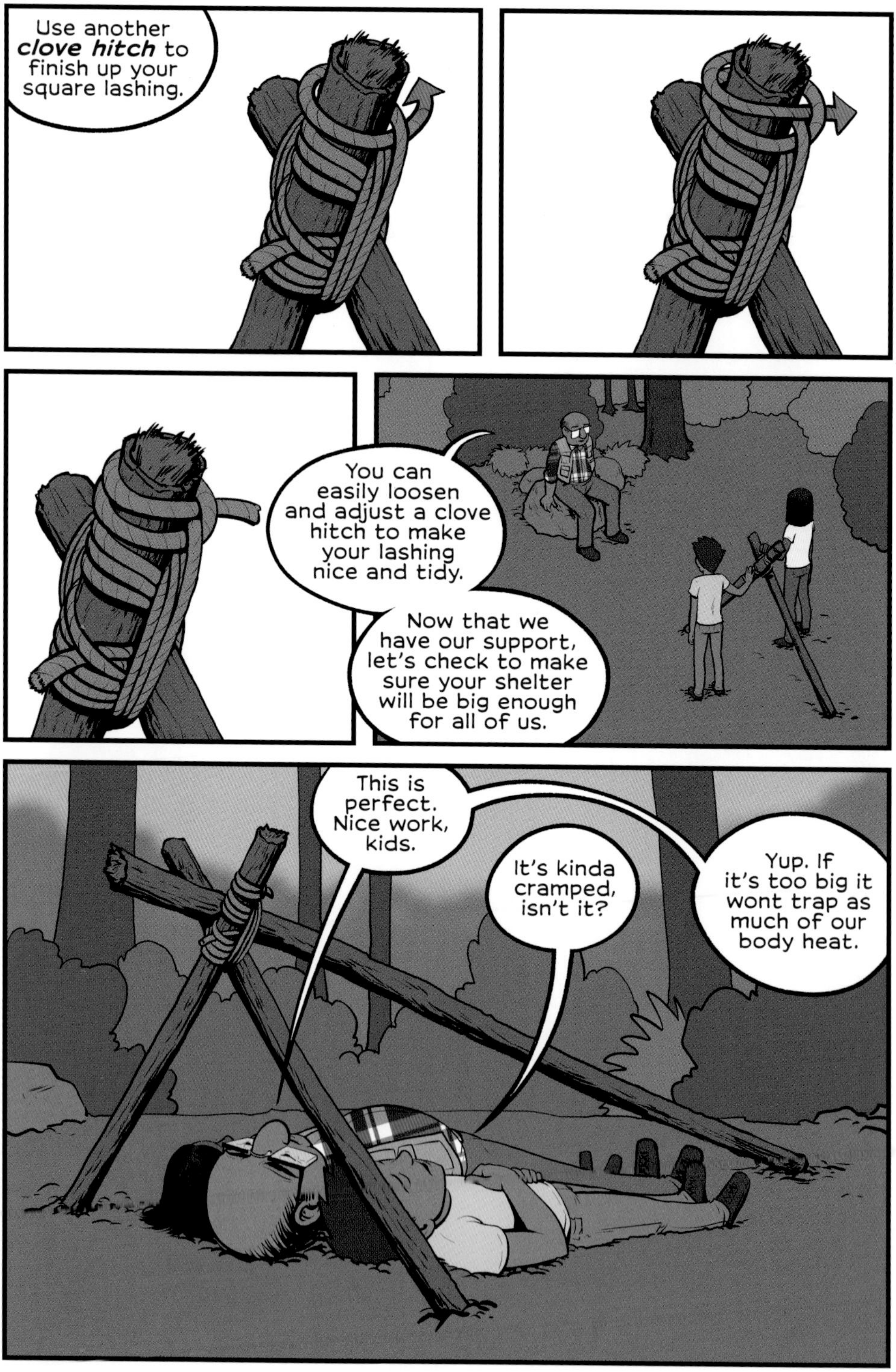
Use another **clove hitch** to finish up your square lashing.
You can easily loosen and adjust a clove hitch to make your lashing nice and tidy.
Now that we have our support, let's check to make sure your shelter will be big enough for all of us.
This is perfect. Nice work, kids.
It's kinda cramped, isn't it?
Yup. If it's too big it wont trap as much of our body heat.

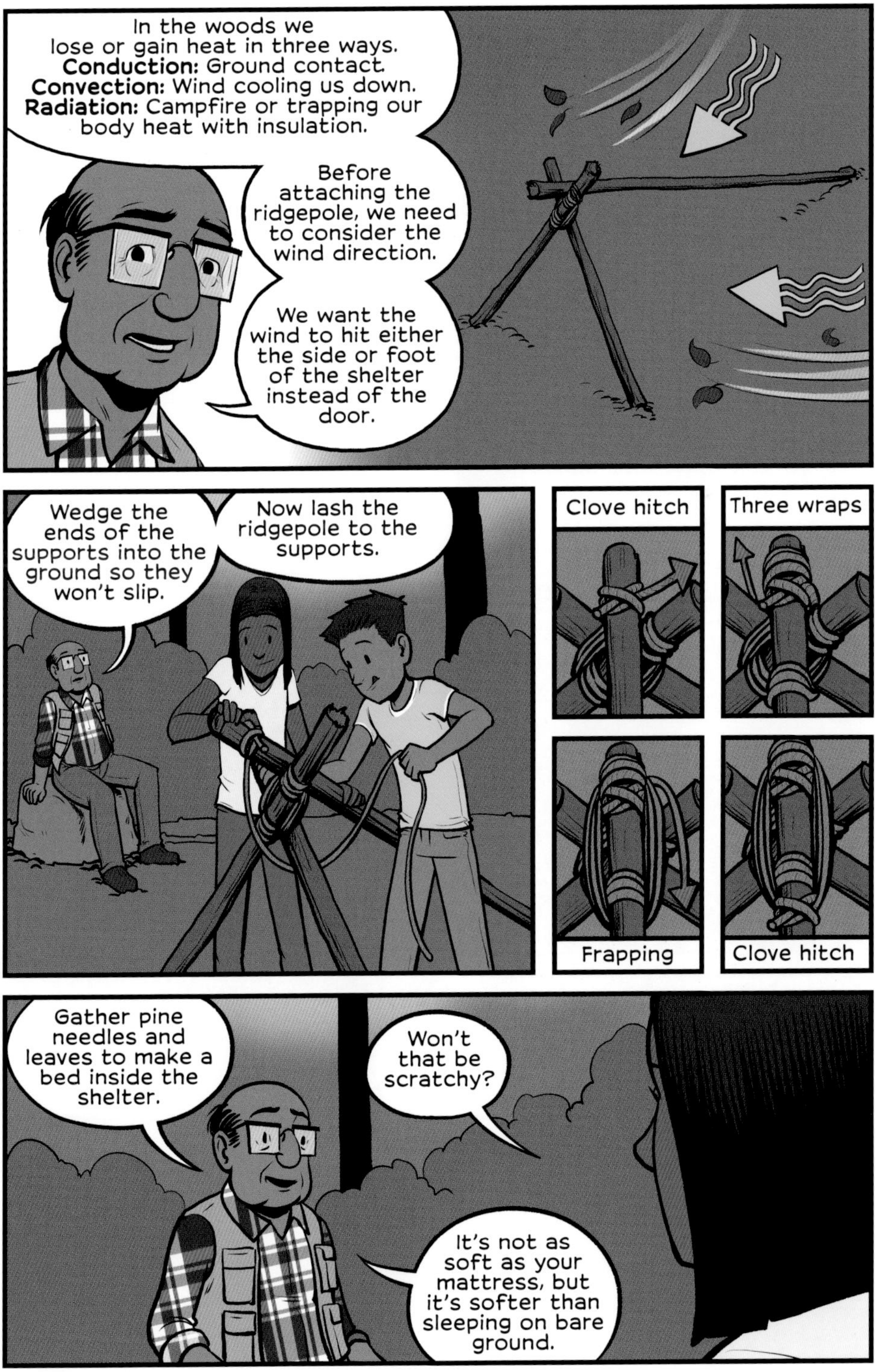
In the woods we lose or gain heat in three ways. **Conduction:** Ground contact. **Convection:** Wind cooling us down. **Radiation:** Campfire or trapping our body heat with insulation.
Before attaching the ridgepole, we need to consider the wind direction.
We want the wind to hit either the side or foot of the shelter instead of the door.
Wedge the ends of the supports into the ground so they won't slip.
Now lash the ridgepole to the supports.
Clove hitch
Three wraps
Frapping
Clove hitch
Gather pine needles and leaves to make a bed inside the shelter.
Won't that be scratchy?
It's not as soft as your mattress, but it's softer than sleeping on bare ground.

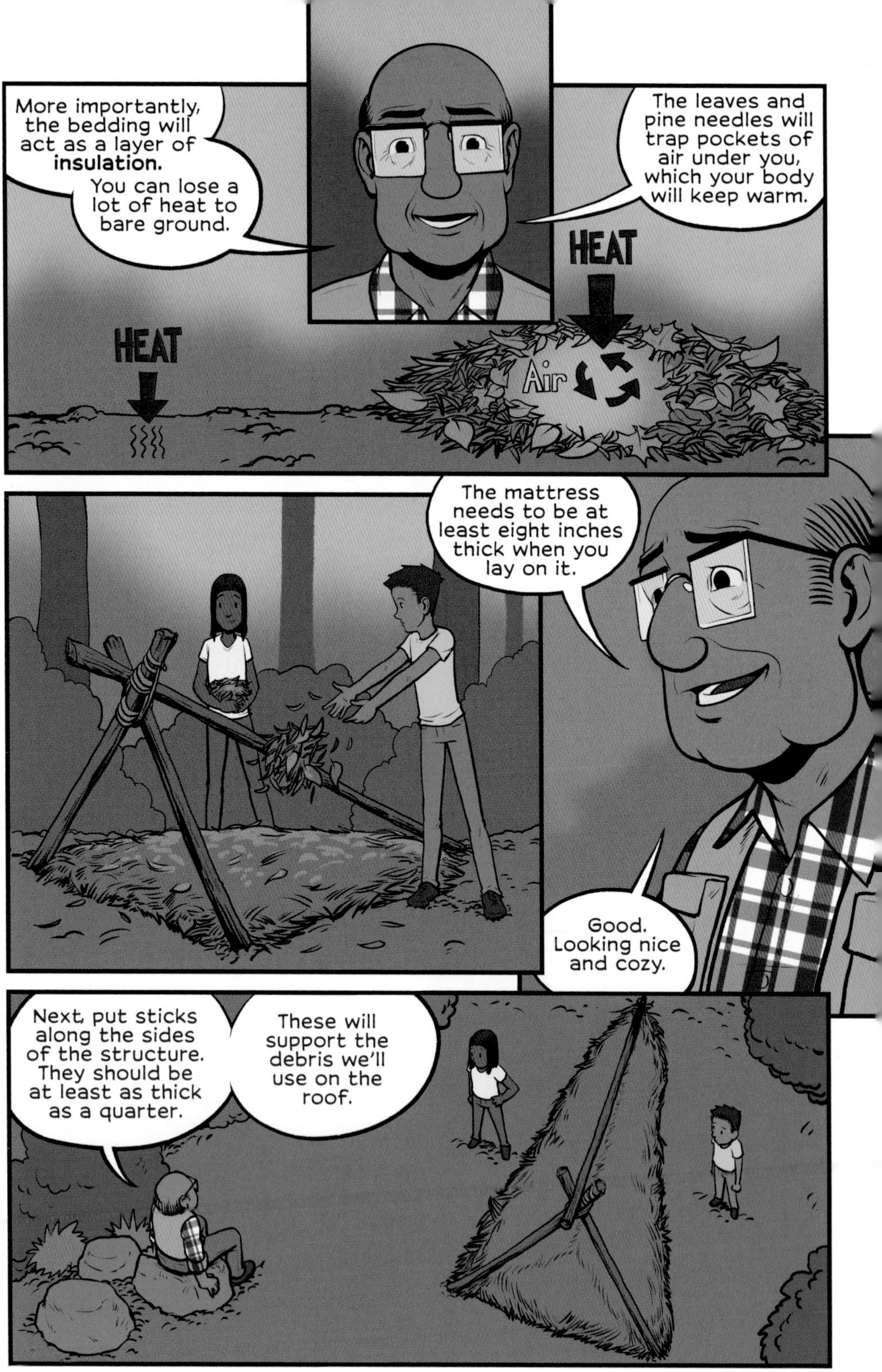
More importantly, the bedding will act as a layer of **insulation.**
You can lose a lot of heat to bare ground.
The leaves and pine needles will trap pockets of air under you, which your body will keep warm.
HEAT
HEAT
Air
The mattress needs to be at least eight inches thick when you lay on it.
Good. Looking nice and cozy.
Next, put sticks along the sides of the structure. They should be at least as thick as a quarter.
These will support the debris we'll use on the roof.

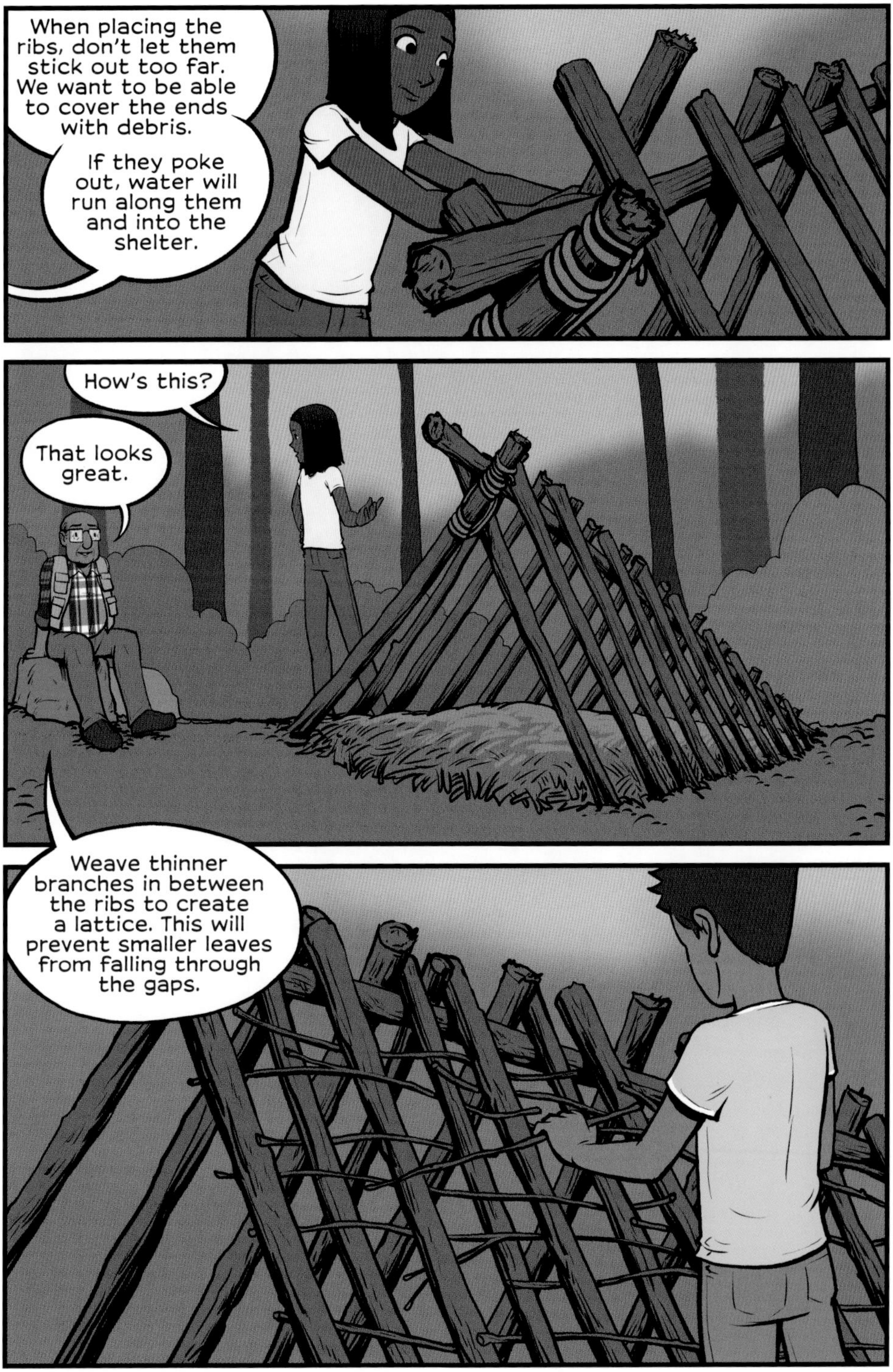

When placing the ribs, don't let them stick out too far. We want to be able to cover the ends with debris.
If they poke out, water will run along them and into the shelter.
How's this?
That looks great.
Weave thinner branches in between the ribs to create a lattice. This will prevent smaller leaves from falling through the gaps.

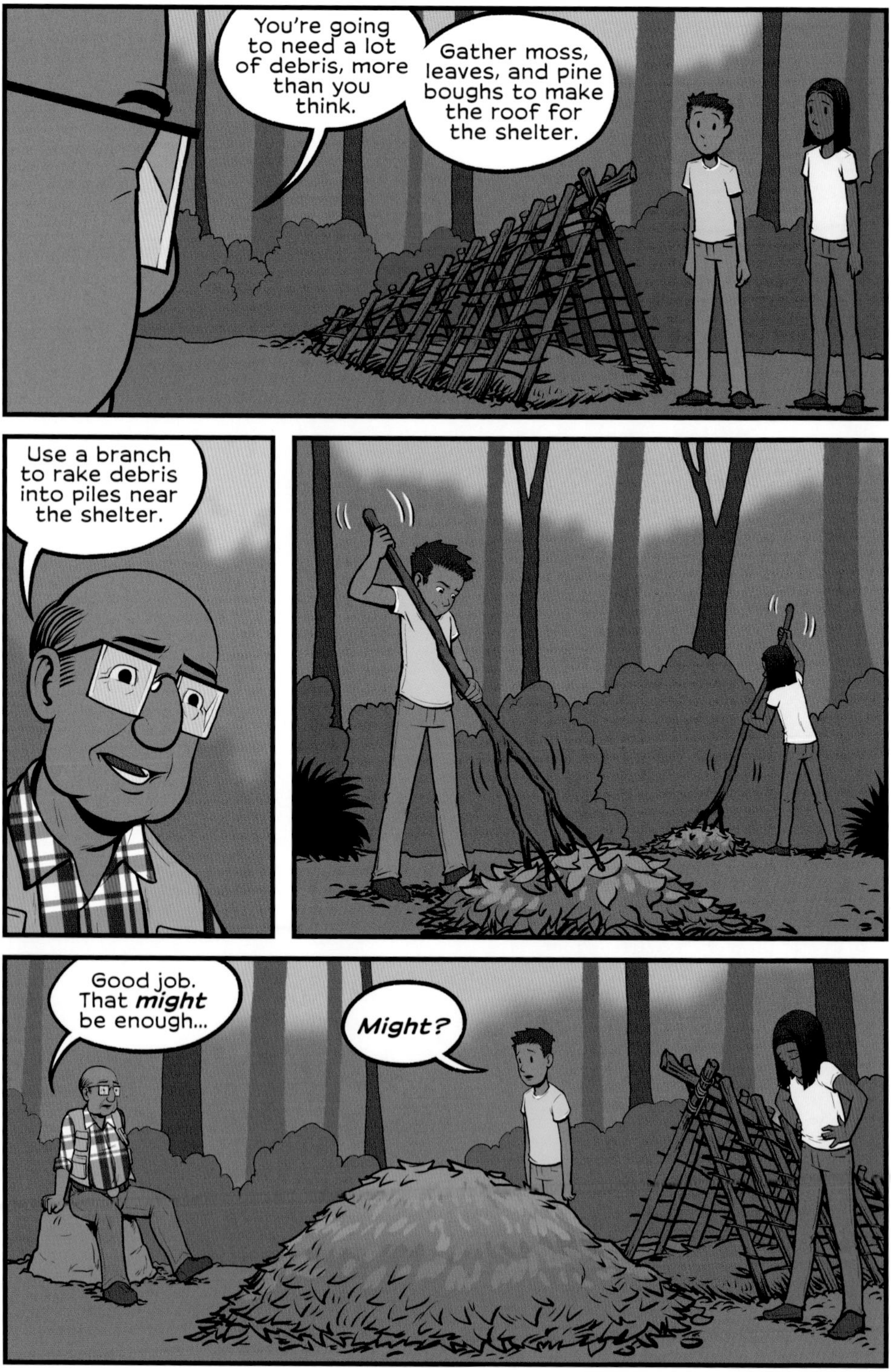
You're going to need a lot of debris, more than you think.
Gather moss, leaves, and pine boughs to make the roof for the shelter.
Use a branch to rake debris into piles near the shelter.
Good job. That ***might*** be enough...
***Might?***

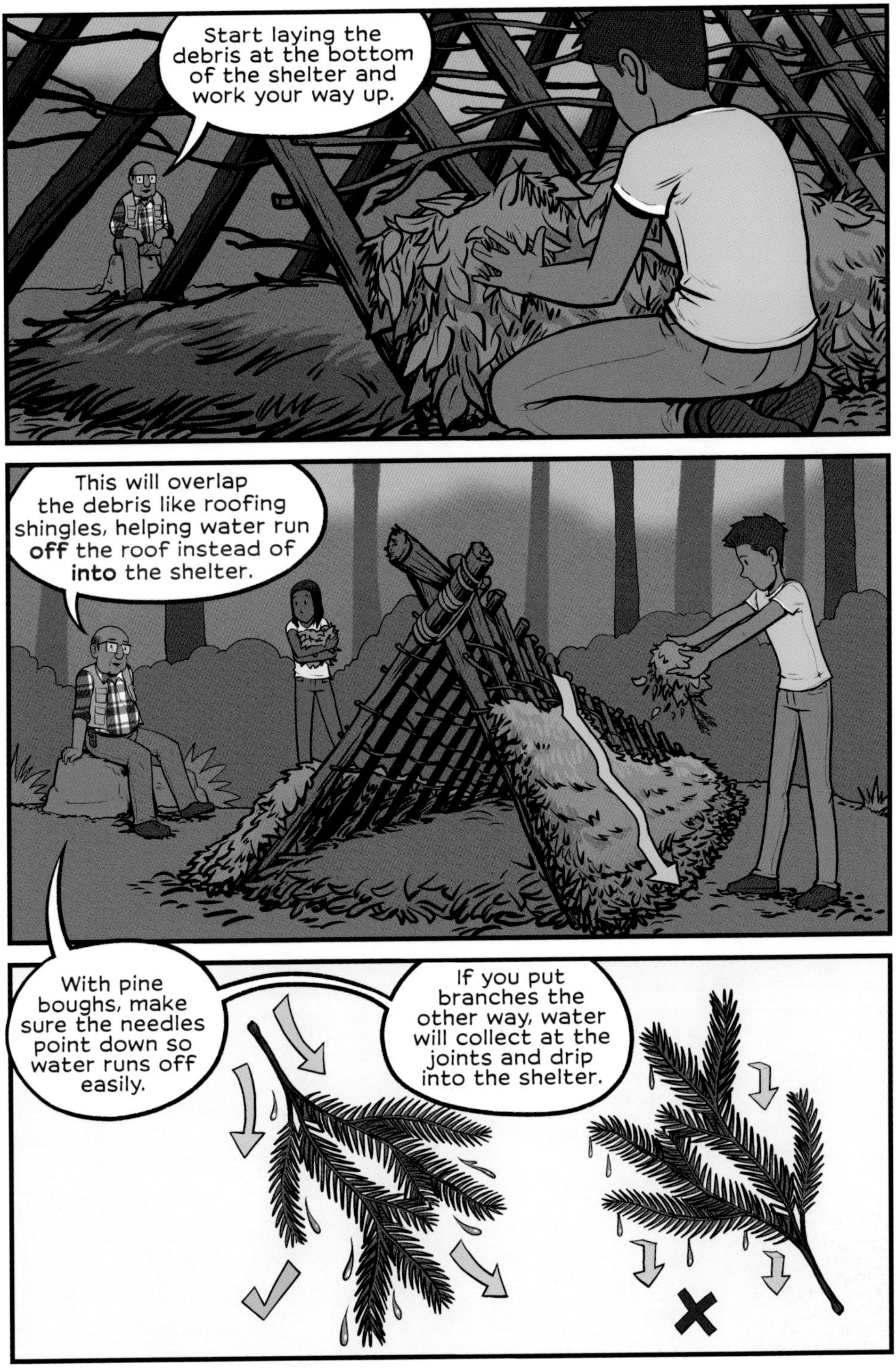
Start laying the debris at the bottom of the shelter and work your way up.
This will overlap the debris like roofing shingles, helping water run **off** the roof instead of **into** the shelter.
With pine boughs, make sure the needles point down so water runs off easily.
If you put branches the other way, water will collect at the joints and drip into the shelter.

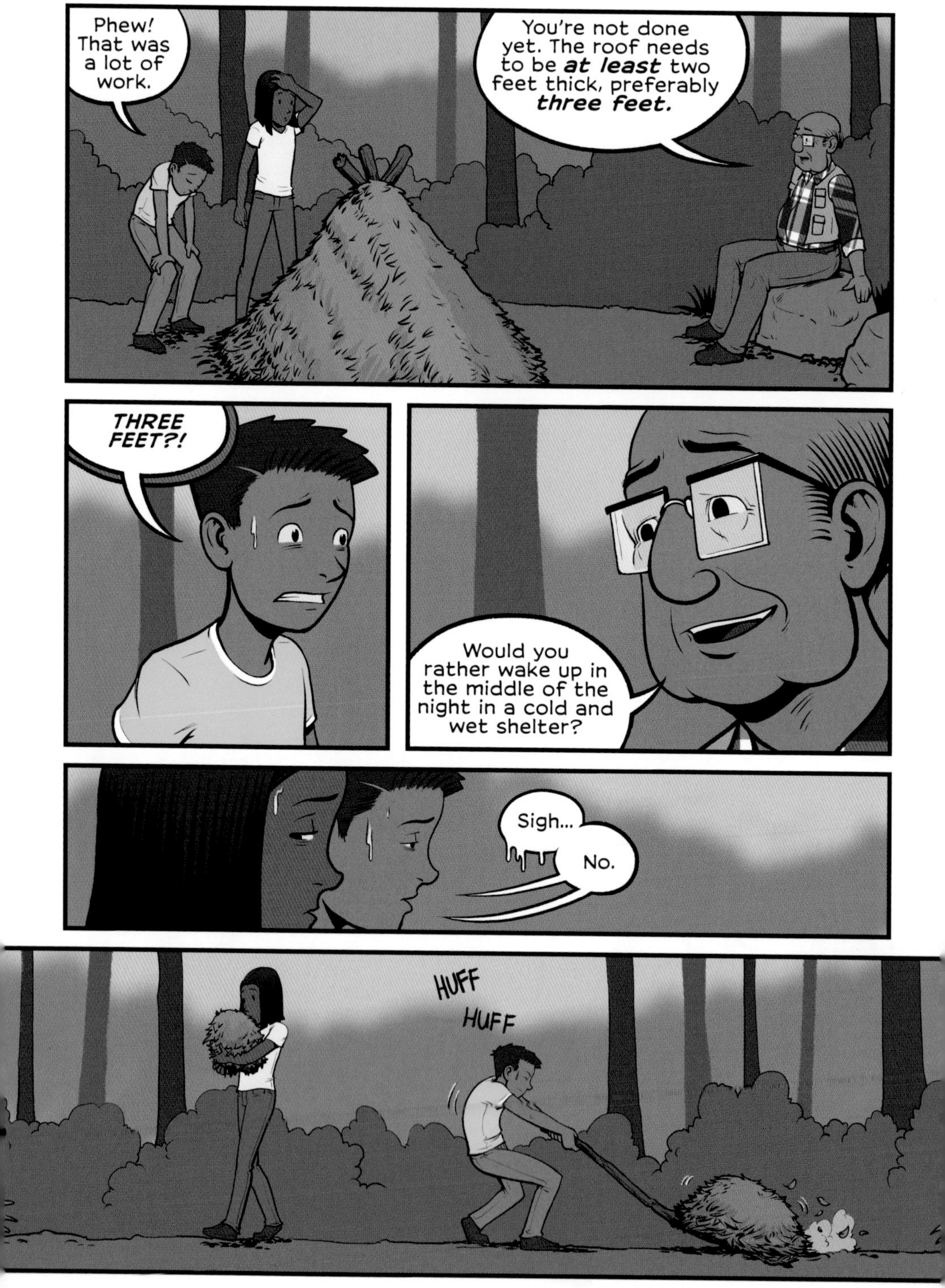
Phew! That was a lot of work.
You're not done yet. The roof needs to be ***at least*** two feet thick, preferably ***three feet.***
***THREE FEET?!***
Would you rather wake up in the middle of the night in a cold and wet shelter?
Sigh...
No.
HUFF
HUFF

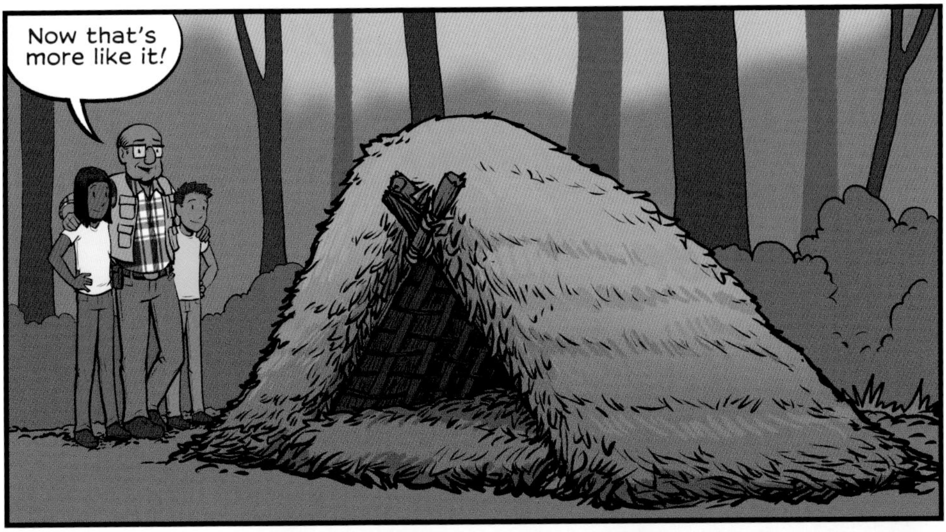
Now that's more like it!

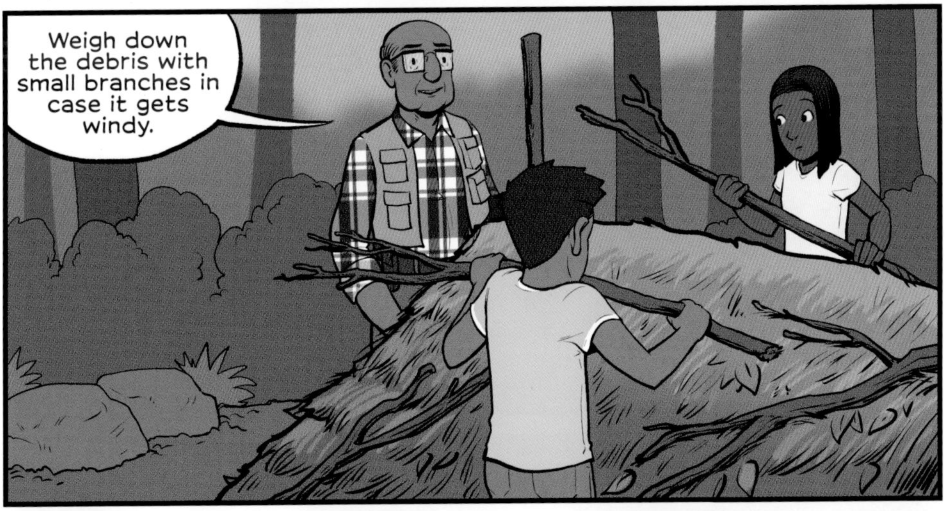
Weigh down the debris with small branches in case it gets windy.

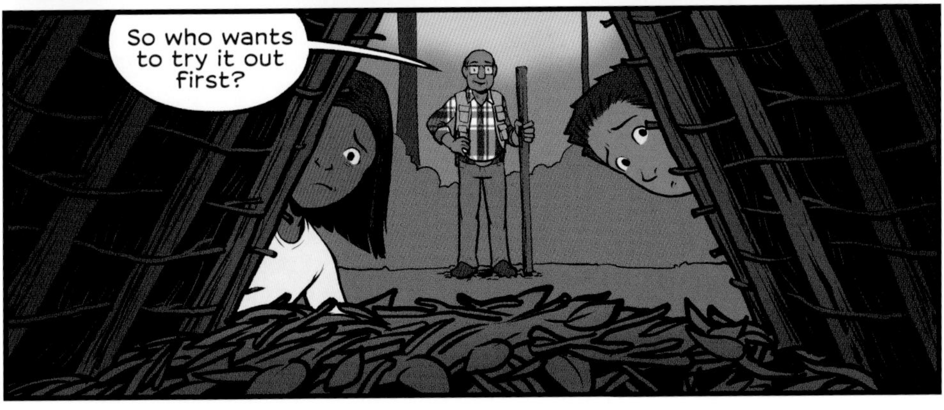
So who wants to try it out first?

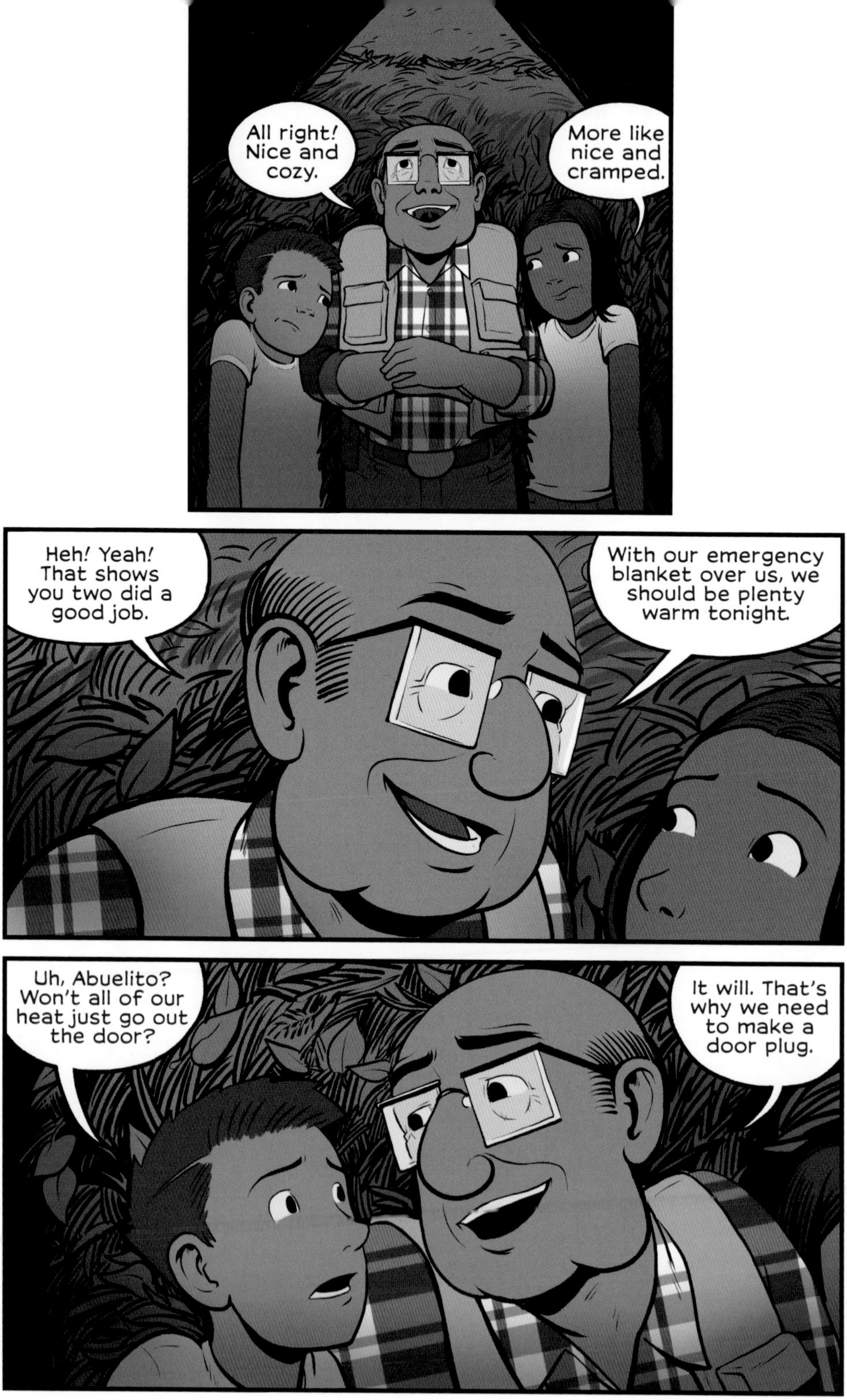
All right! Nice and cozy.
More like nice and cramped.
Heh! Yeah! That shows you two did a good job.
With our emergency blanket over us, we should be plenty warm tonight.
Uh, Abuelito? Won't all of our heat just go out the door?
It will. That's why we need to make a door plug.

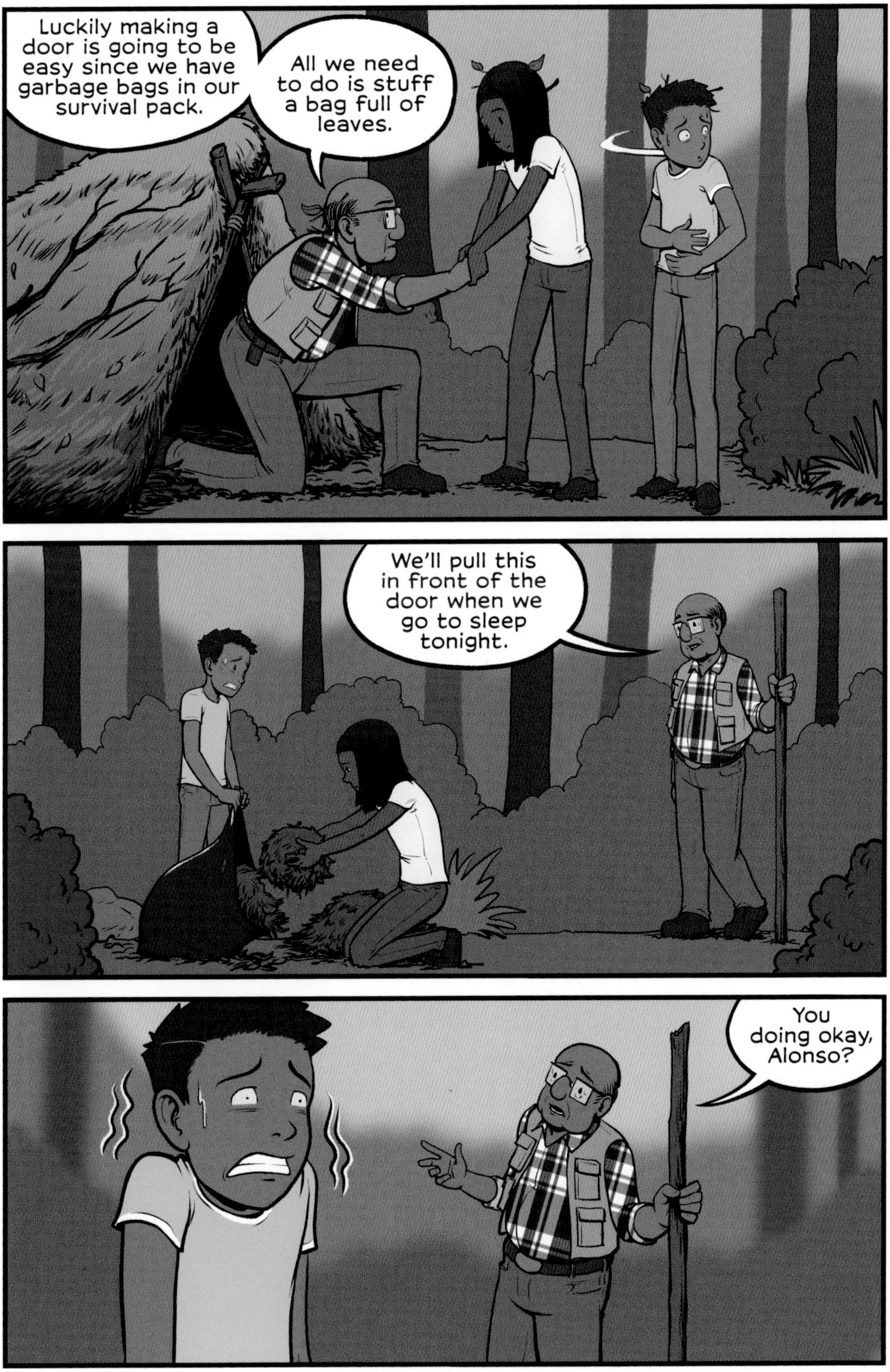
Luckily making a door is going to be easy since we have garbage bags in our survival pack.
All we need to do is stuff a bag full of leaves.
We'll pull this in front of the door when we go to sleep tonight.
You doing okay, Alonso?

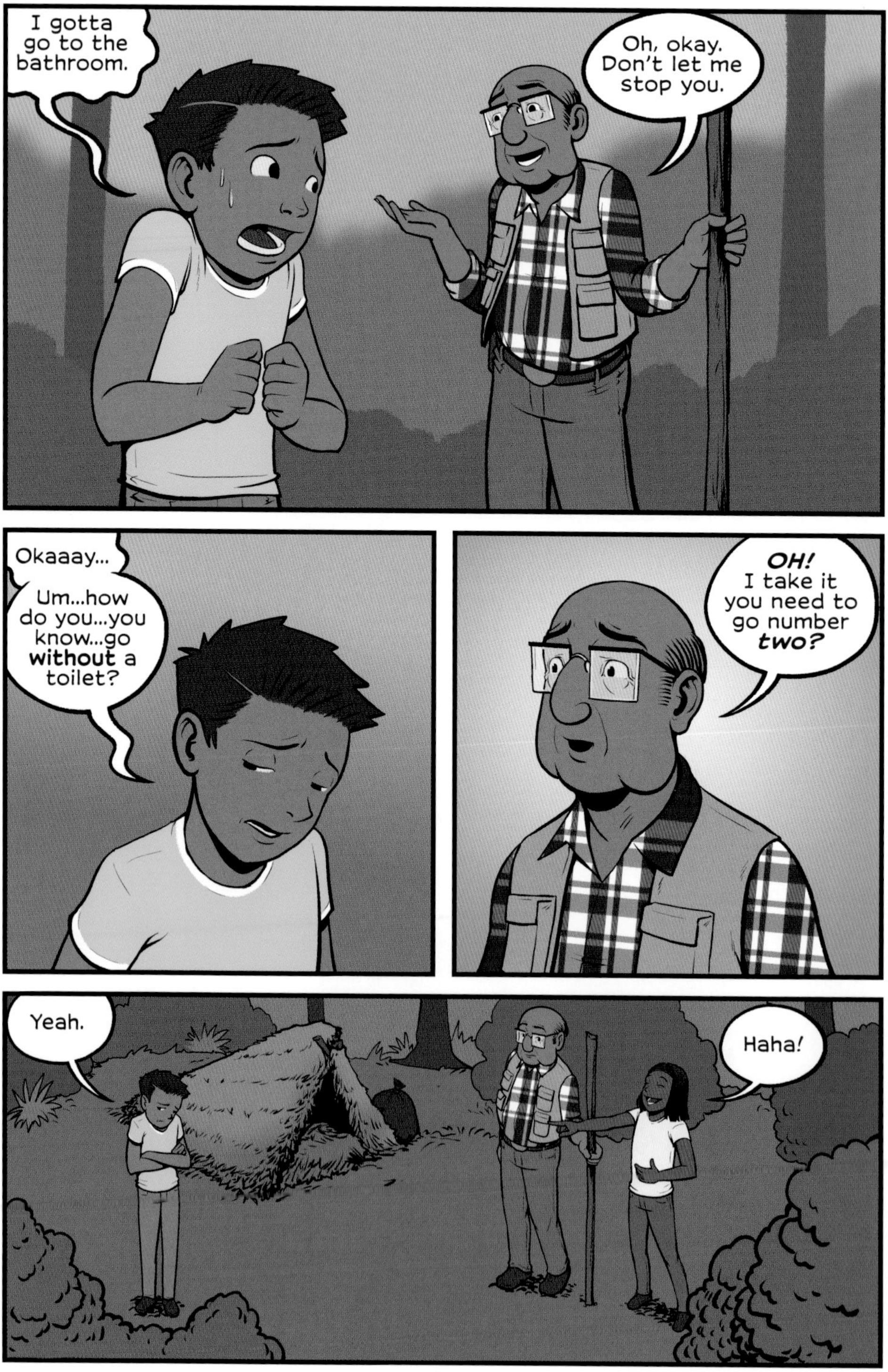
I gotta go to the bathroom.
Oh, okay. Don't let me stop you.
Okaaay...
Um...how do you...you know...go **without** a toilet?
***OH!*** I take it you need to go number ***two?***
Yeah.
Haha!

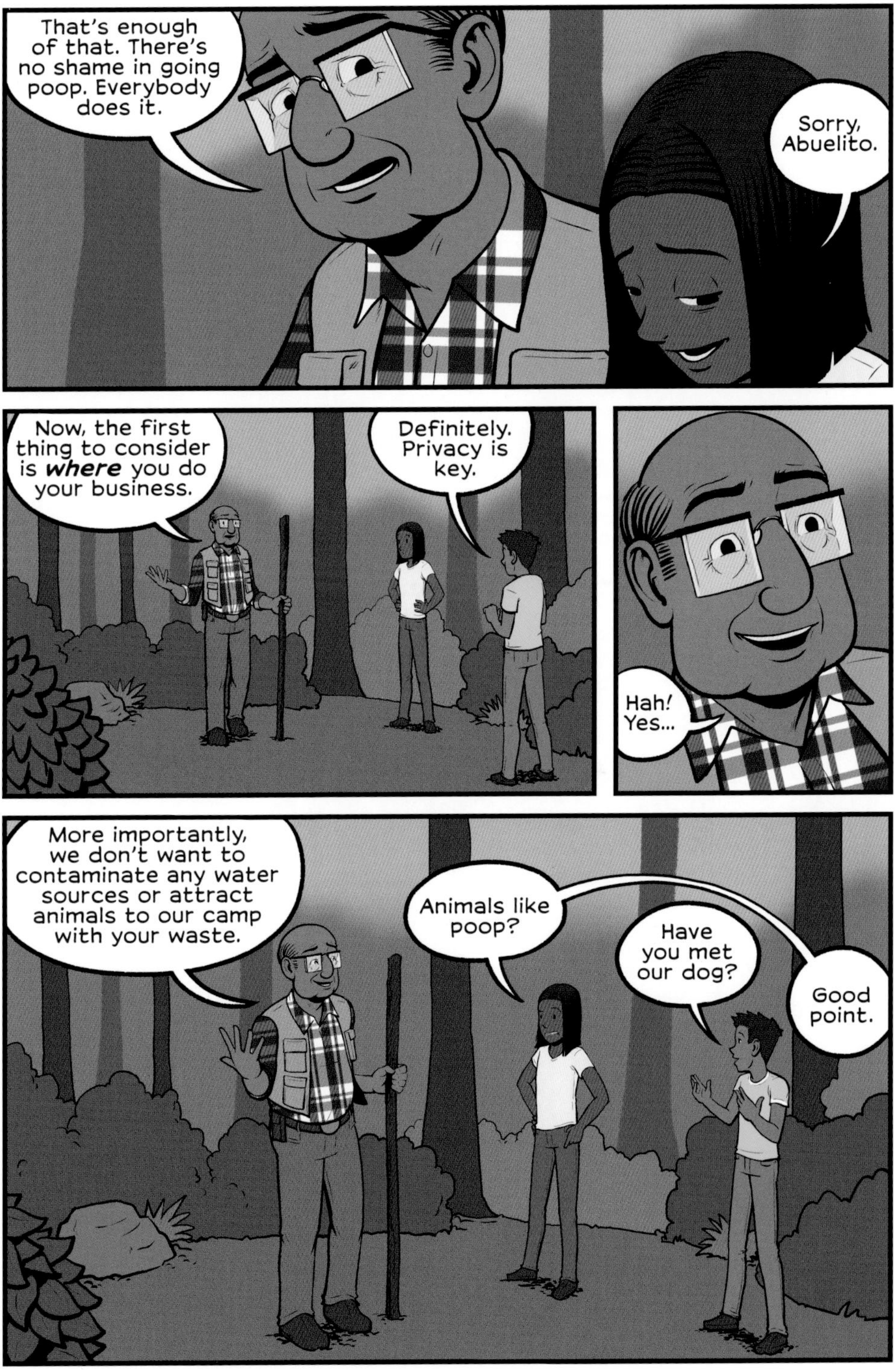
That's enough of that. There's no shame in going poop. Everybody does it.
Sorry, Abuelito.
Now, the first thing to consider is ***where*** you do your business.
Definitely. Privacy is key.
Hah! Yes...
More importantly, we don't want to contaminate any water sources or attract animals to our camp with your waste.
Animals like poop?
Have you met our dog?
Good point.

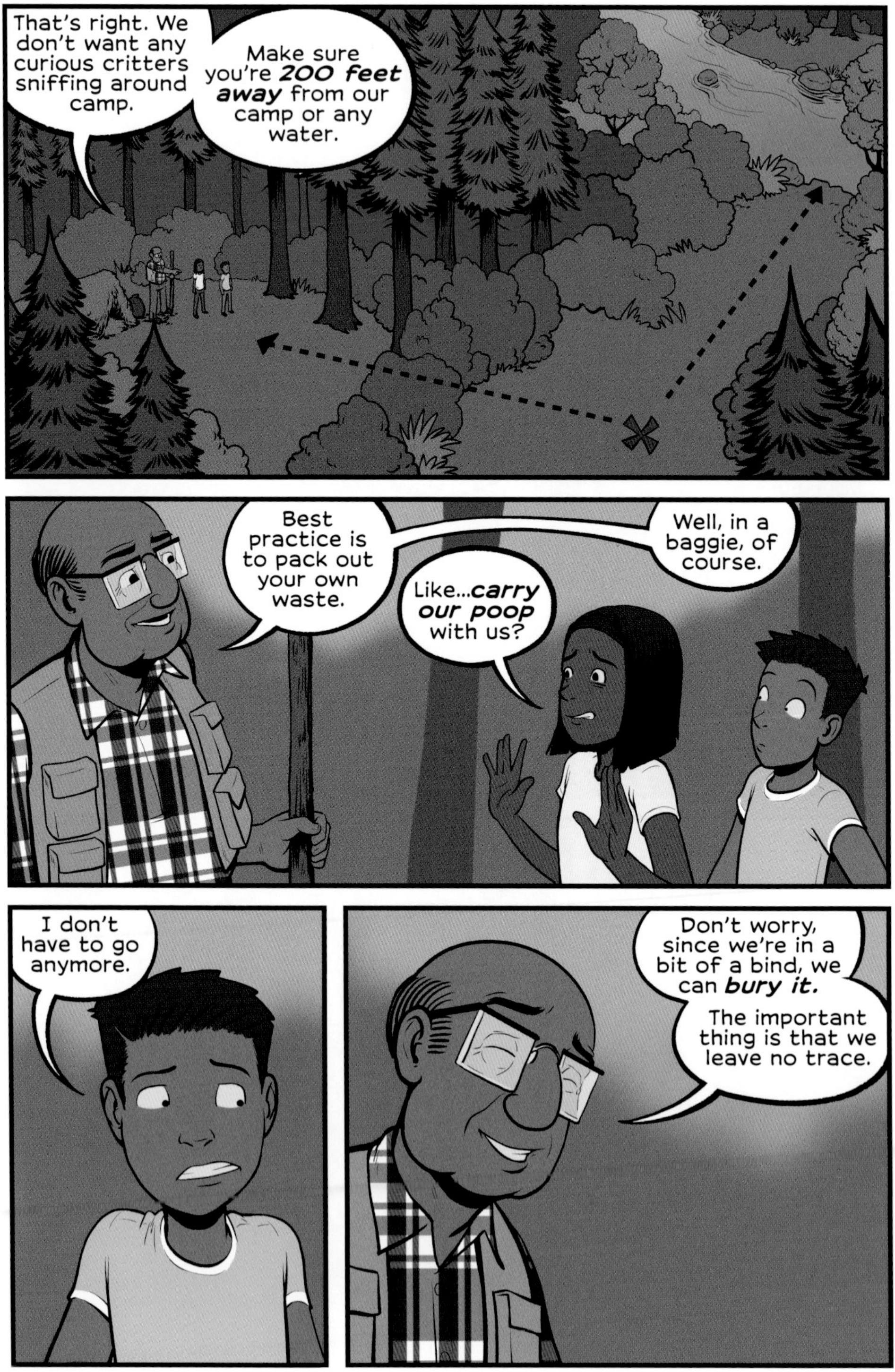
That's right. We don't want any curious critters sniffing around camp.
Make sure you're ***200 feet away*** from our camp or any water.
Best practice is to pack out your own waste.
Like...***carry our poop*** with us?
Well, in a baggie, of course.
I don't have to go anymore.
Don't worry, since we're in a bit of a bind, we can ***bury it.***
The important thing is that we leave no trace.

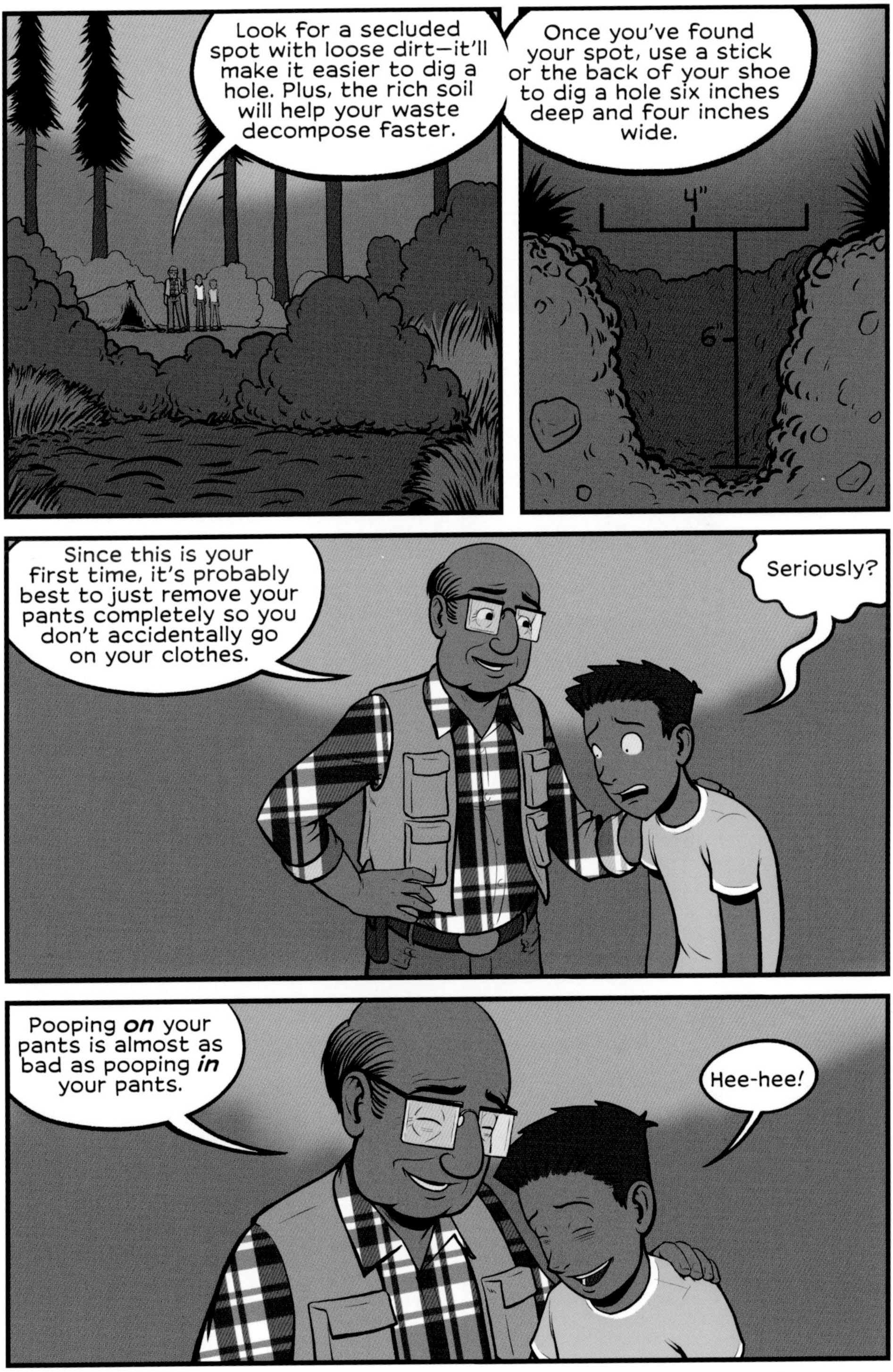
Look for a secluded spot with loose dirt—it'll make it easier to dig a hole. Plus, the rich soil will help your waste decompose faster.
Once you've found your spot, use a stick or the back of your shoe to dig a hole six inches deep and four inches wide.
4"
6"
Since this is your first time, it's probably best to just remove your pants completely so you don't accidentally go on your clothes.
Seriously?
Pooping ***on*** your pants is almost as bad as pooping ***in*** your pants.
Hee-hee!

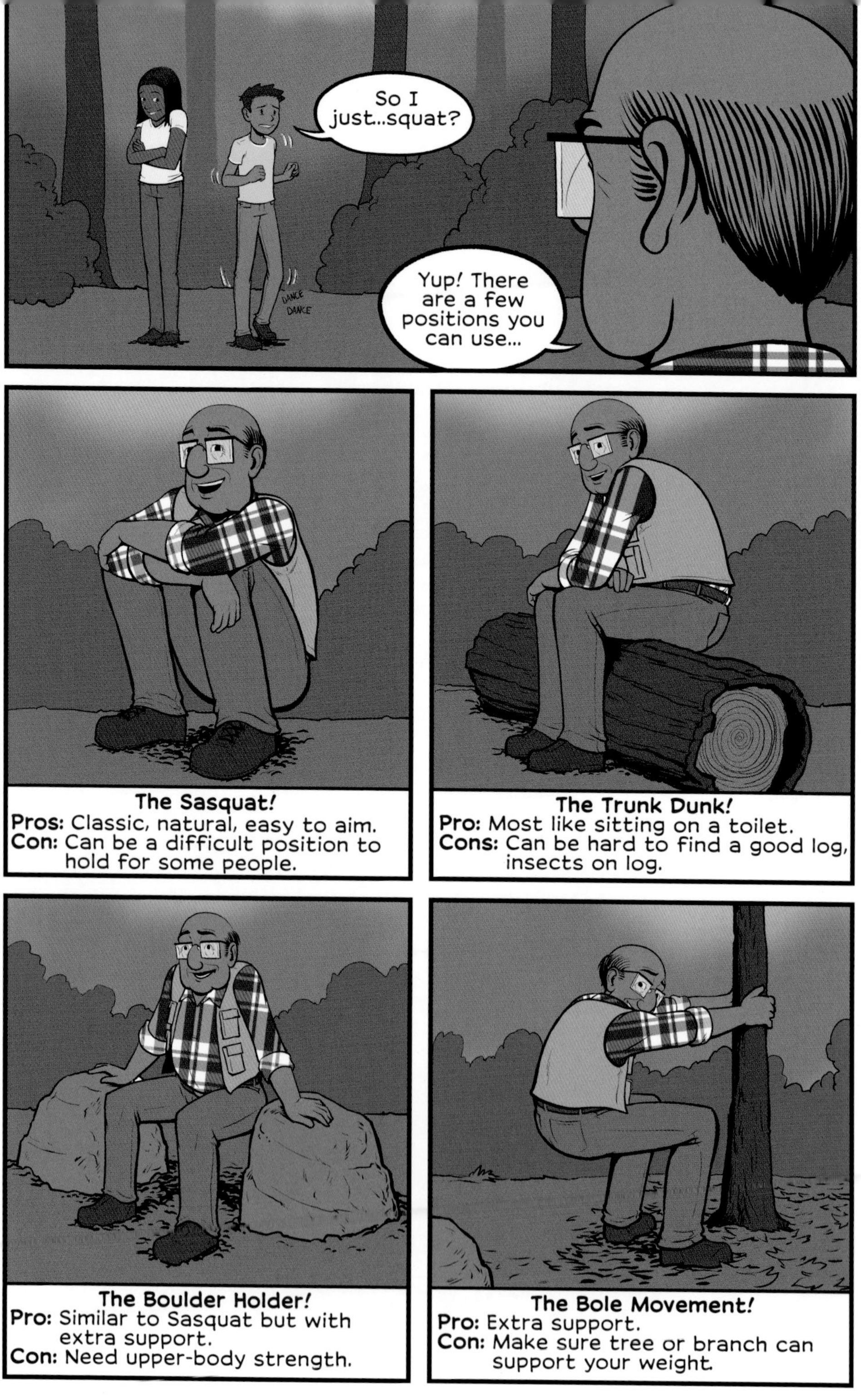
So I just...squat?
DANCE DANCE
Yup! There are a few positions you can use...
The Sasquat!
Pros: Classic, natural, easy to aim.
Con: Can be a difficult position to hold for some people.
The Trunk Dunk!
Pro: Most like sitting on a toilet.
Cons: Can be hard to find a good log, insects on log.
The Boulder Holder!
Pro: Similar to Sasquat but with extra support.
Con: Need upper-body strength.
The Bole Movement!
Pro: Extra support.
Con: Make sure tree or branch can support your weight.

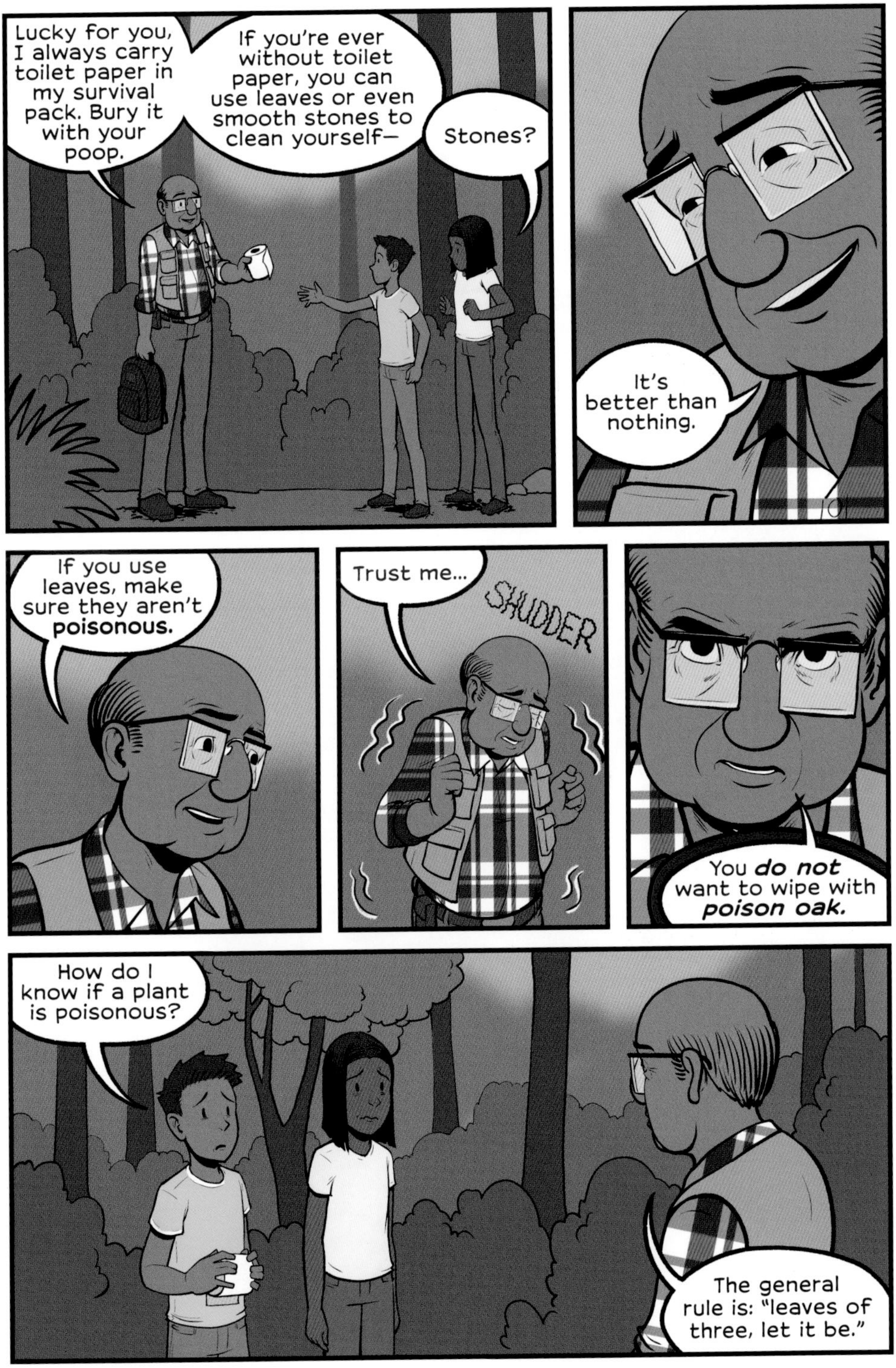
Lucky for you, I always carry toilet paper in my survival pack. Bury it with your poop.
If you're ever without toilet paper, you can use leaves or even smooth stones to clean yourself—
Stones?
It's better than nothing.
If you use leaves, make sure they aren't **poisonous.**
Trust me...
SHUDDER
You ***do not*** want to wipe with ***poison oak.***
How do I know if a plant is poisonous?
The general rule is: "leaves of three, let it be."

**Poison Ivy:**

-Clumps of three leaves with either notched or smooth edges
-Grows as a vine or shrub depending on location
-Color can vary from red, yellow, or shiny green depending on season
-Grows left to right, never side by side

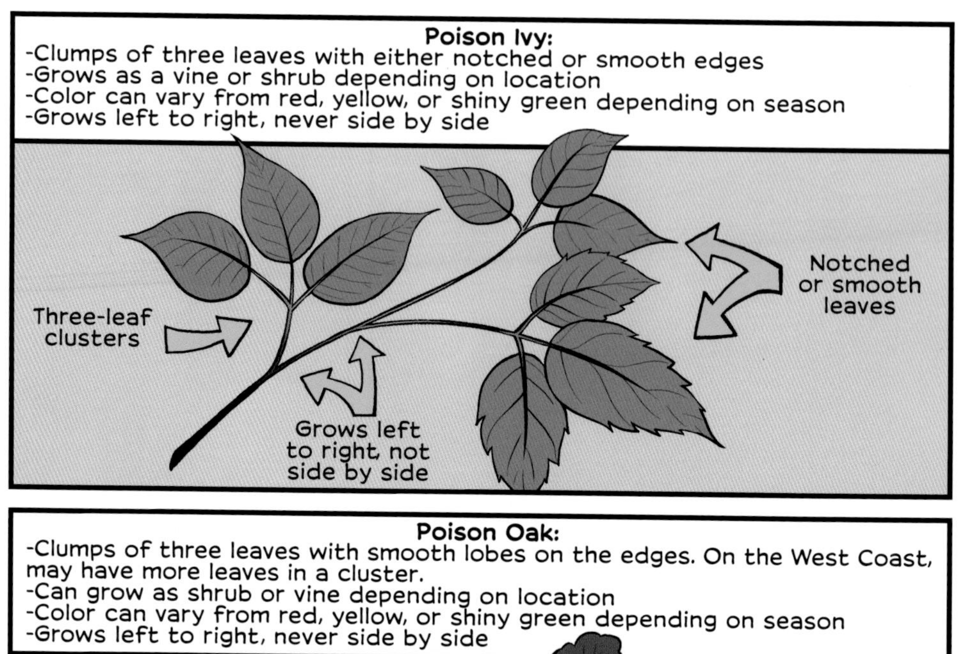
Three-leaf clusters
Grows left to right, not side by side
Notched or smooth leaves

**Poison Oak:**

-Clumps of three leaves with smooth lobes on the edges. On the West Coast, may have more leaves in a cluster.
-Can grow as shrub or vine depending on location
-Color can vary from red, yellow, or shiny green depending on season
-Grows left to right, never side by side

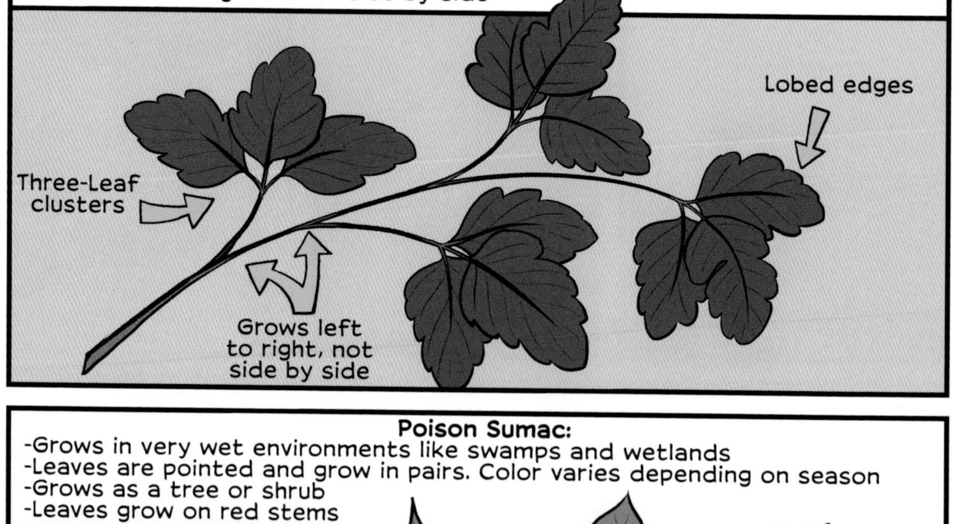
Three-Leaf clusters
Grows left to right, not side by side
Lobed edges

**Poison Sumac:**

-Grows in very wet environments like swamps and wetlands
-Leaves are pointed and grow in pairs. Color varies depending on season
-Grows as a tree or shrub
-Leaves grow on red stems

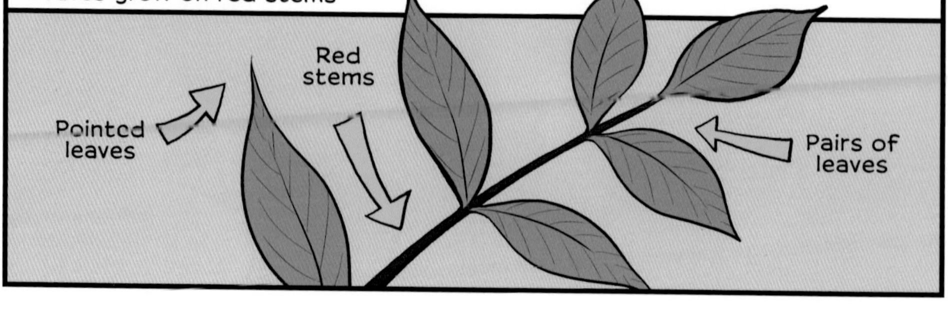
Pointed leaves
Red stems
Pairs of leaves

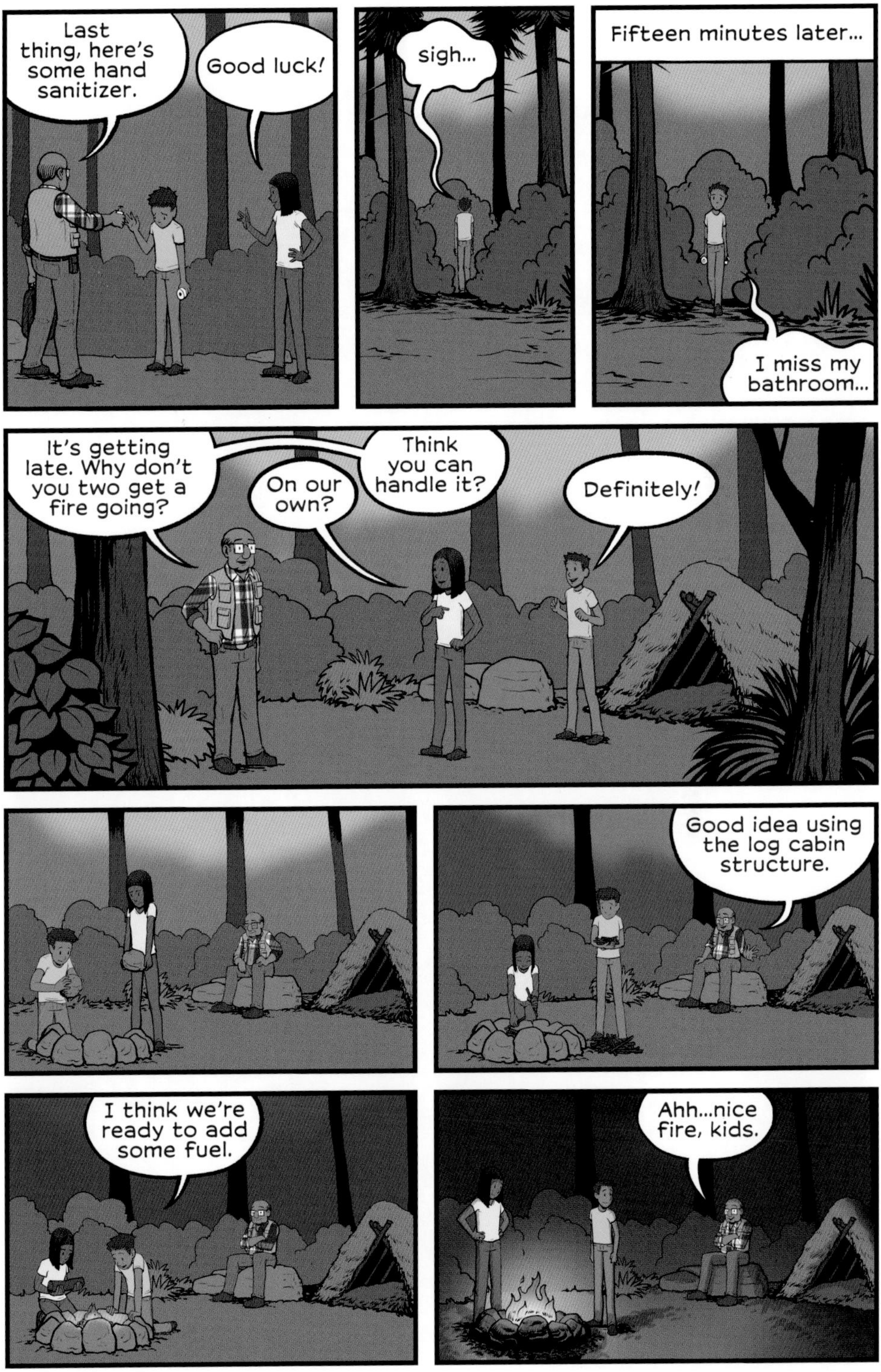
Last thing, here's some hand sanitizer.
Good luck!
sigh...
Fifteen minutes later...
I miss my bathroom...
It's getting late. Why don't you two get a fire going?
On our own?
Think you can handle it?
Definitely!
Good idea using the log cabin structure.
I think we're ready to add some fuel.
Ahh...nice fire, kids.

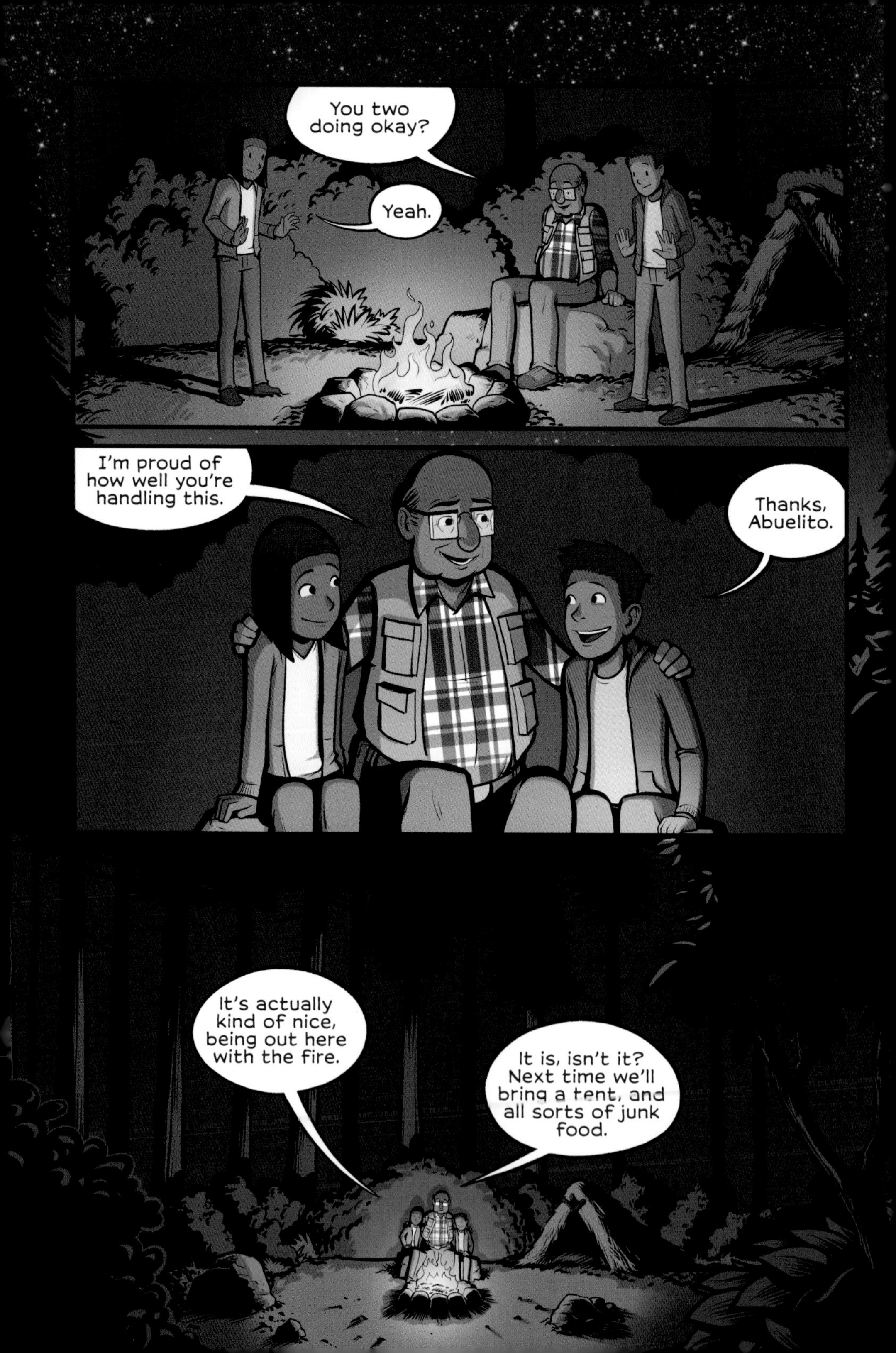
You two doing okay?
Yeah.
I'm proud of how well you're handling this.
Thanks, Abuelito.
It's actually kind of nice, being out here with the fire.
It is, isn't it? Next time we'll bring a tent, and all sorts of junk food.

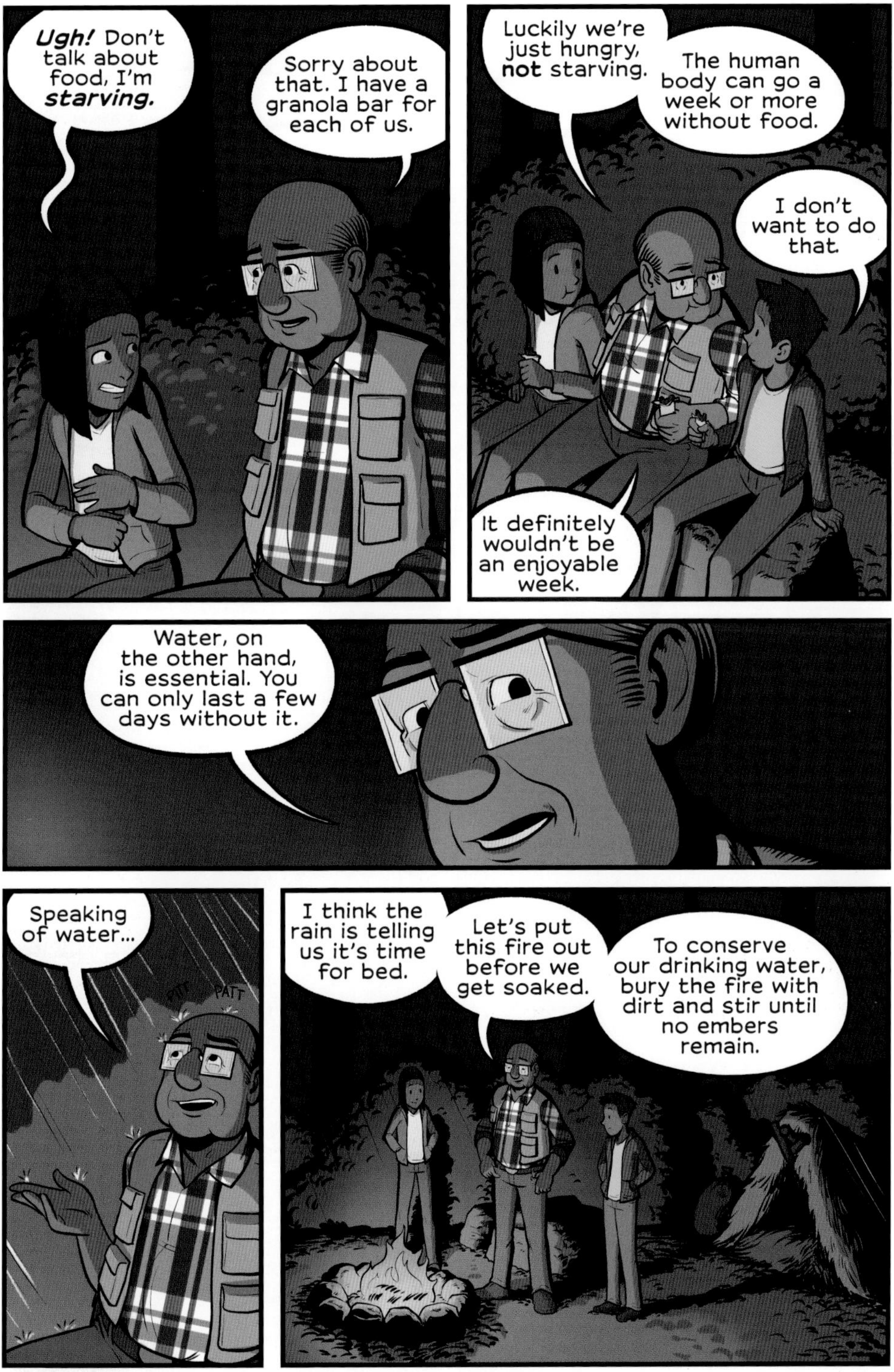
*Ugh!* Don't talk about food, I'm ***starving.***
Sorry about that. I have a granola bar for each of us.
Luckily we're just hungry, **not** starving.
The human body can go a week or more without food.
I don't want to do that.
It definitely wouldn't be an enjoyable week.
Water, on the other hand, is essential. You can only last a few days without it.
Speaking of water...
I think the rain is telling us it's time for bed.
Let's put this fire out before we get soaked.
To conserve our drinking water, bury the fire with dirt and stir until no embers remain.

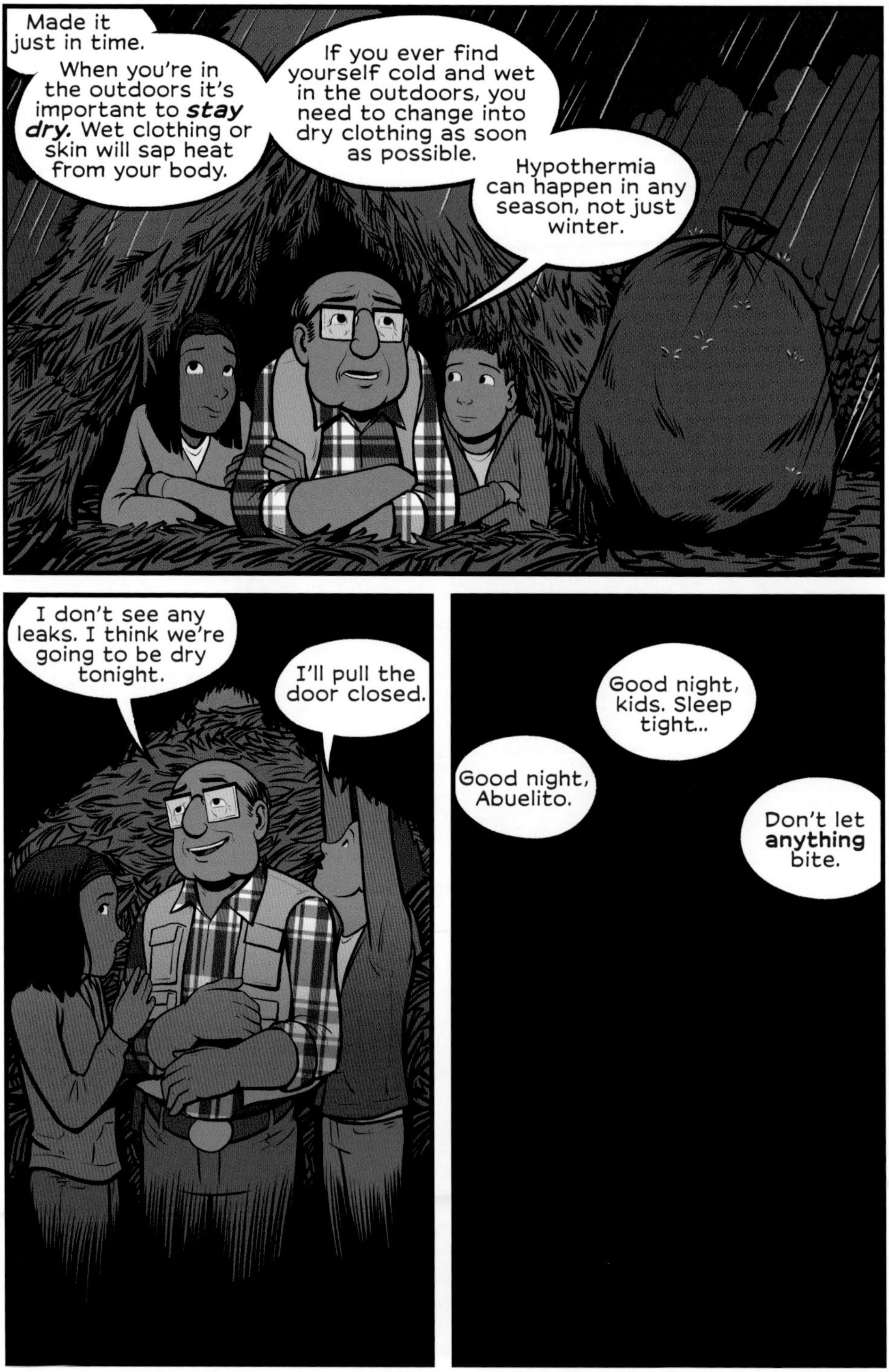
Made it just in time.
When you're in the outdoors it's important to ***stay dry.*** Wet clothing or skin will sap heat from your body.
If you ever find yourself cold and wet in the outdoors, you need to change into dry clothing as soon as possible.
Hypothermia can happen in any season, not just winter.
I don't see any leaks. I think we're going to be dry tonight.
I'll pull the door closed.
Good night, kids. Sleep tight...
Good night, Abuelito.
Don't let **anything** bite.

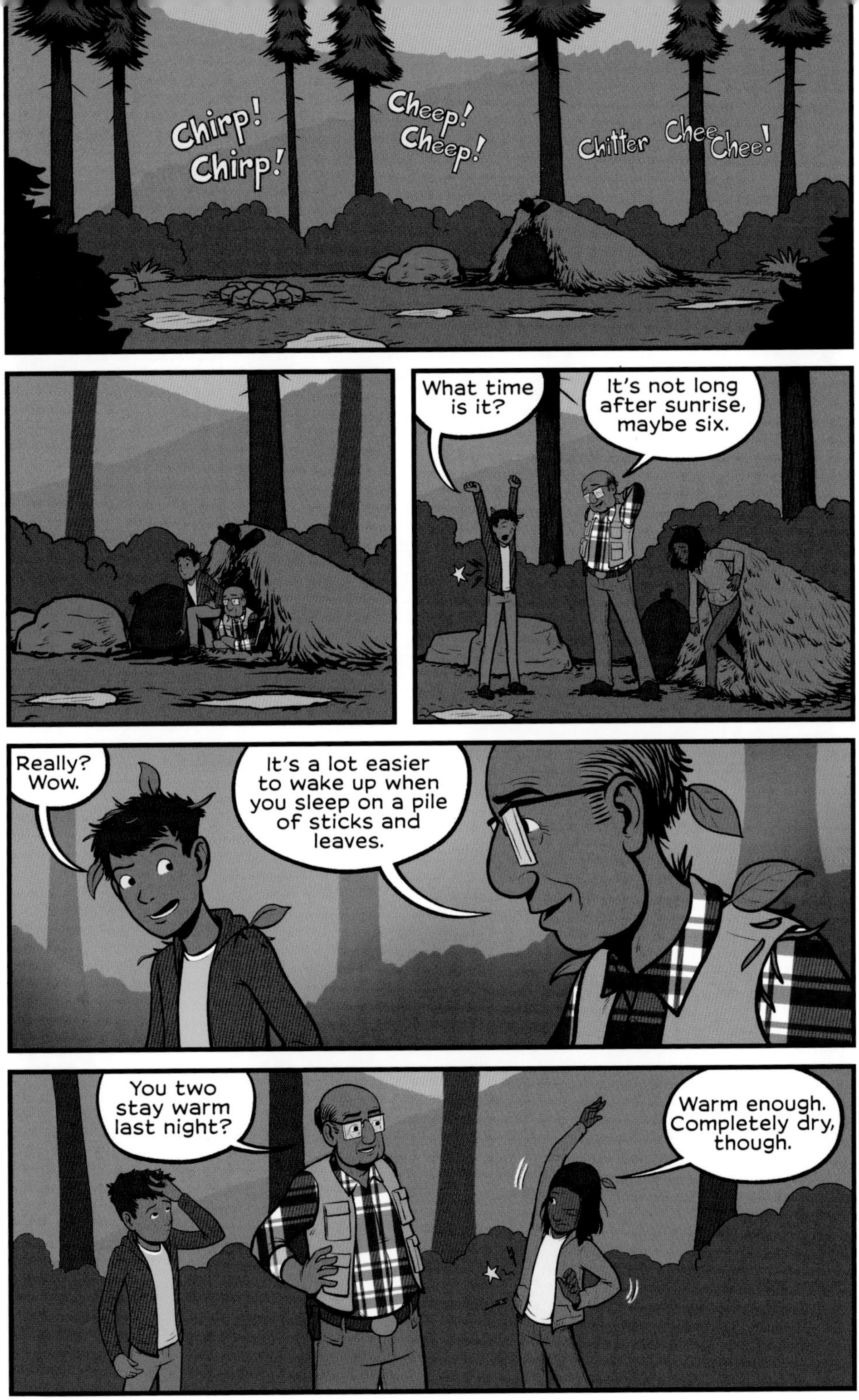
Chirp! Chirp!
Cheep! Cheep!
Chitter Chee Chee!
What time is it?
It's not long after sunrise, maybe six.
Really? Wow.
It's a lot easier to wake up when you sleep on a pile of sticks and leaves.
You two stay warm last night?
Warm enough. Completely dry, though.

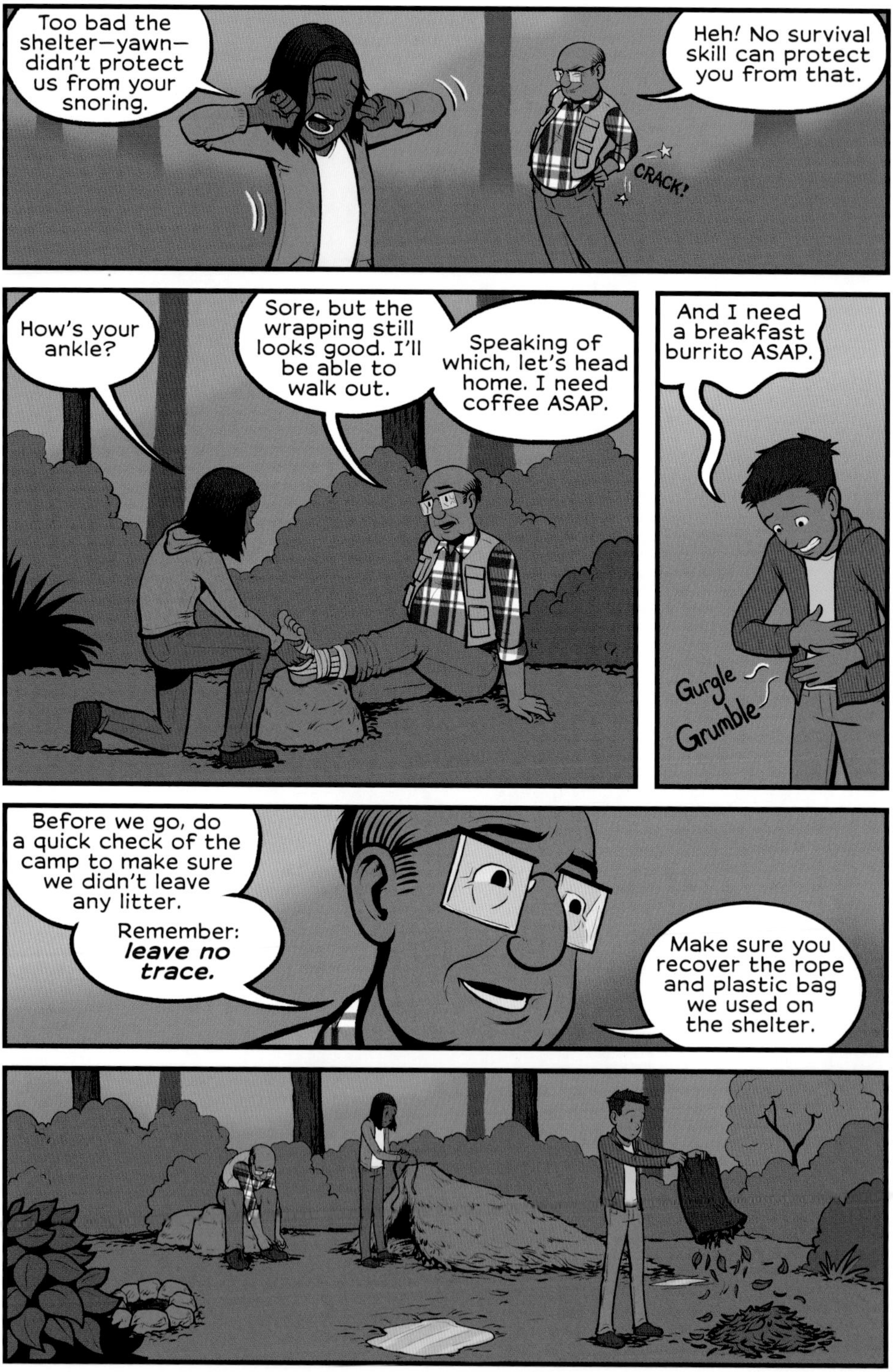
Too bad the shelter—yawn—didn't protect us from your snoring.
Heh! No survival skill can protect you from that.
CRACK!
How's your ankle?
Sore, but the wrapping still looks good. I'll be able to walk out.
Speaking of which, let's head home. I need coffee ASAP.
And I need a breakfast burrito ASAP.
Gurgle
Grumble
Before we go, do a quick check of the camp to make sure we didn't leave any litter.
Remember: ***leave no trace.***
Make sure you recover the rope and plastic bag we used on the shelter.

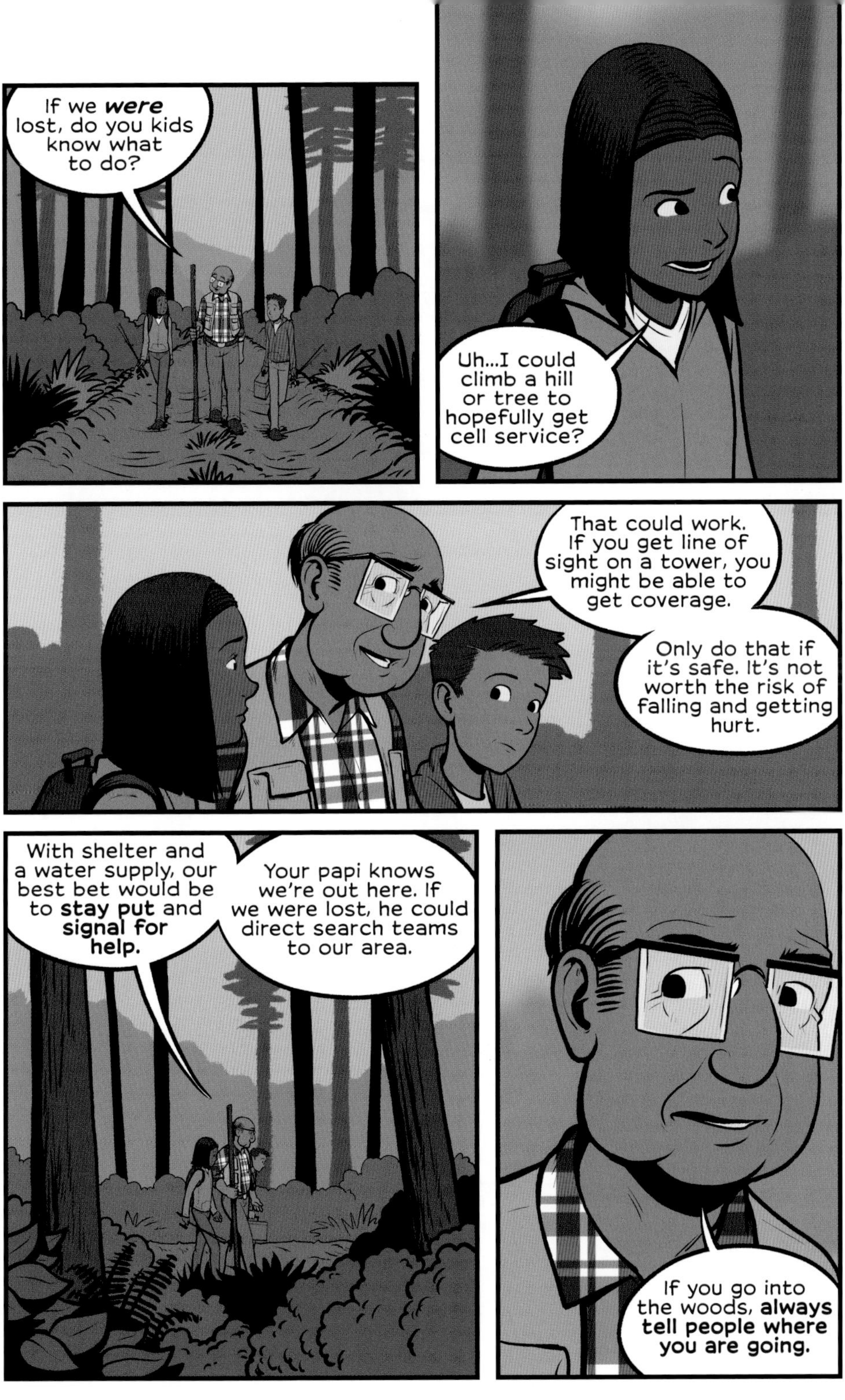
If we ***were*** lost, do you kids know what to do?
Uh...I could climb a hill or tree to hopefully get cell service?
That could work. If you get line of sight on a tower, you might be able to get coverage.
Only do that if it's safe. It's not worth the risk of falling and getting hurt.
With shelter and a water supply, our best bet would be to **stay put** and **signal for help.**
Your papi knows we're out here. If we were lost, he could direct search teams to our area.
If you go into the woods, **always tell people where you are going.**

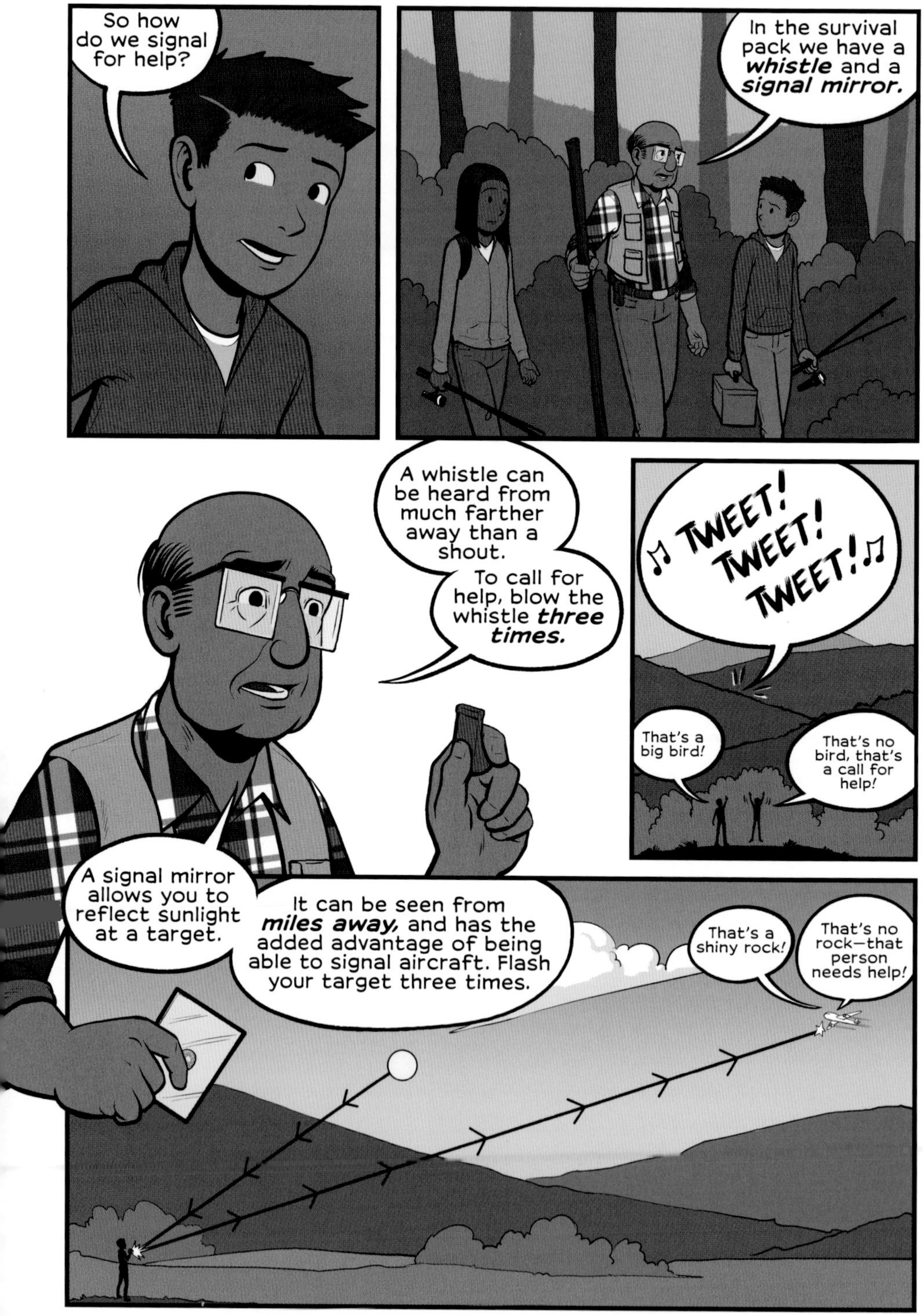
So how do we signal for help?
In the survival pack we have a ***whistle*** and a ***signal mirror.***
A whistle can be heard from much farther away than a shout.
To call for help, blow the whistle ***three times.***
♫ TWEET! TWEET! TWEET! ♫
That's a big bird!
That's no bird, that's a call for help!
A signal mirror allows you to reflect sunlight at a target.
It can be seen from ***miles away,*** and has the added advantage of being able to signal aircraft. Flash your target three times.
That's a shiny rock!
That's no rock—that person needs help!

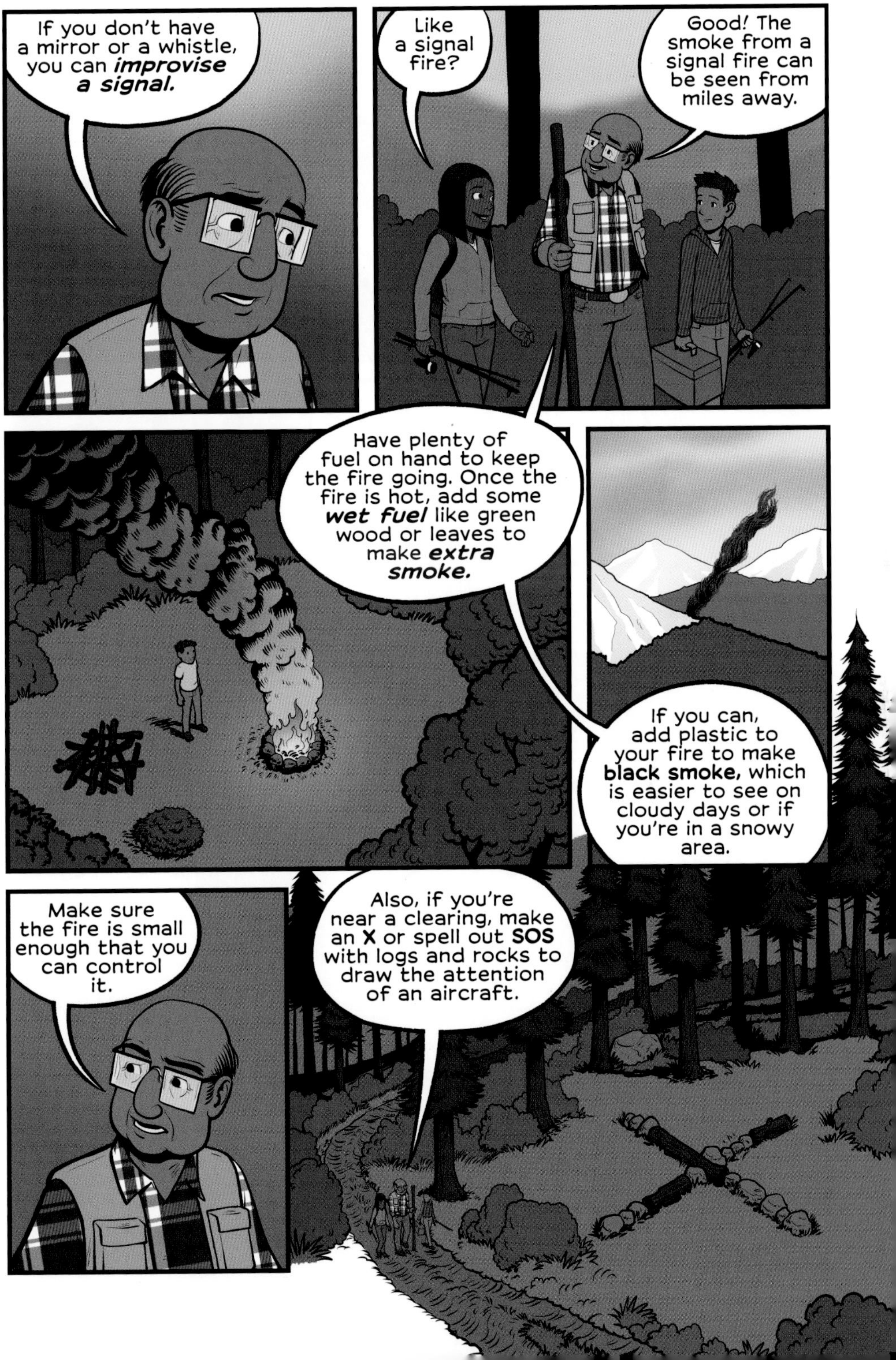
If you don't have a mirror or a whistle, you can *improvise a signal.*
Like a signal fire?
Good! The smoke from a signal fire can be seen from miles away.
Have plenty of fuel on hand to keep the fire going. Once the fire is hot, add some *wet fuel* like green wood or leaves to make *extra smoke.*
If you can, add plastic to your fire to make **black smoke,** which is easier to see on cloudy days or if you're in a snowy area.
Make sure the fire is small enough that you can control it.
Also, if you're near a clearing, make an **X** or spell out **SOS** with logs and rocks to draw the attention of an aircraft.

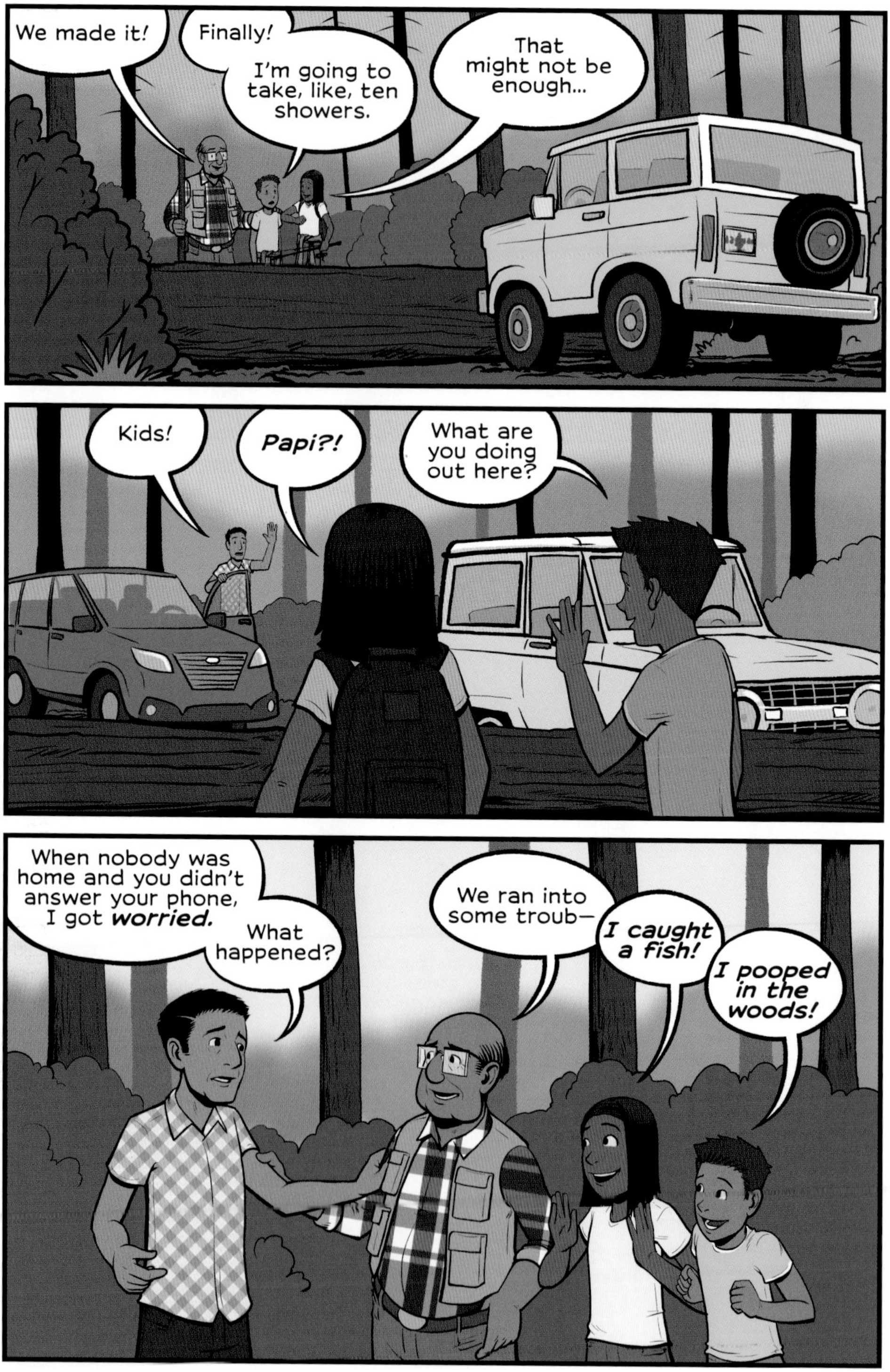
We made it!
Finally!
I'm going to take, like, ten showers.
That might not be enough...
Kids!
Papi?!
What are you doing out here?
When nobody was home and you didn't answer your phone, I got worried.
What happened?
We ran into some troub—
I caught a fish!
I pooped in the woods!

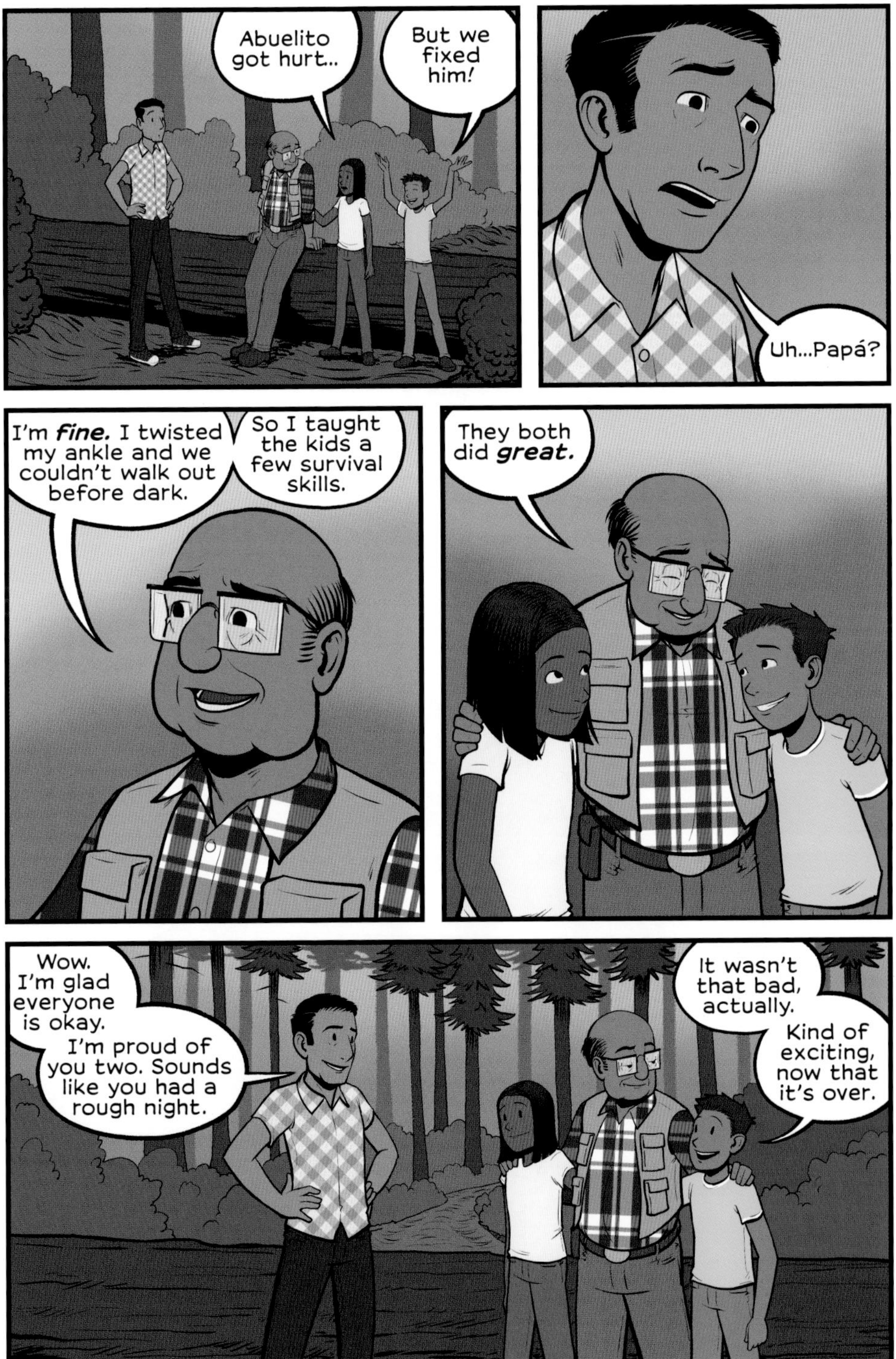
Abuelito got hurt...
But we fixed him!
Uh...Papá?
I'm ***fine.*** I twisted my ankle and we couldn't walk out before dark.
So I taught the kids a few survival skills.
They both did ***great.***
Wow. I'm glad everyone is okay.
I'm proud of you two. Sounds like you had a rough night.
It wasn't that bad, actually.
Kind of exciting, now that it's over.

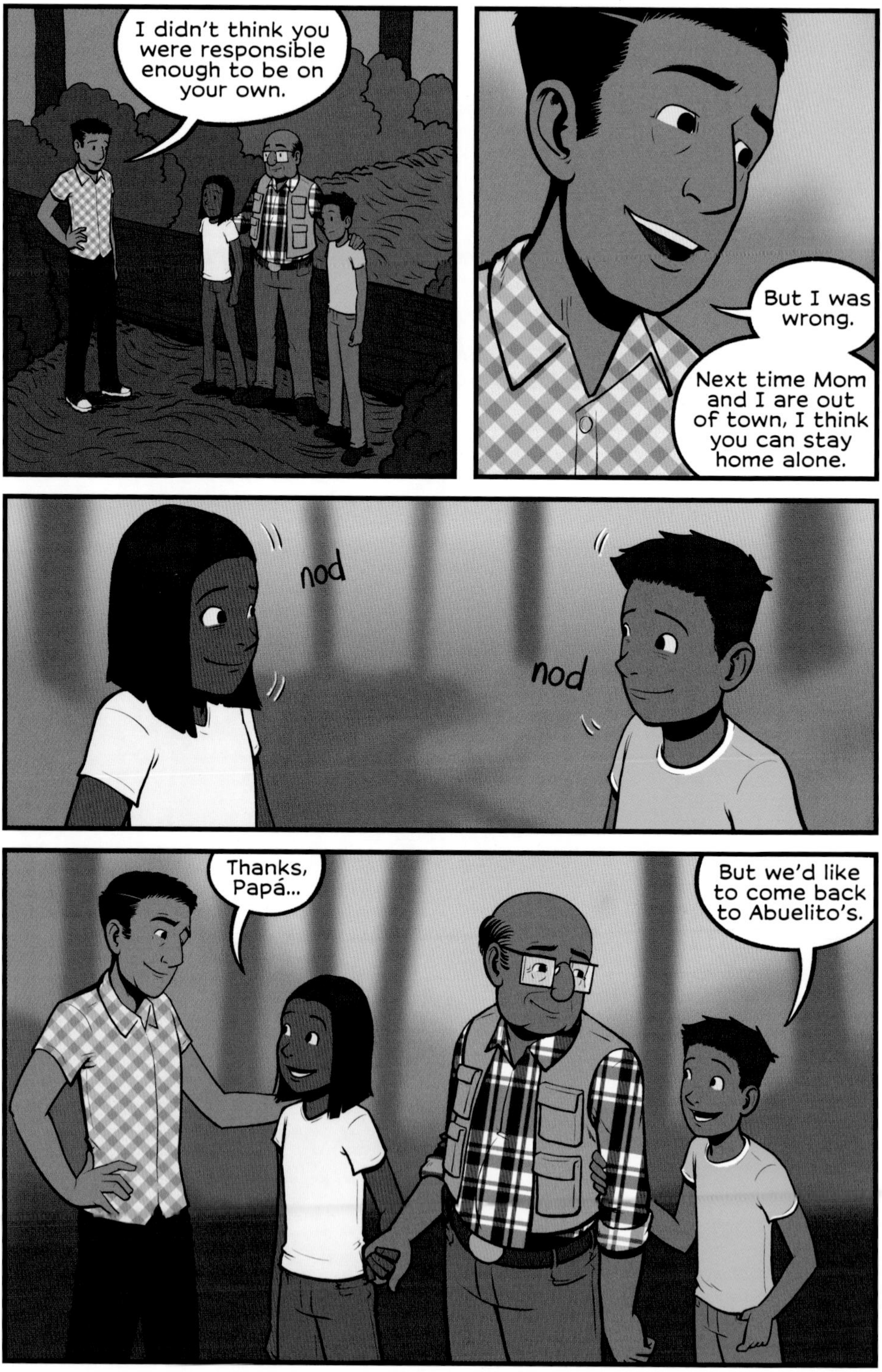

I didn't think you were responsible enough to be on your own.
But I was wrong.
Next time Mom and I are out of town, I think you can stay home alone.
nod
nod
Thanks, Papá...
But we'd like to come back to Abuelito's.

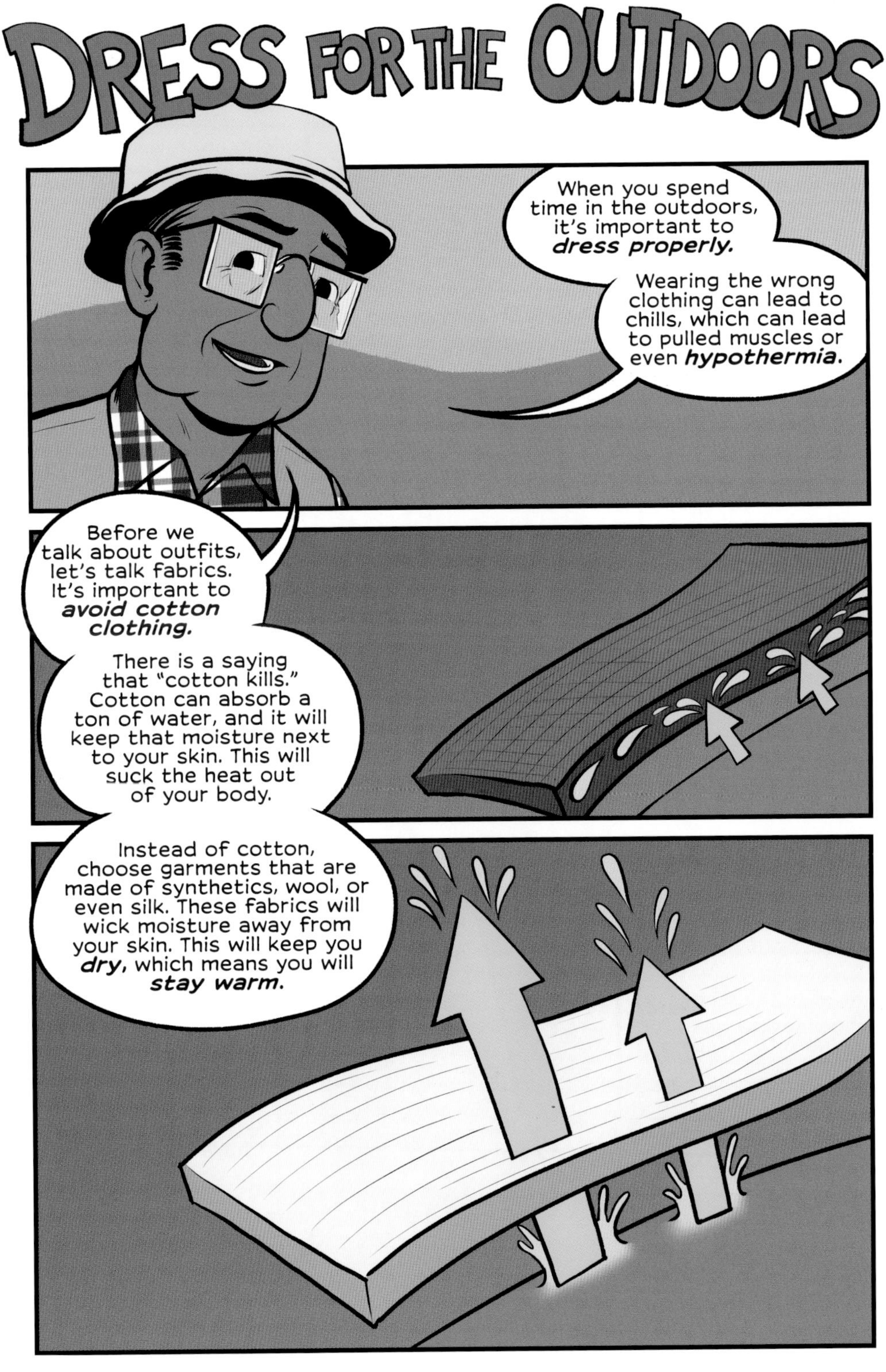
DRESS FOR THE OUTDOORS
When you spend time in the outdoors, it's important to *dress properly.*
Wearing the wrong clothing can lead to chills, which can lead to pulled muscles or even ***hypothermia***.
Before we talk about outfits, let's talk fabrics. It's important to ***avoid cotton clothing.***
There is a saying that "cotton kills." Cotton can absorb a ton of water, and it will keep that moisture next to your skin. This will suck the heat out of your body.
Instead of cotton, choose garments that are made of synthetics, wool, or even silk. These fabrics will wick moisture away from your skin. This will keep you ***dry***, which means you will ***stay warm***.

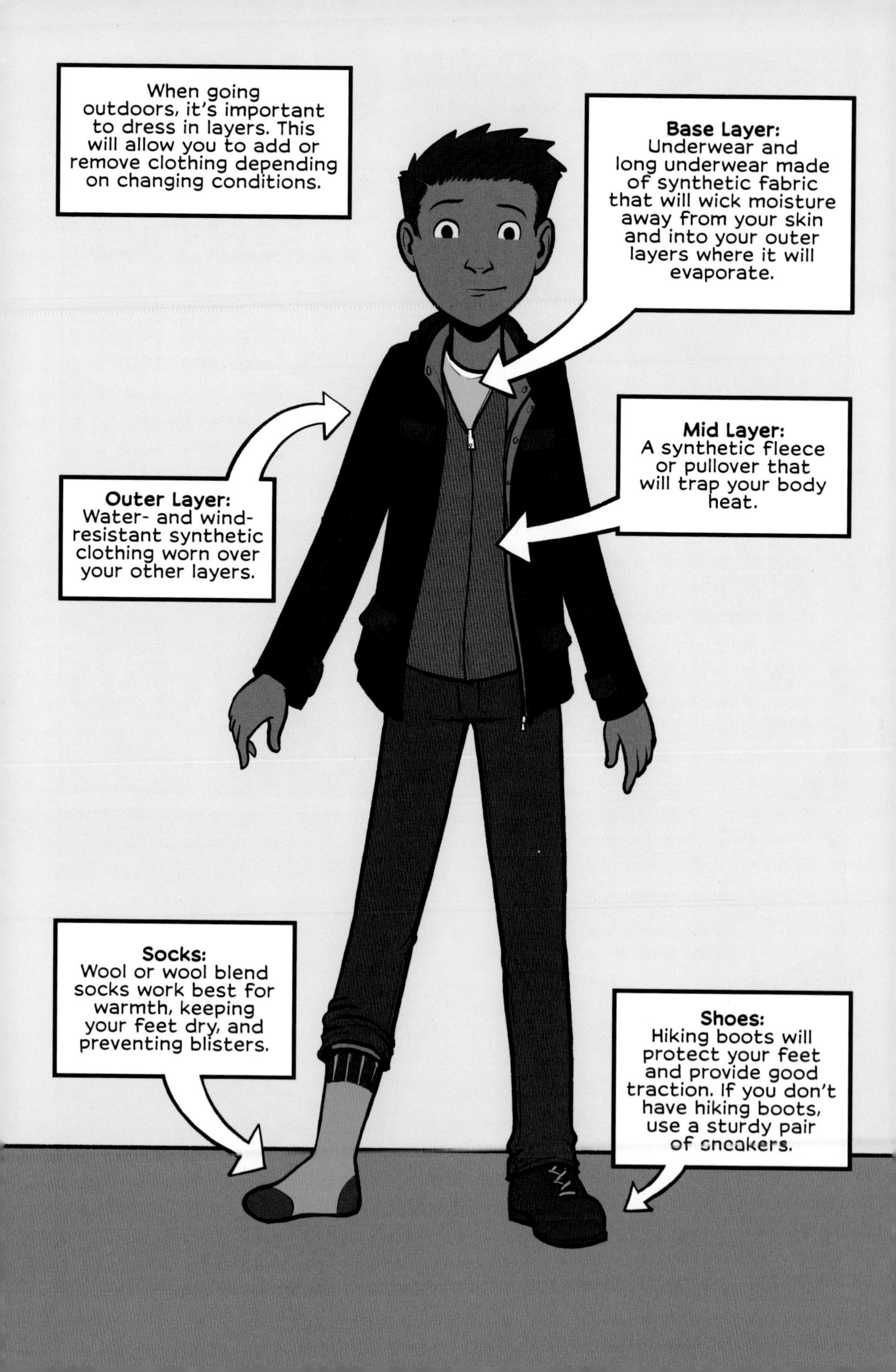
When going outdoors, it's important to dress in layers. This will allow you to add or remove clothing depending on changing conditions.
Base Layer: Underwear and long underwear made of synthetic fabric that will wick moisture away from your skin and into your outer layers where it will evaporate.
Mid Layer: A synthetic fleece or pullover that will trap your body heat.
Outer Layer: Water- and wind-resistant synthetic clothing worn over your other layers.
Socks: Wool or wool blend socks work best for warmth, keeping your feet dry, and preventing blisters.
Shoes: Hiking boots will protect your feet and provide good traction. If you don't have hiking boots, use a sturdy pair of sneakers.

# HYPOTHERMIA

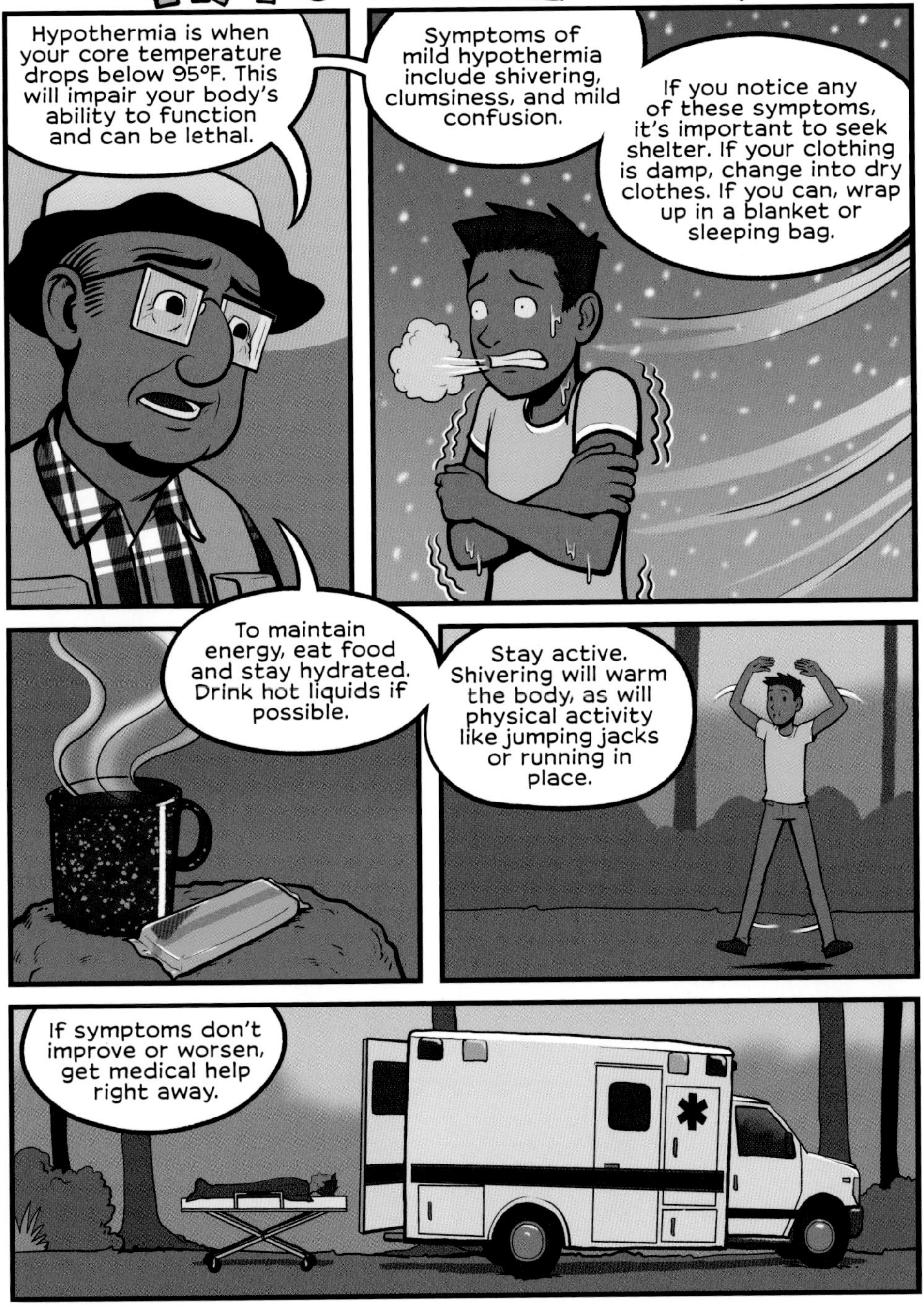

Hypothermia is when your core temperature drops below 95°F. This will impair your body's ability to function and can be lethal.
Symptoms of mild hypothermia include shivering, clumsiness, and mild confusion.
If you notice any of these symptoms, it's important to seek shelter. If your clothing is damp, change into dry clothes. If you can, wrap up in a blanket or sleeping bag.
To maintain energy, eat food and stay hydrated. Drink hot liquids if possible.
Stay active. Shivering will warm the body, as will physical activity like jumping jacks or running in place.
If symptoms don't improve or worsen, get medical help right away.

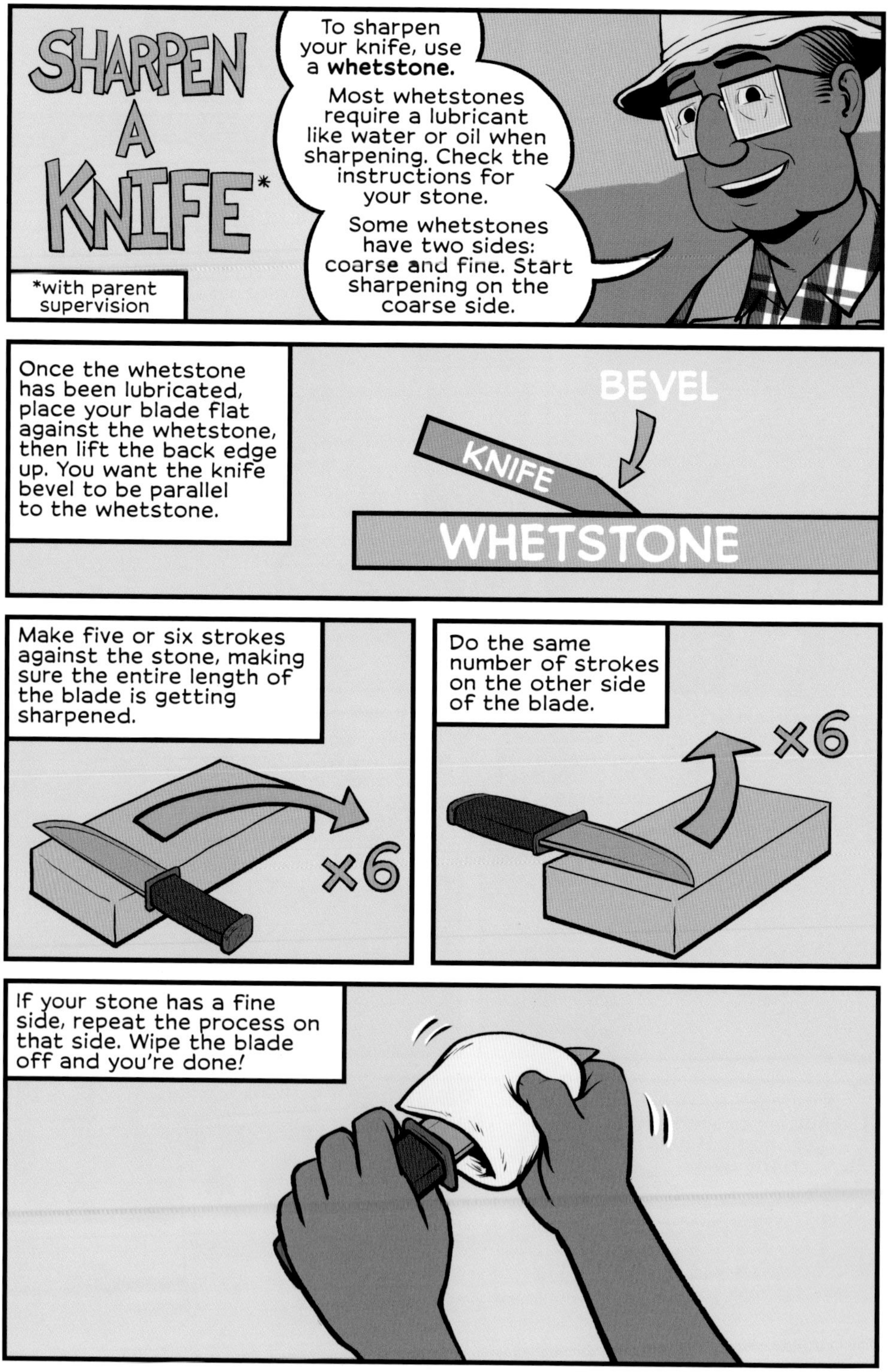
SHARPEN A KNIFE*
*with parent supervision
To sharpen your knife, use a **whetstone.**
Most whetstones require a lubricant like water or oil when sharpening. Check the instructions for your stone.
Some whetstones have two sides: coarse and fine. Start sharpening on the coarse side.
Once the whetstone has been lubricated, place your blade flat against the whetstone, then lift the back edge up. You want the knife bevel to be parallel to the whetstone.
BEVEL
KNIFE
WHETSTONE
Make five or six strokes against the stone, making sure the entire length of the blade is getting sharpened.
×6
Do the same number of strokes on the other side of the blade.
×6
If your stone has a fine side, repeat the process on that side. Wipe the blade off and you're done!

# CELL PHONES in the WILD

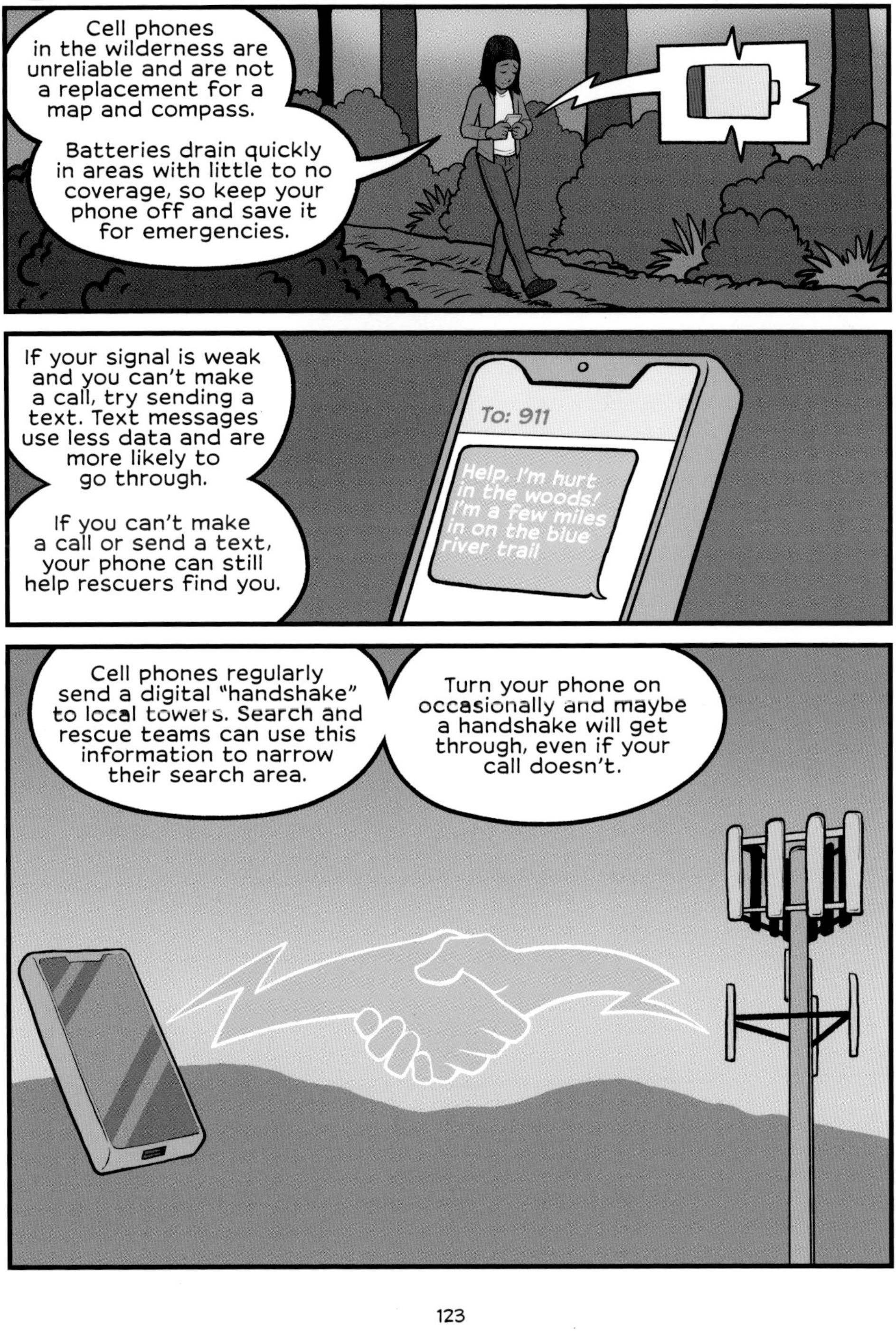

Cell phones in the wilderness are unreliable and are not a replacement for a map and compass.
Batteries drain quickly in areas with little to no coverage, so keep your phone off and save it for emergencies.
If your signal is weak and you can't make a call, try sending a text. Text messages use less data and are more likely to go through.
If you can't make a call or send a text, your phone can still help rescuers find you.
To: 911
Help, I'm hurt in the woods! I'm a few miles in on the blue river trail
Cell phones regularly send a digital "handshake" to local towers. Search and rescue teams can use this information to narrow their search area.
Turn your phone on occasionally and maybe a handshake will get through, even if your call doesn't.

**First Second**

Published by First Second
First Second is an imprint of Roaring Brook Press,
a division of Holtzbrinck Publishing Holdings Limited Partnership
120 Broadway, New York, NY 10271
firstsecondbooks.com
mackids.com

All instructions included in this book are provided as a resource for parents and children.
While all due care has been taken, we recommend that an adult supervise children at
all times when following the instructions in this book. The projects in this book are not
recommended for children three years and under due to potential choking hazard. Neither
the authors nor the publisher accept any responsibility for any loss, injury, or damages
sustained by anyone resulting from the instructions contained in this book.

Library of Congress Control Number: 2020919823

Our books may be purchased in bulk for promotional, educational, or business use.
Please contact your local bookseller or the Macmillan Corporate and Premium Sales Department at
(800) 221-7945 ext. 5442 or by email at MacmillanSpecialMarkets@macmillan.com.

First edition, 2021
Edited by Robyn Chapman, Bethany Bryan, and Alison Wilgus
Cover and interior book design by Molly Johanson
Expert consultation by Dan Wowak of Coalcracker Bushcraft
Printed in China by 1010 Printing International Limited, Kwun Tong, Hong Kong

ISBN 978-1-250-62066-8 (paperback)
3 5 7 9 10 8 6 4

ISBN 978-1-250-62065-1 (hardcover)
1 3 5 7 9 10 8 6 4 2

Drawn digitally in Clip Studio Paint and colored in Photoshop. Lettered with CCSoliloquous

Don't miss your next favorite book from First Second!
For the latest updates go to firstsecondnewsletter.com and sign up for our enewsletter.